DUBLIN
STREETFINDER

Contents

Tourist and travel information 2

Key to map symbols 3

Key to map pages . . . . 4 - 5

Route planning map . . . . 6 - 7

Main Dublin maps . . . . 8 - 57

Central Dublin map . . . . 58 - 59

Guide to central Dublin . . . . . 60 - 79

Index to place names 80

Index to street names . . . . 80 - 96

Tourist and travel information

Air

Dublin Airport
Tel: 01 814 1111.
Web: www.dublin–airport.com
Frequent direct flights operate between Dublin and many airports in Britain, Europe and North America. Internal flights are available to Cork, Donegal, Galway, Kerry, Knock, Shannon & Sligo. Aer Arann **Tel: 0818 210210 (R of I), 0800 587 2324 (UK)** www.aerarannexpress.com & Aer Lingus **Tel: 01 886 8888 (R of I), 0845 084 4444 (UK)** www.aerlingus.com operate the internal routes. Other operators flying into Dublin are British Airways **Tel: 1890 626 747 (R of I), 0870 850 9850 (UK)** www.britishairways.com, Flybe **Tel: 1890 925 532 (R of I), 0871 700 0535 (UK)** www.flybe.com, British Midland **Tel: 01 407 3036 (R of I), 0870 6070 555 (UK)** www.flybmi.com & Ryanair **Tel: 01 609 7800 (R of I), 0871 246 0000 (UK)** www.ryanair.com.

The airport is 12km (8 miles) north of the city centre with Dublin Bus operating many services to and from the airport including the 'Airlink' express coach service operating between the airport, the central bus station in Store Street (Busáras) and the two mainline rail stations, Connolly and Heuston. It runs every 10 - 15 mins (15 - 20 mins on Sundays) between 05.45 and 23.30 from the airport and between 05.15 and 22.50 from O'Connell Street in the centre of Dublin. **Tel: 01 873 4222** www.dublinbus.ie. 'Aircoach' runs between the airport and Dublin City and South Dublin City stopping at major hotels. The 24 hour service operates every 10-20 minutes except from 24.00 and 05.00 when an hourly service operates. **Tel: 01 844 7118** www.aircoach.ie. 'Aerdart' is a bus service operating every 15 minutes between the airport and Howth Junction DART station.

Services at Dublin airport include Travel Information, Tourist Information and Bureau de Change

Passenger and vehicle ferries

Numerous modern ferries and high-speed services with drive-on drive-off facilities cross the Irish Sea to Dublin from Britain (Liverpool, Mostyn, Holyhead), the Isle of Man and France (Cherbourg).

Irish Ferries (Dublin–Holyhead). **Tel: 01 638 3333 / 0818 300 400** or from UK: **08705 17 17 17.**
Web: www.irishferries.com
Email: info@irishferries.ie

Norse Merchant Ferries (Dublin–Birkenhead). **Tel: 01 819 2999** or from UK: **0870 600 4321.**
Web: www.norsemerchant.com

P & O Irish Sea (Dublin–Liverpool).
Tel: 1800 409 049 or from UK: **0870 24 24 777.**
Web: www.poirishsea.com

Isle of Man Steam Packet Company/Sea Containers (Dublin–Douglas).
Tel: 1800 80 50 55 or from UK: **08705 523 523.**
Web: www.steam–packet.com

Stena Line
(Dún Laoghaire–Holyhead & Dublin–Holyhead).
Tel: 01 204 7777
or from UK: **08705 70 70 70.**
Web: www.stenaline.co.uk
Email: info.ie@stenaline.com

Dublin Port and Dún Laoghaire have bus and taxi services to the city centre although on busy sailings it may be prudent to pre-book a taxi. The ferry terminal at Dún Laoghaire is also linked to the city by the DART rail service with a 20 minute journey time.

Tourist information

Dublin Tourism Centre, Suffolk Street. **Tel: 01 605 7700.** Open: (July and August) Mon–Sat 09.00–19.00, (Sept–June) Mon–Sat 09.00–17.30. Open Sun & bank holidays 10.30–15.00; closed 25 & 26 Dec & 1 Jan.
Formerly St. Andrew's Church, the centre provides details of visitor attractions and events in the city as well as acting as a ticket and accommodation bureau. Transport and tour information, exchange facilities and a café are also on hand.
Other tourist information and reservation centres in Dublin (walk-in only) are located at:
Dublin Airport. Open: Mon–Sun 08.00–22.00. Open bank holidays except 25 & 26 Dec & 1 Jan.
Dún Laoghaire Ferry Terminal. Open: Mon–Sat 10.00–18.00, closed 13.00-14.00. Open bank holidays except 25 & 26 Dec & 1 Jan.

Baggott Street Bridge. Open: Mon–Fri 09.30–17.00, closed 12.00-12.30. Closed bank holidays.
For accommodation reservations in Dublin and Ireland contact Ireland Reservations. Tel from within Ireland: **1800 363 626**; from within UK: **008 002 580 2580.**

Official tourism website for Dublin:
Web: www.visitdublin.com
Email: information@dublintourism.ie
or reservations@dublintourism.ie

Irish Tourist Board Website:
Web: www.ireland.ie

Department of Environment, Heritage & Local Government:
Web: www.heritageireland.ie
Email: info@heritageireland.ie

Key to map symbols ③

M1 /	Motorway / under construction	P	Car park
	Tunnelled motorway	■ Garda	Garda Síochána (police) station
N6	National primary road	🇮	Tourist information centre
N55	National secondary road	+	Church
R95	Regional road	■ PO ■ Lib	Public service building (appropriate name shown)
	Other road		Leisure / Tourism
	Track		Shopping
	Ferry		Administration / Law
	Administrative boundary		Health / Hospital
24	Postcode number		Education
	Postal boundary		Notable building
	Railway / Station		Built up area
JERVIS	Dublin Luas tramway / Station		Park / Garden / Sports ground / Public open space
	Bus / Coach station	† †	Cemetery
	Lake / River		Golf course

```
0                    ¼              ½ mile
0         0.25       0.5      0.75      1 km
```

Scale 1:15,840 4 inches (10.2cm) to 1 mile / 6.3cm to 1km

Published by Collins
An imprint of HarperCollins*Publishers*
77-85 Fulham Palace Road, Hammersmith, London W6 8JB

www.collins.co.uk

Copyright © HarperCollins*Publishers* Ltd 2005
Collins® is a registered trademark of HarperCollins*Publishers* Limited
Mapping generated from Collins Bartholomew digital databases

Based on Ordnance Survey Ireland by permission of the Government. © Government of Ireland.

All rights reserved. No part of this publication may be reproduced, stored in a retrieval system, or transmitted, in any form or by
any means, electronic, mechanical, photocopying, recording or otherwise, without the prior written permission of the publisher and
copyright owners.
The contents of this publication are believed correct at the time of printing. Nevertheless, the publisher can accept no responsibility
for errors or omissions, changes in the detail given, or for any expense or loss thereby caused.

The representation of a road, track or footpath is no evidence of a right of way.

Printed in Hong Kong
RI11894   NDB
e-mail: roadcheck@harpercollins.co.uk

Ward

Pinkeen

Tolka

N3

Kilbride

Coolquoy

Chapelmidway

SW

Ward

Skephubble

Baytownpark

N2

Killshane

St.
Margaret's

Dunboyne

Ballymacoll

Clonee

Corduff

M50

Finglas

Kilgraigue

Rathleek

Blanchardstown

8 - 9

10 - 11

Clonsilla

Castleknock

Glasnevin

M4

Leixlip

Liffey

Clondalkin

Toll

6

26 - 27

24 - 25

Phoenix
Park

N3

Celbridge

N4

Lucan

Palmerston

7

Chapelizod

32 - 33

34 - 35

N4

Stacumny

Grand

Canal

Coolfitch

Hazelhatch

Milltown

Clondalkin

9

40 - 41

42 - 43

Crumlin

N7

N81

Newcastle

Brownsbarn

Kingswood

10

48 - 49

50 - 51

Ardclough

Athgoe

Saggart

TALLAGHT

11

Oughterard

Rathcoole

12

M50

Redgap

Friarstown

Rockbroo

N81

Raheen

Porterstown

Brittas

Thornberry

Kilteel

Monaspick

Cunard

Rathmore

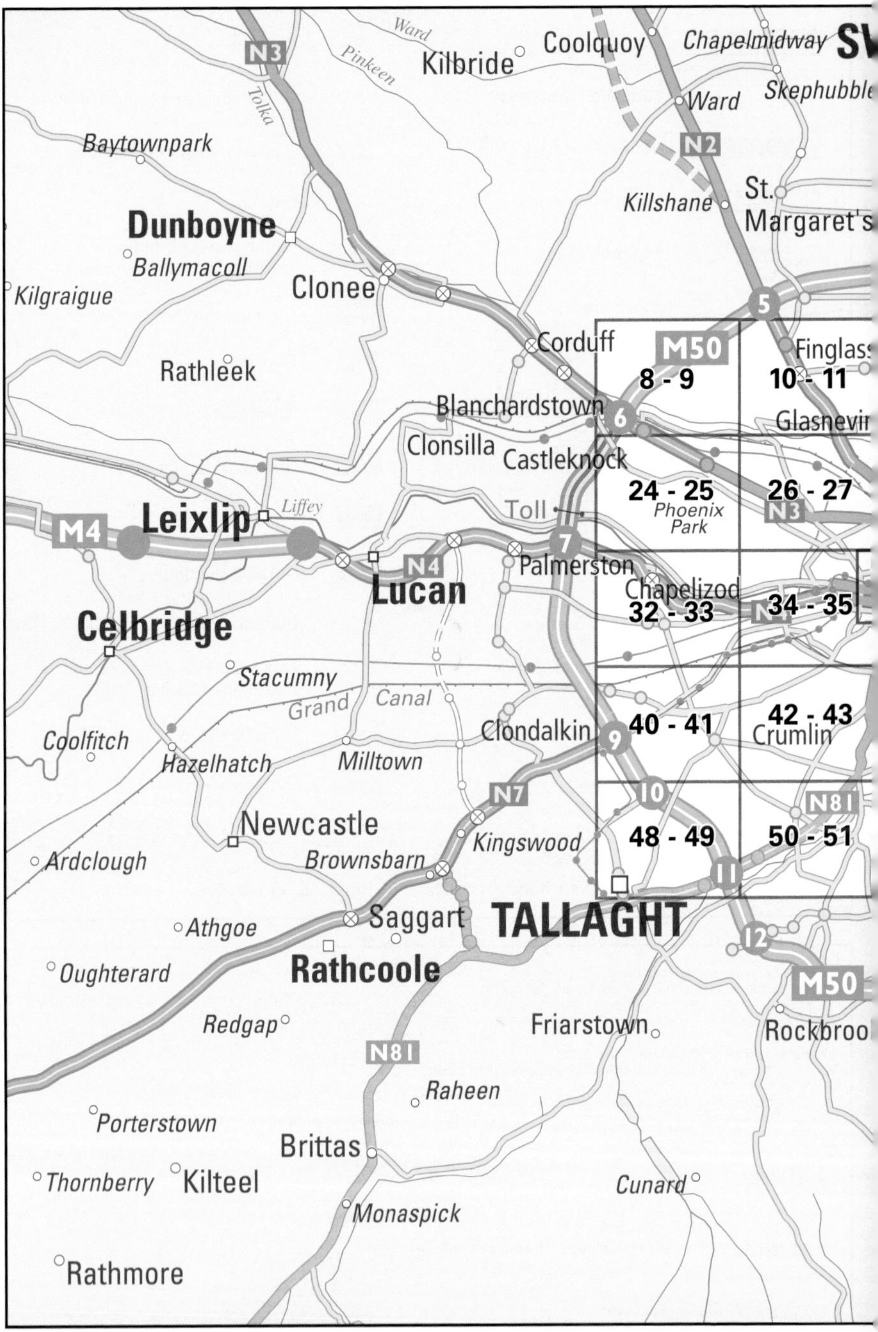

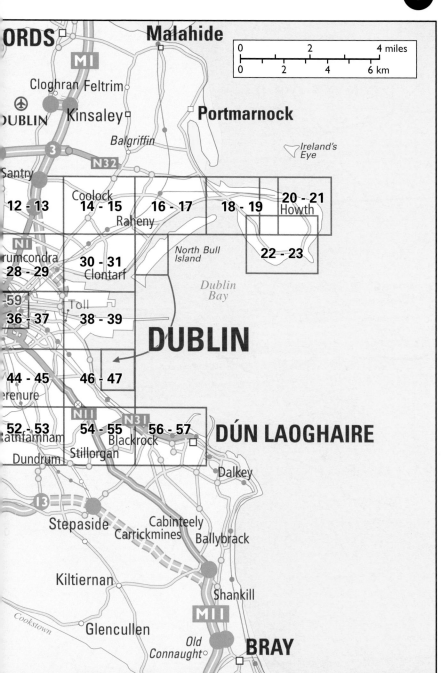

Route planning map ⑦

Scale

0 — 3 — 6 — 9 miles
0 — 5 — 10 — 15 km

Road distances shown in blue
are in miles

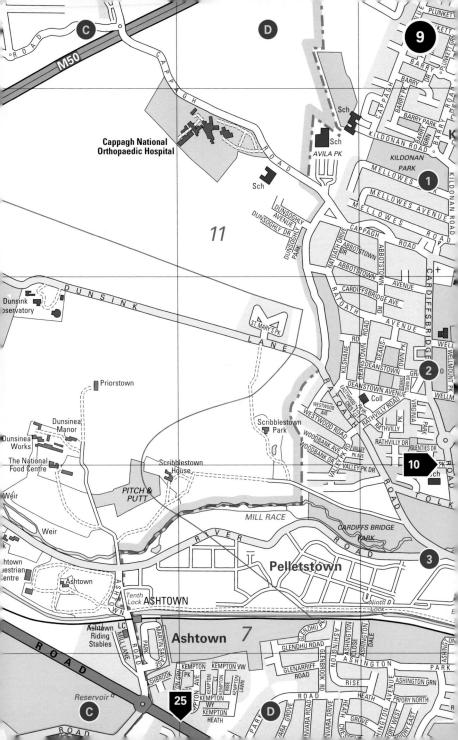

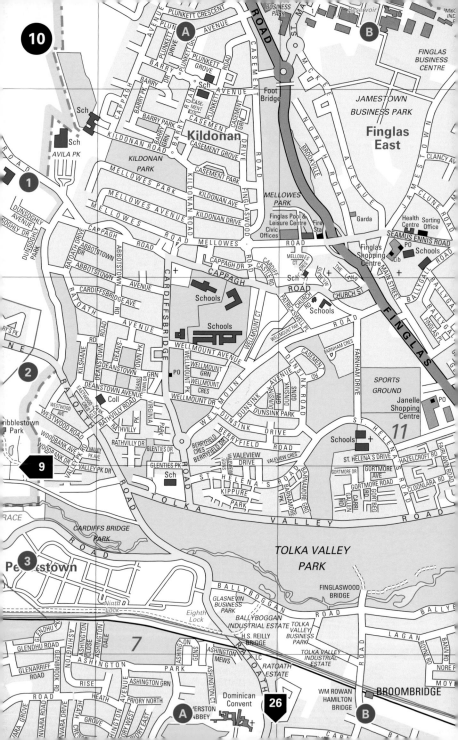

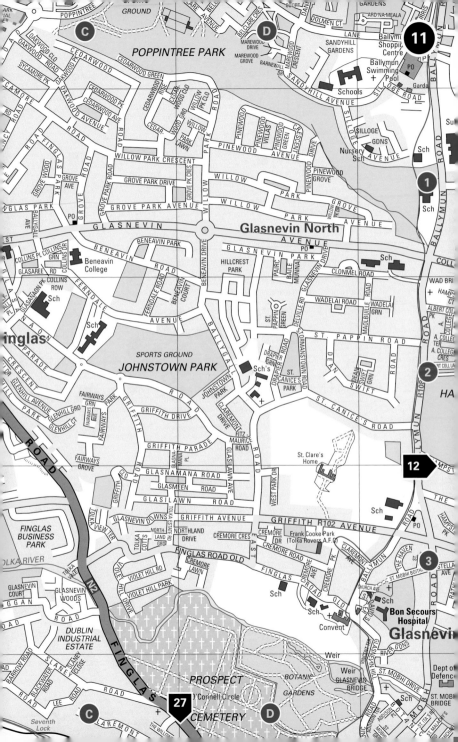

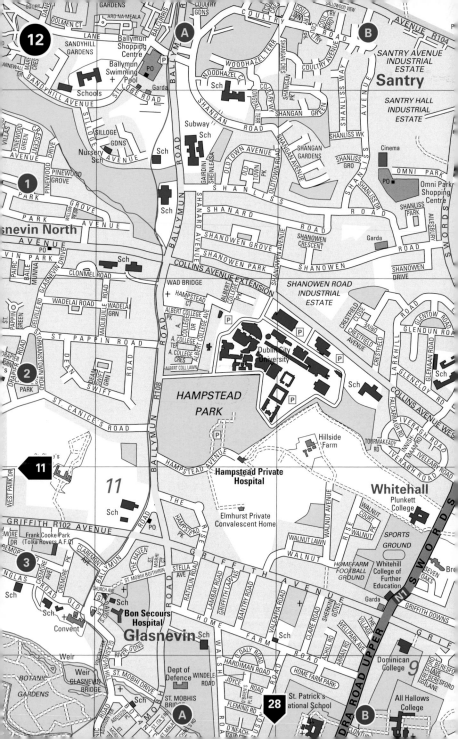

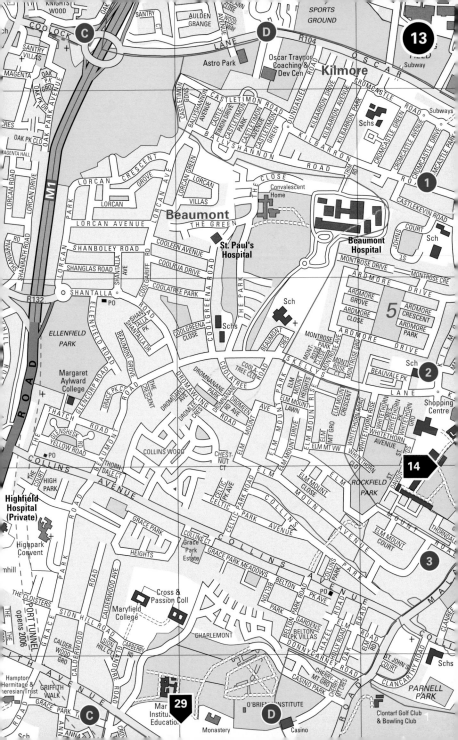

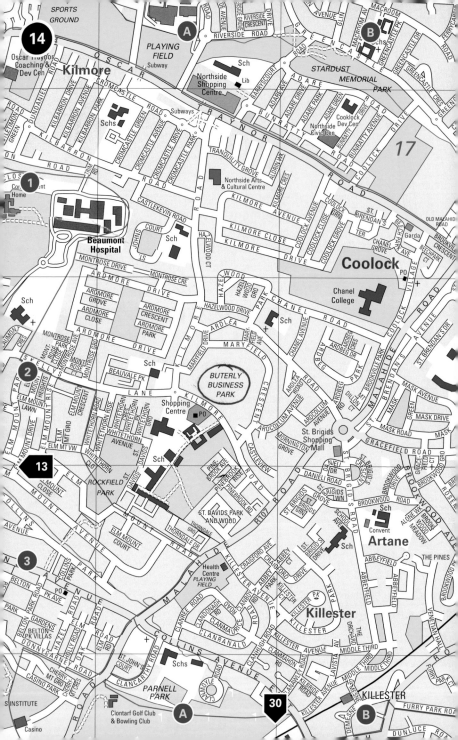

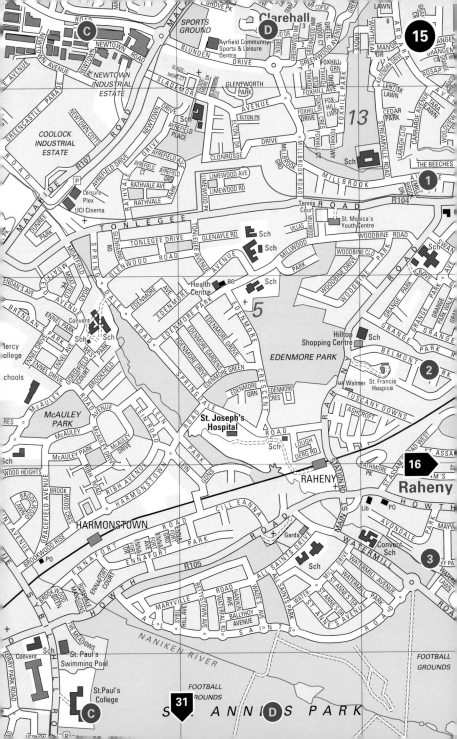

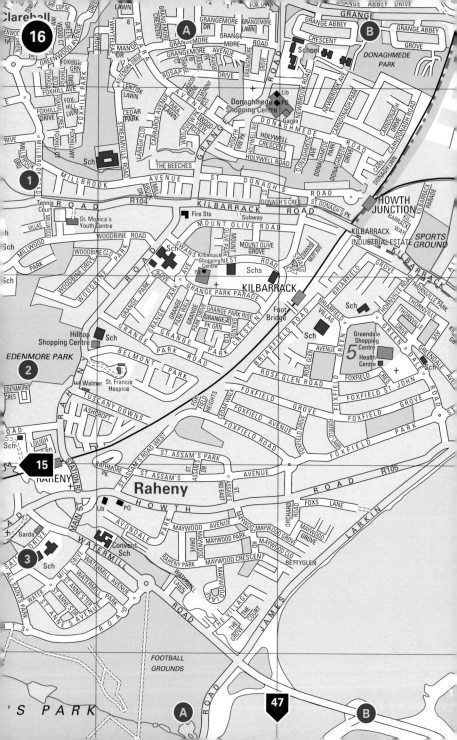

C

D

School

GRANGE PARK

LAW

GRANGE PARK

ADMIRAL

NOLAN

COLLEGE STREET

MAIN

STRAND

PO
Lib

2

ROAD

GRANGE

ROAD

Youth
Club

BROOKSTONE RD

GEORGIAN
HAMLET

Sch

STREET

WARRENHOUSE ROAD

PARADE

GRANGE AVENUE

GRANGE BRI

PO

SEAGRANGE AV

SEAGRANGE

DUBLIN

Sch

4

Grave
Yard

Nursing
Home

ROAD

GRANGE CLOSE

GRANGE DRIVE

Racecourse
Shopping Centre

SEAGRANGE

SEAGRANGE
PARK

TUSCANY PARK

MEADOWBROOK AVENUE

MEADOWBROOK
CLOSE

MEADOWS

Sch

TURNBERRY

WARREN

GREEN

BALDOYLE
INDUSTRIAL
ESTATE

13

MARIAN PARK

ABBEY PARK

Moyclare
DRIVE

MOYCLARE

MOYCLARE
PARK

BURROWFIELD

JAMES MCCORMACK

ROAD

EXPRESS

GRANGE   WAY

SEACLIFF AVENUE

SEACLIFF DR

PARKVALE

Sch

MOYCLARE ROAD

MOYCLARE
GDNS

LC

SEACLIFF RD

BAYSIDE

MOYCLARE CLO

1

VERBENA LAWNS

BAYSIDE BOULEVARD

BAYSIDE WALK

SUTTON

BALDOYLE ROAD

RAILWAY AVENUE

THE
CRES

ROAD

VERBENA
PK

VERBENA
GRO

BAYSIDE BOULEVARD

BAYSIDE SQ NORTH

SUTTON
PARK

SEAFIELD
CT

BINN

EADAIR

Sch

AVENUE

SARTO LAWN

BAYSIDE SQ NORTH

SUTTON PARK

SUTTON
PARK
LAWNS

ALDEN PARK

VERBENA

SARTO

PARK

BAYSIDE SQ WEST

PO

BAYSIDE SQ

SUTTON GROVE

SUTTON
COURT

TX DRIVE

VERBENA AVENUE

SARTO ROAD

SARTO
PARK

BAYSIDE SQ SOUTH

SUTTON DOWNS

KILBARRACK
CEMETERY

R105

ROAD

Kilbarrack

R104 ROAD

RONCALLI ROAD

FACELLI

SARTO ROAD

BAYSIDE BOULEVARD S

JAMES
JOYCE CT

DUBLIN

S U T T O N   S

BARRACK
GARDENS

BARRACK AVENUE

DEL VAL AVE

DEL VAL CT

BEACH VIEW

HILLSIDE VIEW

ROSSEM

2

ARGARET'S AVENUE

ISLAND VIEW

ROAD

18

N o r t h   B u l l   I s l a n d

ST. ANNE'S GOLF COURSE

Nature Reserve
and Bird Sanctuary

3

Clubhouse

C

D

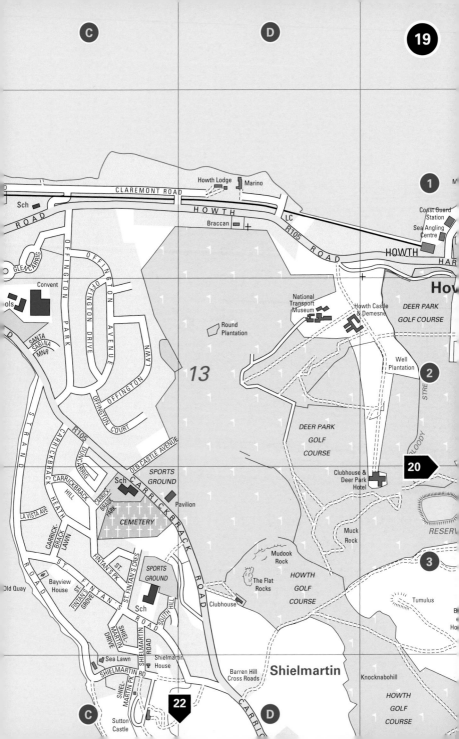

CLAREMONT ROAD

Howth Lodge Marino

Sch

HOWTH

ROAD

GLEN CARRIG

Braccan

LC

R105

HOWTH

Coast Guard
Station

Sea Angling
Centre

ROAD

Convent

OFFINGTON PARK

OFFINGTON DRIVE

OFFINGTON AVENUE

ools

SANTA
SABINA
MNR

OFFINGTON LAWN

Round
Plantation

National
Transport
Museum

Howth Castle
& Demesne

DEER PARK
GOLF COURSE

Hov

Ho

D

OFFINGTON COURT

13

Well
Plantation

2

STRAND

R105

CARRICKBRACK

DUNCARRIG

Old Castle Avenue

CARRICKBRACK

HEATH

HILL

LA VISTA AVE

CARRICK-
BRACK
LAWN

ROAD

CARRICKBRACK

CARRICK-
BRACK
PARK

Sch

SPORTS
GROUND

Pavilion

CEMETERY

DEER PARK

GOLF

COURSE

Clubhouse &
Deer Park
Hotel

BLOODY

20

ROAD

ST. FINTAN'S PK.

ST.
FINTAN'S GROVE

ST. FINTAN'S
ST. FINTAN'S CRES.

SPORTS
GROUND

Sch

Muck
Rock

RESER

3

Old Quay

Bayview
House

SHIEL-
MARTIN
DRIVE

SHIELMARTIN
ROAD

SOUTH HILL

Mudook
Rock

The Flat
Rocks

HOWTH

GOLF

COURSE

Tumulus

B

Ho

Clubhouse

Sea Lawn

Shielmartin
House

SHIELMARTIN RD.

SHIEL-
MARTIN PK.

Barren Hill
Cross Roads

Shielmartin

Knocknabohill

CARRIC

HOWTH

GOLF

COURSE

Sutton
Castle

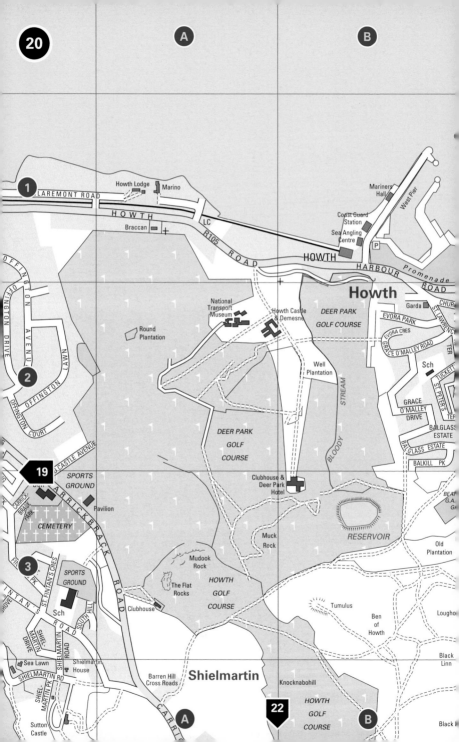

A

B

Howth Lodge   Marino

1 LAREMONT ROAD

Mariners'
Hall   West Pier

H O W T H

Coast Guard
Station

Braccan   LC

R105 ROAD   Sea Angling
Centre   P

HOWTH

HARBOUR   Promenade

Howth   ROAD

OFFINGTON DRIVE

National Transport
Museum   Howth Castle
& Demesne   DEER PARK
GOLF COURSE   Garda   CHUR

EVORA PARK   ST LAWRENCE TER

Round
Plantation   EVORA CRES

GRACE O'MALLEY ROAD

OFFINGTON AVENUE

2
Well
Plantation   Sch   TUCKETT

ST PETERS TER

BLOODY STREAM

GRACE
O'MALLEY
DRIVE

BALGLASS
ESTATE

BALGLASS ESTATE

OFFINGTON COURT

DEER PARK
GOLF
COURSE

BALKILL PK

CASTLE AVENUE

19 SPORTS
GROUND

CARRICKBRACK PARK

CARRICKBRACK ROAD

Pavilion

Clubhouse &
Deer Park
Hotel

BEAT
G.A.
Gr

RESERVOIR

CEMETERY

Muck
Rock

Old
Plantation

3 SPORTS
GROUND

FINT ST FINTAN'S CRES

Mudook
Rock

The Flat
Rocks

HOWTH
GOLF
COURSE

Tumulus

Ben
of
Howth

Lougho

Sch

SOUTH HILL

Clubhouse

FINTAN ROAD

SHIELMARTIN DRIVE

SHIEL MARTIN PK

Sea Lawn

Shielmartin
House

Black
Linn

SHIELMARTIN RD

Barren Hill
Cross Roads

Shielmartin

Knocknabohill

Black L

SHIEL-
MARTIN CRES

CARRIG

Sutton
Castle

A

22

HOWTH
GOLF
COURSE

B

Black l

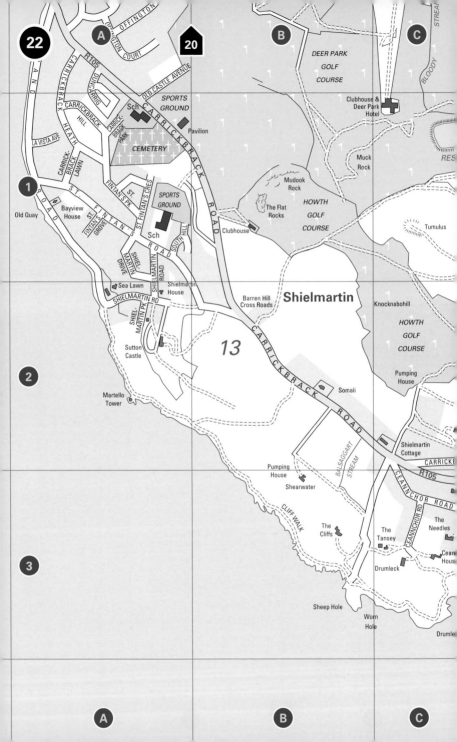

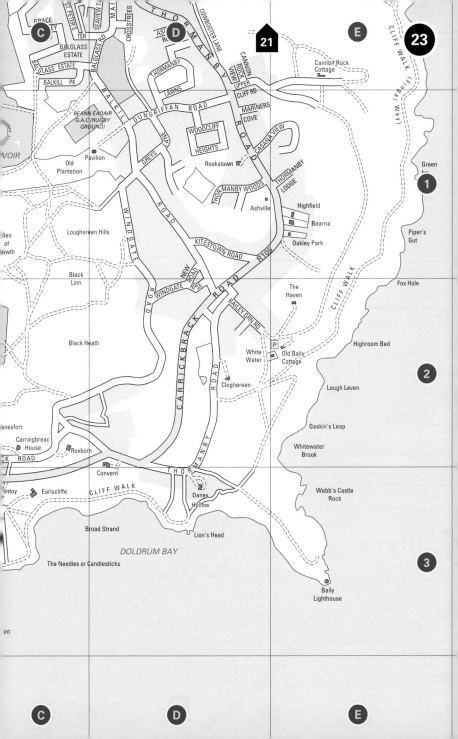

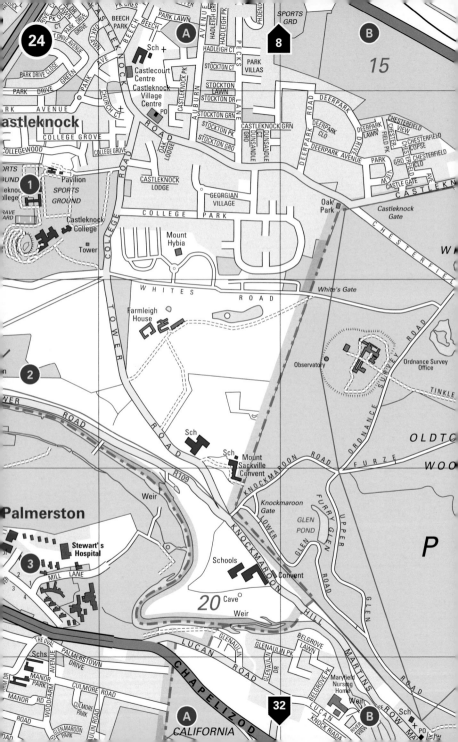

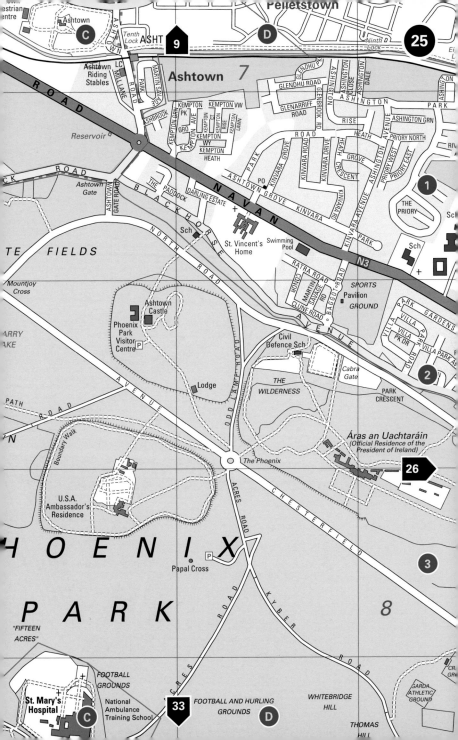

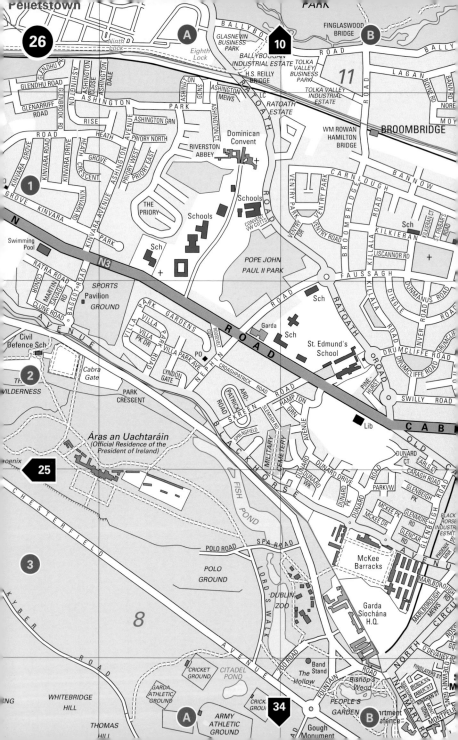

Pelletstown

26

A

10

FINGLASWOOD BRIDGE

B

BALLYBOGGAN
GLASNEVIN BUSINESS PARK
BALLYBOGGAN INDUSTRIAL ESTATE
H.S. REILLY BRIDGE
TOLKA VALLEY BUSINESS PARK

11

TOLKA VALLEY INDUSTRIAL ESTATE

BROOMBRIDGE

WM ROWAN HAMILTON BRIDGE

Ninth Lock
Eighth Lock

GLENDHU RD
GLENDHU ROAD
GLENARRIFF ROAD
GLENBROOK RD

ASHINGTON CLOSE
ASHINGTON DALE

ASHINGTON

ASHINGTON RISE
HEATH
GROVE
CRESCENT

KINVARA GROVE
KINVARA ROAD
KINVARA DRIVE

1

KINVARA

GROVE

KINVARA AVENUE

PARK

ASHINGTON AVENUE
PRIORY NORTH
PRIORY WEST
PRIORY EAST
ASHINGTON GRN

ASHINGTON CT
ASHINGTON MEWS

ASHINGTON
GDNS

LC
LC

RATOATH
ESTATE

Dominican Convent
RIVERSTON ABBEY

Schools

CONVENT VW COTTS

Swimming Pool

N

N3

THE PRIORY

Schools

Sch

Pope John Paul II Park

Sch

CARNLOUGH

VENTRY PARK
VENTRY DR
VENTRY PARK
VENTRY ROAD

BROOMBRIDGE ROAD

KILLALA
KILKIERAN

Sch

KILKIERAN CT
ST. FINBAR'S
LISCANNOR RD

FAUSSAGH

DINGLE
KILLALA ROAD
INVER ROAD
DUNMANUS ROAD

RATRA ROAD
MARTIN SAVAGE
CLUNE ROAD
BAGGOT ROAD

SPORTS
Pavilion
GROUND

PARK GARDENS
VILLA
VILLA
VILLA PK DR
VILLA PARK RD
VILLA PARK AVE

ROSSMORE
CROAGHPATRICK ROAD

Garda
Sch

Sch

St. Edmund's School

DRUMCLIFFE ROAD
DRUMCLIFFE RD

SWILLY ROAD

2

THE WILDERNESS

Civil Defence Sch

Cabra Gate

PARK CRESCENT

LYNDON GATE

PATRICK'S
SCREEN ARD.

SPRINGFIELD

MILITARY CEMETERY

SLEMISH RD

HAMPTON GRN

PINE HURST

Lib

CAB

25

Áras an Uachtaráin
(Official Residence of the President of Ireland)

BLACKHORSE

AVENUE

DUNARD AVENUE
DUNARD RD
DUNARD WK

DUNARD DRIVE
DUNARD PK
DUNARD

PARKVW

OLD

DUNARD CT
EARLS CT
CARAGH ROAD
GLENBEIGH PK

MCKEE PK
MCKEE DR

GLENMORE RD
GLENCAR RD

BLACK HORSE INDUSTRIAL ESTATE

Phoenix

3

CHESTERFIELD

FISH POND

SPA ROAD

POLO ROAD

POLO GROUND

LORD'S WALK

DUBLIN ZOO

McKee Barracks

Garda Síochána H.Q.

MARLBOROUGH RD
MARLBOROUGH MEWS

PHOENIX

CIRCU

8

KYBER

ROAD

AVENUE

ZOO ROAD

Band Stand
The Hollow

Bishop's Wood

FOUNTAIN ROAD

NORTH

INFIRMARY

O'DEVANEY GDNS

RINDLASTER'S
STANHOPE ST

BLACKHALL PL

ASHER'S
MONTPELI

WHITEBRIDGE HILL

CRICKET GROUND

GARDA ATHLETIC GROUND

CITADEL POND

CRICK. GROU

A

THOMAS HILL

ARMY ATHLETIC GROUND

34

PEOPLE'S GARDEN

Gough Monument

B

Department Defence

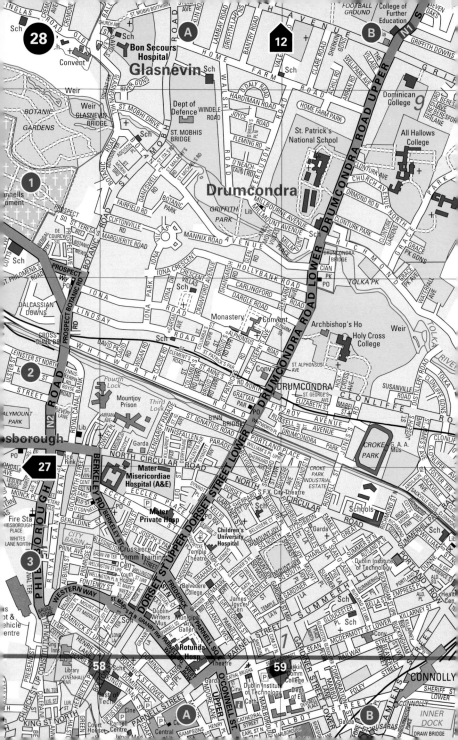

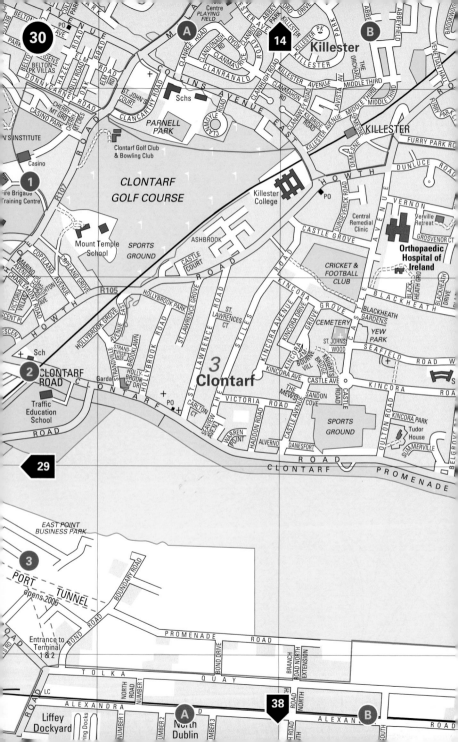

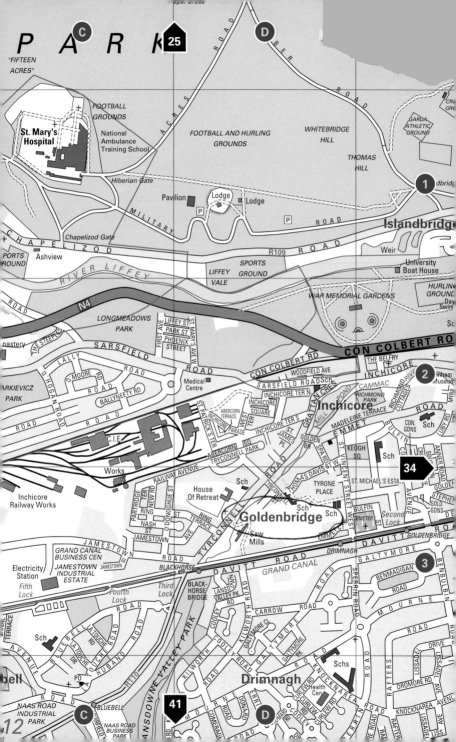

P A R k

"FIFTEEN
ACRES"

FOOTBALL
GROUNDS

St. Mary's
Hospital

National
Ambulance
Training School

A C R E S

FOOTBALL AND HURLING
GROUNDS

WHITEBRIDGE
HILL

GARDA
ATHLETIC
GROUND

CRE

THOMAS
HILL

Hiberian Gate

Chapelizod Gate

C H A P E L I Z O D

MILITARY

Pavilion

Lodge

Lodge

P

P

ROAD

1

dbridge

Islandbridge

Weir

PORTS
ROUND

Ashview

R109

ROAD

University
Boat House

RIVER LIFFEY

LIFFEY
VALE

SPORTS
GROUND

WAR MEMORIAL GARDENS

HURLING
GROUND
Day
Swim

ROAD

N4

nastery

The Steeples

LONGMEADOWS
PARK

FIRST AVE

LIFFEY ST.
PARK ST.
PHOENIX STREET

ST. MARY'S AVE

CON COLBERT RO

CON COLBERT RD

THE BELFRY

INCHICORE

inham
Museum

2

SARSFIELD

ROAD

WOODFIELD AVE

SARSFIELD ROAD

Sch

CAMMAC

LALLY

ROAD

MOORE

ROAD

BALLYNEETY RD

ROAD

HOGAN ROAD

ARKIEVICZ
PARK

ROAD

Medical
Centre

INCHICORE TER N.

Inchicore

INCHICORE TER S.

POND

Sch

RICHMOND
PARK

RICHMOND
COTTAGES

Sch

CON.
GDNS

ROAD

ABERCORN
TERRACE

INCHICORE
SQUARE

ST. PATRICK'S TER.

INCHICORE PARADE

INCHICORE TER.

ST.
JAMES
PL.

GRATTAN CRES

MADELEINE TERRACE

EMMET

BULFIN

ANNER ROAD

ROAD

C.I.E.

ABERCORN
SQ

TRYCONNELL PARK

GOLDEN
BR

SPAR RD

KEOGH
SQ

ST. VINCENT STREET WEST

ST. MICHAEL'S ESTATE

BULFIN
GDNS

Sch

Works

Inchicore
Railway Works

RAILWAY AVENUE

ODOGHUE ST.

House
Of Retreat

Sch

TRYCONNELL

THOMAS DAVIS ST.

TYRONE
PLACE

CEMETERY

Second
Lock

34

AVENUE

GOLD
GDNS

PARTRIDGE
TER.

RING
TER.

NASH
ST.

Sch

RING
TERRACE

Sch

Saw
Mills

EMMET

Goldenbridge

ROAD

Goldenbridge

JAMESTOWN

ST.

JAMESTOWN

AVE

TYRCONNELL

DAVITT

ROAD

DRIMNAGH

GALTYMORE

Electricity
Station
Fifth
Lock

GRAND CANAL
BUSINESS CEN

JAMESTOWN
INDUSTRIAL
ESTATE

JAMESTOWN

ROAD

BLACKHORSE

DAVITT

ROAD

GRAND CANAL

ROAD

BENMADIGAN

Road

3

GALTYMORE

SPERRIN ROAD

MOURNE

BENBULBIN RO

Fourth
Lock

Third
Lock

BLACK-
HORSE
BRIDGE

LANSD-
VALLEY PK
RD

CARROW

ROAD

ROAD

ROAD

ROAD

TERRACE

Sch

BLUEBELL

LATOUCHE
RD

LATOUCHE
DR

HUBAND

ROAD

ROAD

RITO

LANSDOWNE VALLEY PARK

KILWORTH

ROAD

COOLEY

ROAD

KILWORTH CL

GALTYMORE CL

COOLEY

ROAD

CARROW

ROAD

STEPHEN
GOLD
GDNS

DRIVE

LISSADE

DROMORE RD

KNOCKNAREA

ROAD

RAFTERS

ROAD

KNOCKNAGH

LISSADEL

bell

AVENUE

PO

BLUEBELL

NAAS ROAD
INDUSTRIAL
PARK

C

NAAS ROAD
BUSINESS
PARK

MOD

COMERAGH

CURLEW

ERRIGAL

ROAD

Drimnagh

COOLEY

Schs

Health
Cen

KNOCKNAREA

CURLEW

ERRIGAL ROAD

FERTIN ROAD

ROAD

DROMORE

LISSADE

D

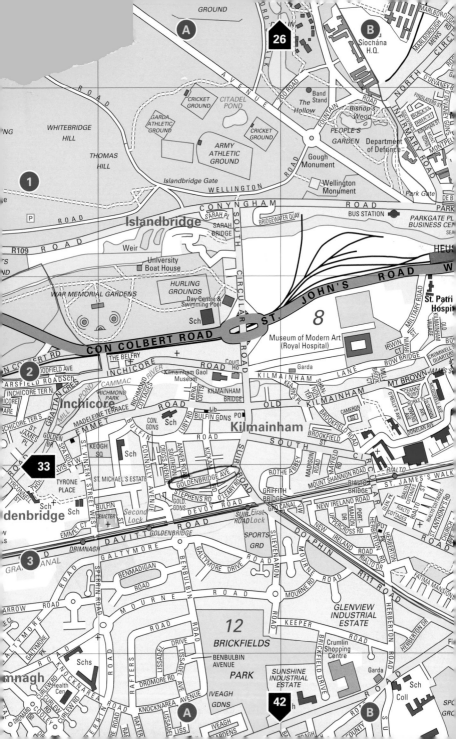

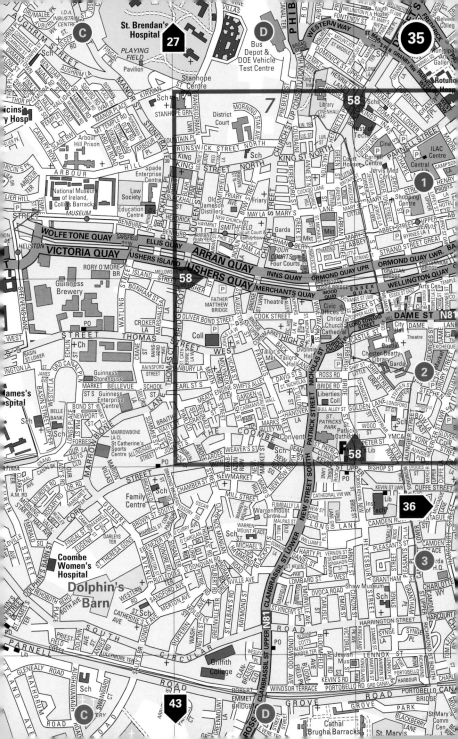

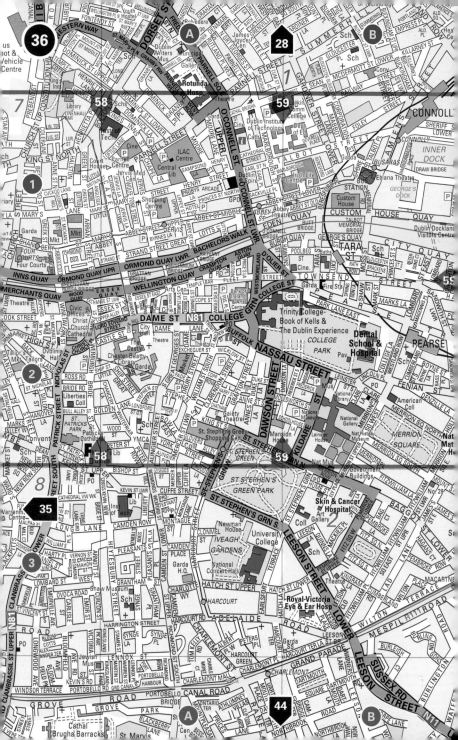

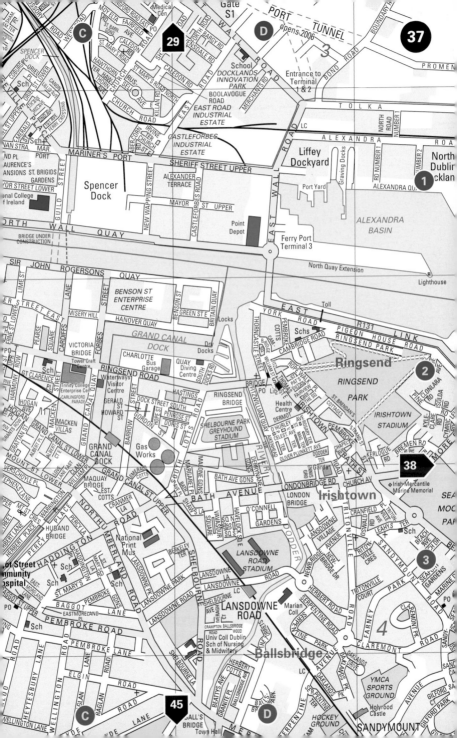

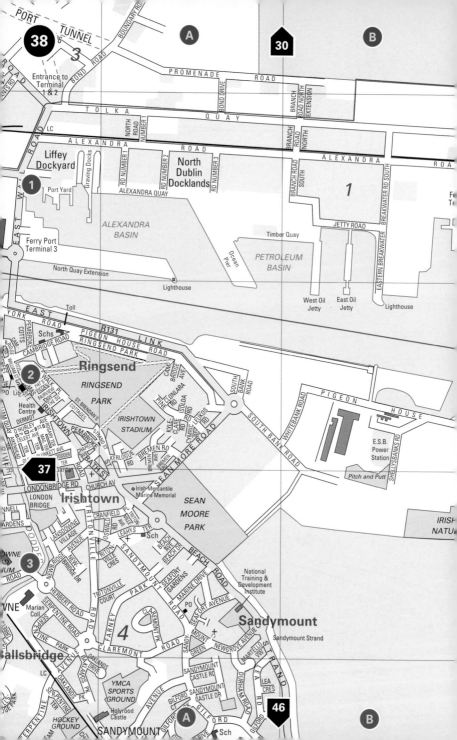

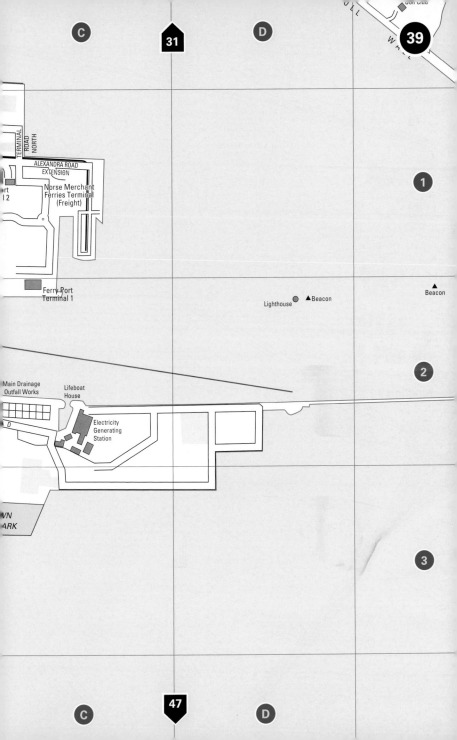

C
D
31
39

TERMINAL
ROAD
NORTH

ALEXANDRA ROAD
EXTENSION

Norse Merchant
Ferries Terminal
(Freight)

1

Ferry Port
Terminal 1

Lighthouse ● ▲Beacon   ▲
                              Beacon

2

Main Drainage
Outfall Works

Lifeboat
House

D

Electricity
Generating
Station

WN
ARK

3

C
D
47

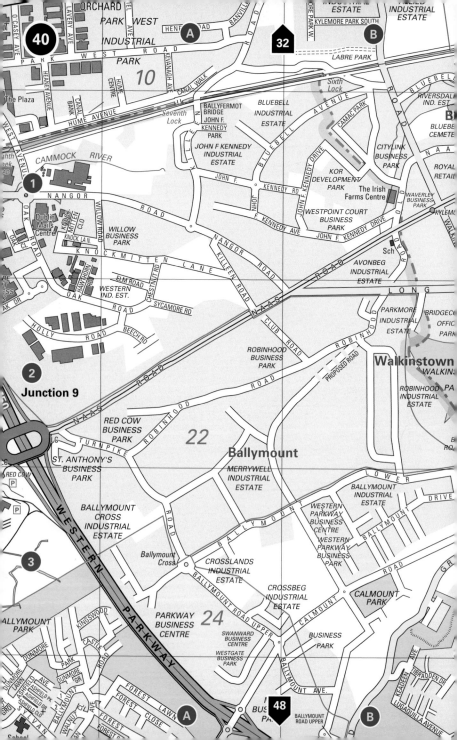

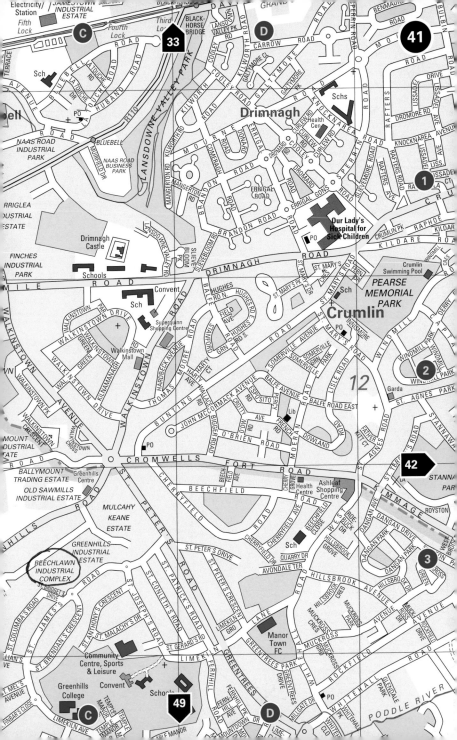

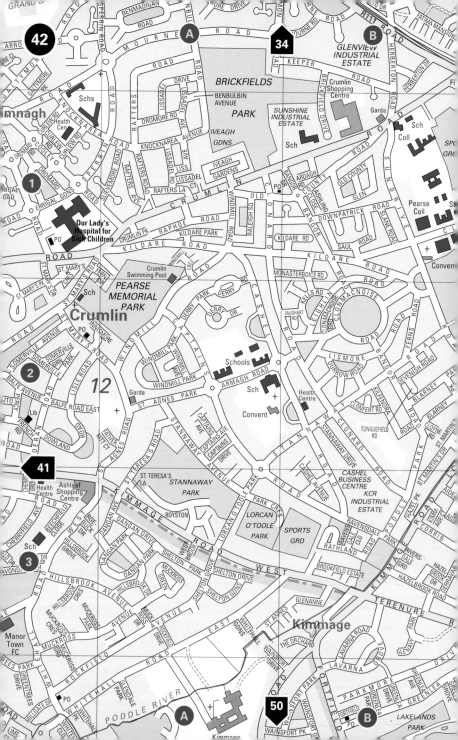

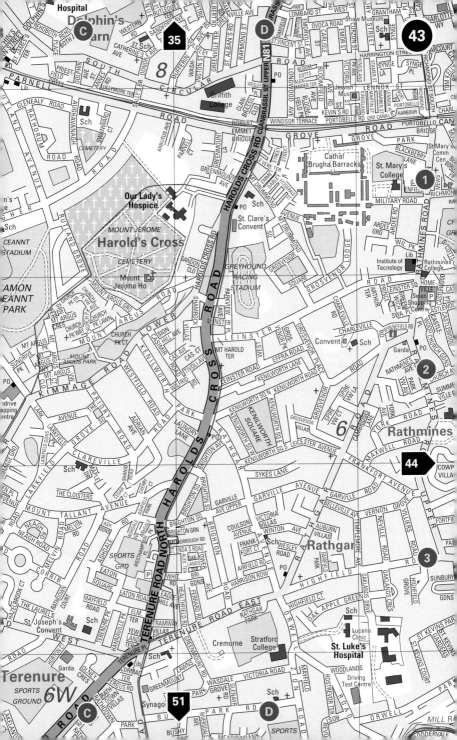

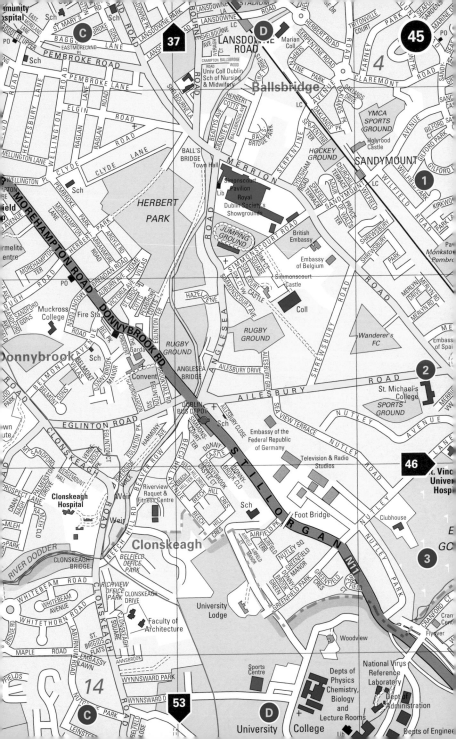

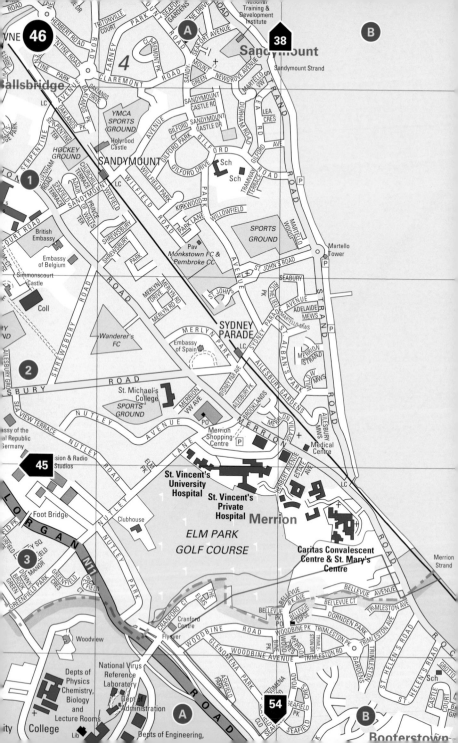

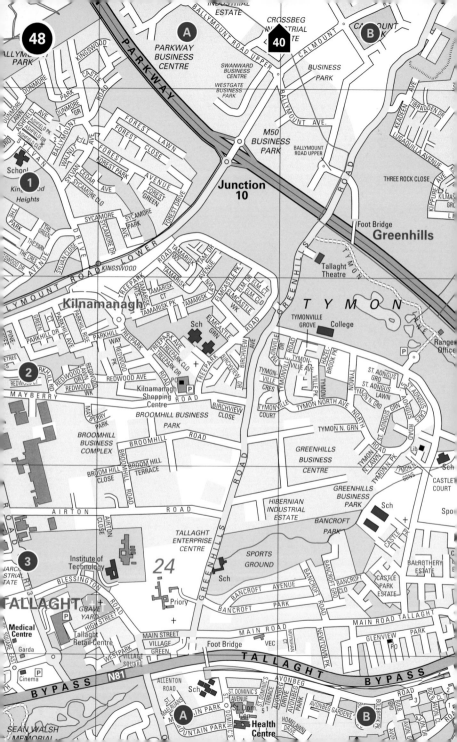

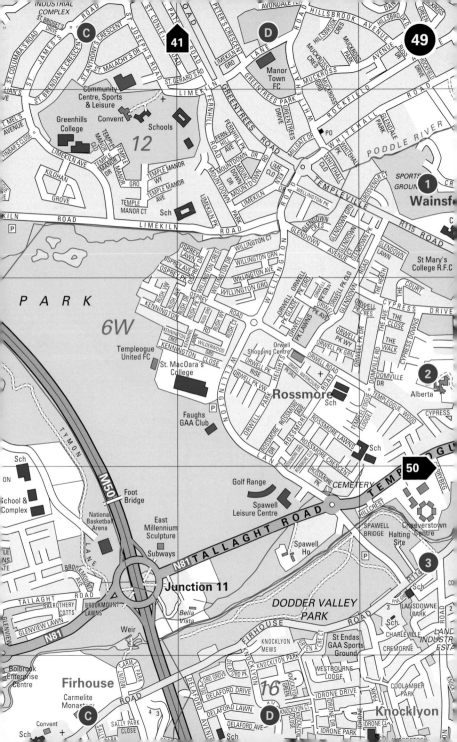

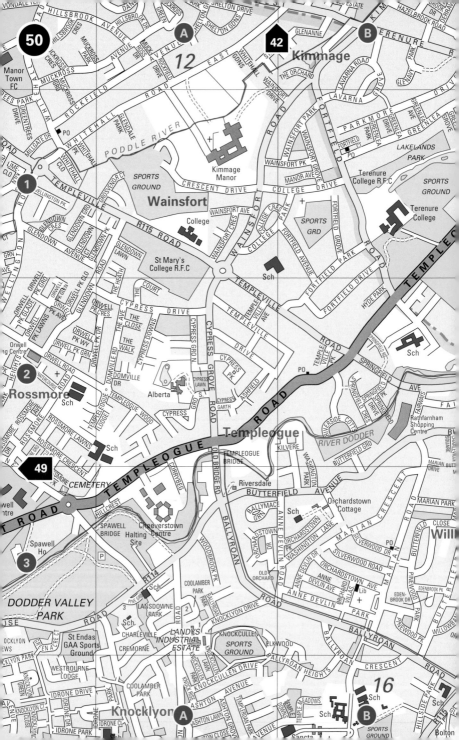

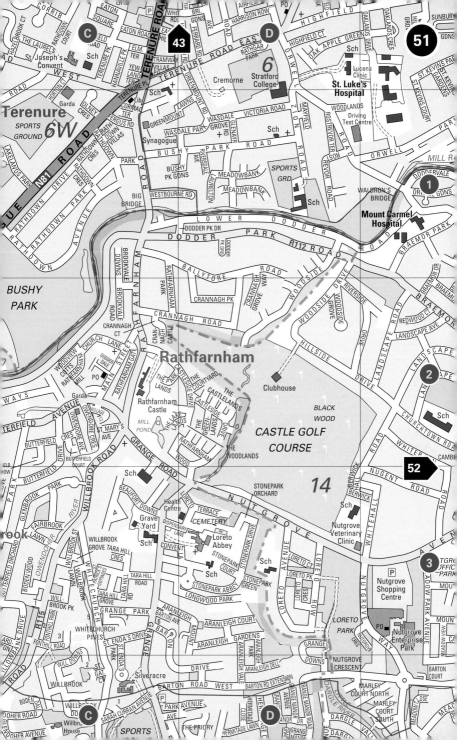

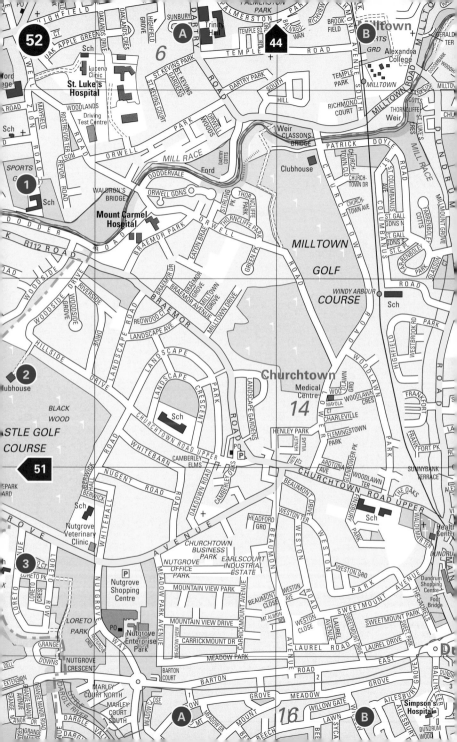

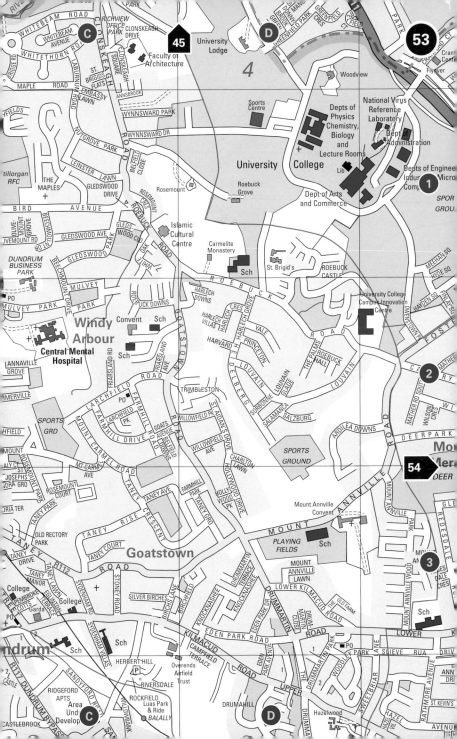

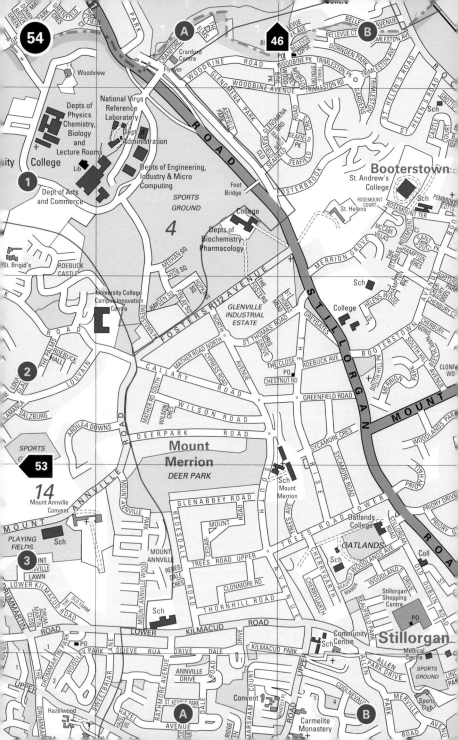

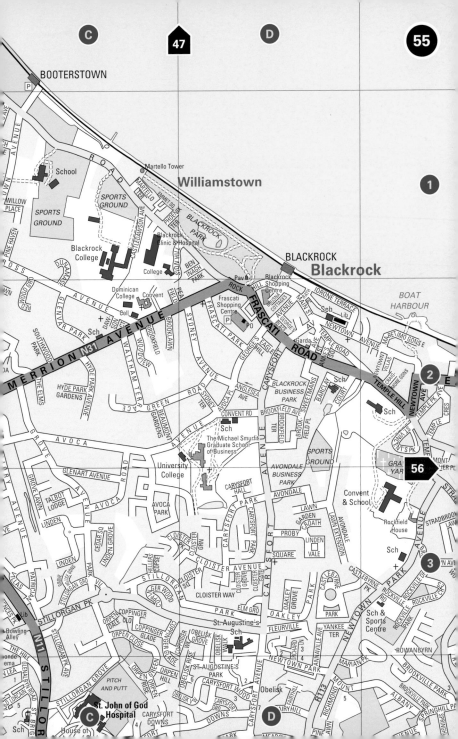

Lighthouse

Lighthouse

MARINA WEST BREAKWATER

WEST PIER

Automatic
Weather
Station

Captain Boyds
Memorial

DÚN LAOGHAIRE HARBOUR

MARINA EAST BREAKWATER

EAST PIER

Traders
Wharf

Jetties

Old
Pier

Old
Coastguard
Station

Car Ferry
Terminal

Band
Stand

Marine
Activity
Centre

OLD
HARBOUR

HARBOUR ROAD

Yacht
Club

DÚN
LAOGHAIRE

Mail Boat or
Carlisle Pier

Geographical
Pointer

OLD DUNLEARY RD   DUNLEARY RD   CROFTON ROAD

DUNLEARY HILL

CUMBERLAND
ST

CLARENCE

CROFTON
CROFTON TER

GEORGE'S PLACE

CHARLEMONT AVE

RNLI

LONGFORD PLACE

DE VESCI
GARDENS

DUNLEARY HILL

BARRETT
ST

SMITHS
VILLAS

YORK
TERRACE

GEORGE'S STREET LOWER

Town Hall

Yacht
Club

LOPERTON

THE SLOPES

WILLOW
BANK

IMC Cinema

ROSARY
GDNS

ROSARY
GDNS E

Library

St. Michael's
Hospital

Pavilion
Theatre

Coll

Lifeboat
Station

VESEY GARDENS

Shopping
Centre

MARINE RD

EBLANA AVE

Reservoir

HALPIN TER

VESEY PLACE

NORTHCOTE
AVE

DOMINICK ST

CROSS AVENUE

GEORGE'S STREET UPPER

PO

Shopping
Centre

ADELAIDE ST

MELLIFONT AVE

QUEEN'S ROAD

WINDSOR TER   NEWTOWNSMITH

DUN
LAOGHAIRE

KNAPTON
PARK

KNAPTON
LAWN

TIVOLI
AVE

TERRACE NORTH

Community
Training
Workshop

DESMOND AVE

WOLFE TONE AVE

MULGRAVE STREET

NORTHUMBERLAND AVE

SYDENHAM
MEWS

Sch & Coll

LA

CLARINDA
TER

Garda

MARINE
TER

CLARINDA
PARK WEST

PARK RD

CLARINDA
PARK NORTH

ROSMEEN GDNS

ROSMEEN PARK

PARK RD

SUMMERHILL ROAD

HADDINGTON TER

PEOPLE'S
PARK

MARINE ROAD

SCOTSMAN'S
BAY

College

MONKSTOWN
PARK

PATRICK

MOUNT TOWN ROAD UPPER

Monkstown
Castle

TIVOLI TERRACE EAST

TIVOLI ROAD

ST JOHN'S

MULGRAVE

CORRIG

District
Court

CROSTHWAITE PARK WEST

CLARINDA
MANOR

CROSTHWAITE PARK SOUTH

ROYAL TERRACE WEST

CROSTHWAITE PARK EAST

GLENAGEARY

Nursing
Home

TIVOLI TERRACE SOUTH

TIVOLI
PK

TIVOLI
ROAD

PRIM
ROSE
HILL

EGLINTON PK

Turkish
Consulate

Clubhouse

Sch

CORRIG
ROAD

ROYAL TERRACE EAST

CROSTHWAITE
PARK

Consulate

SANDYCOVE
GLASTHULE

EDEN PK

EDEN ROAD UPPER

EDEN TER

EDEN ROAD LOWER

GLASTHULE ROAD

LINK RD

MARINE
RD

HUDSON

GLANDORE PARK

MOUNT WOOD

ST PATRICK'S

DÚN LAOGHAIRE
GOLF COURSE

ROYAL TERRACE WEST

Nursing
Home

Sch

College

19 20

Pav

BEAU

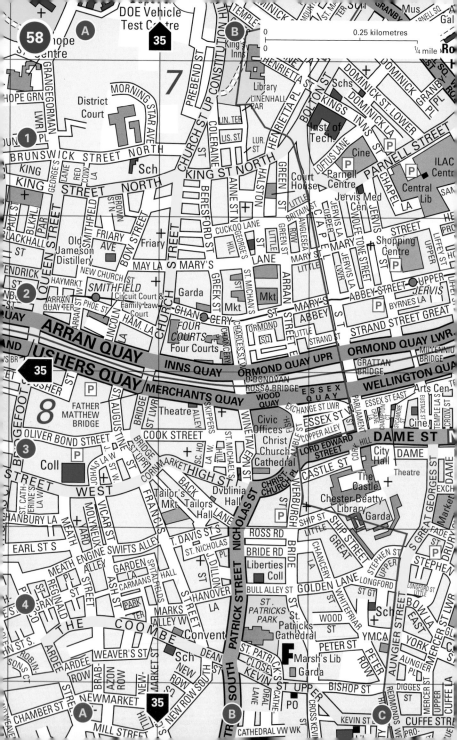

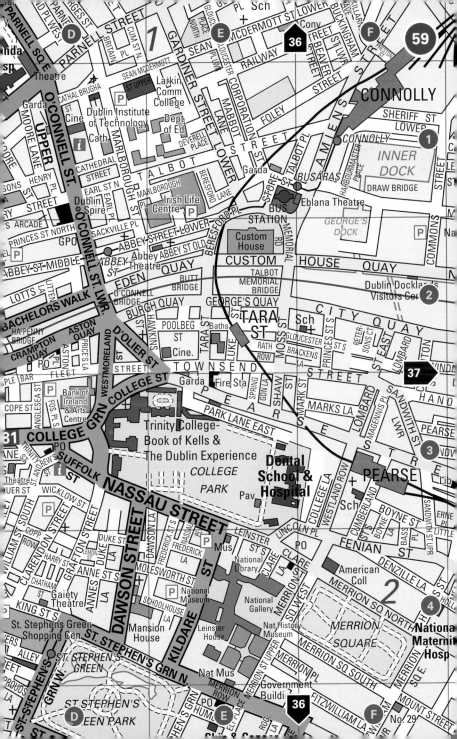

History

The ford over the River Liffey has been important since Celtic times and there was a thriving Christian community here from the 5thC, following their conversion by St Patrick in AD448. Marauding Vikings landed here in AD840, established a garrison port by the Dark Pool or Dubbh Linn, and within a few years had built a fortified town on the high ground above the estuary. Originally a base for raiding sorties, Dublin soon became a flourishing trading port as well, until Viking dominance was curtailed following a defeat by Brian Boru at the Battle of Clontarf in 1014.

Many of the Vikings had inter-married with the Irish and converted to Christianity but they were finally driven out by the Anglo-Normans under Strongbow, who took Dublin by storm and executed the Viking leader Hasculf. In 1170 Henry II arrived in Dublin, defeated Strongbow and received the submission of the Irish chieftains on the site of College Green. Henry granted the city by charter to the citizens of Bristol, thereby establishing English authority in Ireland.

The city and surrounding area, established as the seat of English government and protected by an enclosing wall and strategic castles, was known as The Pale. Frequently attacked during the 12thC and 13thC by the Irish clans based in the Wicklow Mountains, it was assaulted unsuccessfully by Edward Bruce in 1316. The city witnessed the crowning of Lambert Simnel, pretender to the English throne, in Christ Church in 1486. Unmoved by the rebellion of 'Silken' Thomas Fitzgerald in 1534, the inhabitants remained loyal to the English crown, supporting King Charles during the Civil Wars. Parliamentarians captured Dublin in 1647 and at this time the city was in decline. Following the Restoration of Charles I, however, Dublin underwent a great economic and architectural expansion.

By the end of the 17thC Dublin had become a flourishing commercial centre and during the following century the city was transformed into one of the most beautiful Georgian cities in Europe. The 'Wide Streets Commission' was established in 1757 and in 1773 the Paving Board was formed. New, elegantly spacious streets and squares were planned and palatial town houses built. In 1783 the Irish Parliament led by Henry Grattan was granted a short-lived autonomy but there was growing political unrest, which erupted in the unsuccessful uprising of 1798. Lord Edward Fitzgerald died of wounds sustained resisting arrest and in 1800 the detested Act of Union was established and the fortunes of the city began to wane.

With government now in London, few of the noblemen required their fine mansions and many returned to their country estates or left for London. Bitterness increased; in 1803 the Lord Chief Justice was assassinated and Robert Emmet, the leader of an abortive insurrection, was hanged. The newspaper The Nation was established by Charles Gavan Duffy in 1842, the heyday of the Repeal Movement. Daniel O'Connell was elected Lord Mayor in 1841 but only three years later he was interned in Richmond Gaol for campaigning for the repeal of the Union and the restoration of Grattan's 'Irish Parliament'. In 1873 the first great Home Rule Conference was held and in 1879 the Land League was formed, whose leaders, including Parnell and Davitt, were imprisoned as a consequence. In 1882 the new Chief Secretary, Lord Frederick Cavendish, and his Under-Secretary were assassinated in Phoenix Park by the Invincibles, a new terrorist organisation.

As the campaign for Home Rule gathered momentum, the Gaelic League, which started the Irish literary renaissance, was established by Douglas Hyde and Eóin MacNeill in 1893. Conceived as a means of reviving interest in the Irish language and traditional Irish life, the Gaelic League was also responsible for a remarkable literary revival resulting in the formation of the Abbey Theatre in 1904, where plays by J M Synge, Sean O'Casey and W B Yeats, amongst others, were performed.

In 1905 the Sinn Fein movement was formed, in 1909 the Irish Transport and General Workers Union was set up under the leadership of James Connolly, and in 1913 there was a massive strike, paralysing the city. The Irish Volunteers came into being in 1914, largely to combat the Ulster Volunteers who had been raised by Edward Carson in January 1913 to defend the right of Ulster to remain united with Great Britain. In 1916 the Irish Volunteers seized the General Post Office in Lower O'Connell Street as their headquarters and the Easter Rising had begun. It was quickly crushed, but so brutally that public conscience, clearly appalled, overwhelmingly elected Sinn Fein at the general election of December 1918 with Eamon de Valera as the new president.

Whilst the Dublin faction was openly in support of the guerrilla bands operating across the country, the Ulster Unionists set up their own provisional government, and the ambushes and assassinations which characterised the Anglo-Irish War, featuring the notorious Black and Tans, began· in bloody earnest. The war ended in the truce of July 1921. Despite the ratification of the Irish Free State in January 1922, a large and dissatisfied faction of leaders in the Irish movement took up arms against their former comrades and seized the Four Courts, which they held for two months. The subsequent shelling ordered by the new Dublin Government destroyed much of O'Connell Street but by the 1930s Dublin was emerging as a modern capital city and most of the public buildings had been restored.

Visiting Dublin

Passports

Citizens of the European Union need either a valid national identity card or passport to enter the Republic of Ireland. It is recommended that visitors from the UK bring a passport as a means of identification. Nationals of other countries require a passport and may require a visa. Enquiries should be made with a travel agent or Irish Embassy before travelling. The address of the Irish Embassy in London is 17 Grosvenor Place, SW1X 7HR.
Tel: 020 7235 2171 & (020 7225 7700 Passport/Visa)
Web: www.irlgov.ie

Banks

In February 2002 the Irish Punt (IEP) was withdrawn from circulation and the Euro (€) became the Irish unit of currency.
Banks open Monday–Friday from 10.00–16.00 and in Dublin most branches remain open until 17.00 on Thursdays. Major banks have 24 hour ATM machines which accept Plus and Cirrus symbols. Most credit cards, including all those with the Eurocard symbol, are widely accepted in shops, petrol stations, restaurants and hotels. Personal cheques from banks outside the Republic of Ireland are not accepted in the country without prior arrangement.

Bureaux de Change

Banks and Bureaux de Change generally offer the best exchange rates, although post offices, hotels, travel agents and some department stores offer exchange facilities.
There is a Bureau de Change at Dublin Airport and Dún Laoghaire ferry terminal. Dublin Airport also has a 24 hour Bank of Ireland foreign currency note exchanger and multi-currency Pass machines. Foreign exchange facilities are also to be found at the central bus station (Busáras) and Connolly railway station.

Language

English is spoken by everyone in Ireland. The country is officially bilingual with Irish (Gaelic) also spoken.

Customs and excise

The Republic of Ireland is a member of the European Union and, in accordance with EU regulations, travellers within the Community can import 90 litres of wine, 110 litres of duty paid beer and 800 cigarettes without question. Duty free sales of goods amongst European community members are now abolished. There are restrictions on taking certain food items into Ireland and checks should be made beforehand with the Irish Embassy or travel agent. Pets may not be brought into the country unless travelling from the UK, all other animals entering the country have to undergo quarantine.

Emergency

If you are involved in an emergency and require the services of the Police, Fire Brigade, Ambulance Service, or Coastguard, dial 999.

Medical treatment

Visitors to Ireland from European Community countries are entitled to free treatment by a general practitioner, medicines on prescription and treatment on a public ward in a hospital. British citizens need only show some form of identification such as a passport or driving licence to the doctor or hospital and request treatment under the EU health agreement. Visitors from other EU countries need to present form EIII (available from social security offices prior to departure). Health Insurance is recommended for visitors from outside the EU. No inoculations are required for travellers to Ireland.

Disabled visitors

The Irish Wheelchair association can offer advice and can arrange wheelchair hire. Tel: 01 818 6400 (Mon–Fri 09.00–17.00).
Web: www.iwa.ie
Irish Rail publishes a 'Guide for Mobility Impaired Passengers' which details the accessibility of all railway and DART stations. Obtainable at all manned stations or from the Access and Liaison officer, tel: 01 703 2634. Most of the Dublin Bus fleet is low floor easy access, and the buses run by Bus Éireann – Ireland's national bus company – are largely wheelchair accessible. Discounts on many ferry sailings from Britain are available to disabled drivers who wish to take their own car to Ireland. Drivers should contact the Disabled Drivers' Association or Motor Club in Britain to obtain the relevant form. This form should then be sent to the ferry company.

Phones

Most calls are dialled direct with cheaper call charge rates between 18.00 and 08.00 Mon–Fri and all day Saturday, Sunday and bank holidays. The dialling code for Dublin is 01 and so for calls within Dublin omit 01 at the beginning of a number. To dial Dublin from abroad dial the access code for Ireland (00353) plus the area code for Dublin (01) but omit the zero. For directory enquiries, including Northern Ireland, dial 11811; for Great Britain or International numbers dial 11818. For operator assistance dial 10 (Ireland and UK) or 114 for the international operator. Card phones are cheaper than payphones and are widely available. Callcards are obtainable at post offices, newsagents and supermarkets. Mobile phones can be brought into Ireland but visitors need to ensure their phone company has a roaming agreement with the Irish network operators.

Transport

Driving

Driving is on the left-hand side of the road in Ireland as in the UK; at roundabouts give way to traffic from the right. All drivers and front seat passengers must wear seat belts, and rear belts if they are fitted. Children under twelve must have a suitable restraint. Helmets are compulsory for motorcyclists. The maximum speed limit is 97kph (60mph) outside urban areas and the motorway speed limit is 110kph (70mph). In urban areas the limit is usually 50kph (30mph). There are on-the-spot fines for speeding and drink driving laws are strict. Parking infringements are taken seriously and illegally parked cars in Dublin City are liable to be clamped or towed away to the Corporation pound with a recovery charge payable.

Distances and speed limits are now both measured in kilometres (speed limit signs changed on 20th January 2005). Place names are generally in English and Irish. Unleaded petrol and diesel are widely available. Recorded weather information is available for Dublin by calling the Meteorological Service Tel: 1550 123 854. There is a charge for this call.

Car hire

Car hire is readily available in Dublin, although in July and August there is a high demand and it is best to book in advance. You must have held a full licence for 2 years and be under 70 and over 23. Some companies make exceptions to this but charges may be higher. A full valid driving licence of your country of residence (which you must have held for at least two years without endorsements) must be presented at the time of hiring.

Most international car rental companies have offices in Dublin and cars can also be hired at the airport and Dún Laoghaire ferry terminal. The cost of hire will depend on the type of car and time of year and it is worthwhile shopping around. It is important, however, to check the insurance details and ensure Collision Damage Waiver is included. A deposit is usually payable at the time of booking or before you drive away. Fly-drive or rail-sail-drive packages arranged by travel agents or the air and ferry companies can be an economical and easy way of hiring a car.

Public transport

Dublin is linked with the cities and towns of Ireland by a network of rail and bus services overseen by Córas Iompair Éireann (CIE), which is Ireland's National Transport Authority. The CIE organises Iarnód Éireann (Irish Rail), Bus Éireann (Irish Bus) and Dublin Bus. Bus and rail timetables can be bought at most newsagents. Unlimited use period tickets are available for use on rail and/or bus services.

Bus and coach travel

Dublin Bus (Bus Átha Cliath) operates the public bus services in Dublin and the surrounding area. Pre-paid tickets can be bought for periods of time ranging from one day to one month and are good value for money. They can be bought at any of the many bus ticket agencies in the city, from the CIE information desk at Dublin Airport or at Dublin Bus head office at 59 O'Connell Street Upper. Many routes operate an exact fare only policy. Dublin Bus also operates late night services (Nitelink) to most suburban areas on Thursdays, Fridays and Saturdays, links to the ferry ports and railway stations, and also sightseeing tours.
Open Mon–Sat 09.00–19.00.
Tel: 01 872 0000 or 01 873 4222
Web: www.dublinbus.ie has details of routes, timetables, and special tickets.

National bus services between Dublin, Dublin Airport and other major cities and towns are provided by Irish Bus (Bus Éireann) and many private companies. Bus Éireann also operate combined bus and ferry services between Britain and Ireland.
Dublin Bus Station (Bus Áras), Store Street.
Tel: 01 836 6111
Web: www.buseireann.ie
Scheduled daily hop-on hop-off city sightseeing tours are operated by Gray Line, Guide Friday and City Sightseeing. Buses depart every 10-20 minutes from 09.30-17.30; also available are seasonal half and full day excursions further afield including to Newgrange and the Boyne Valley, Powerscourt Gardens, Glendalough and

Wicklow. 3 & 4 day trips to Kerry and Dingle are also available. Information and tickets from the Desk 1 at the Dublin Tourism Centre, Suffolk Street.
Tel: 01 605 7705
Web: www.irishcitytours.com
Email: info@irishcitytours.com

Taxis
Taxis are available at taxi ranks or by phoning one of the many radio-linked taxi companies. There are numerous taxi ranks including ones on O'Connell Street, Dame Street, and St. Stephen's Green West.
Taxi companies are listed in the Golden Pages classified telephone directory.

Rail travel
Dublin Connolly and Dublin Heuston are the two mainline railway stations and Irish Rail (Iarnród Éireann) operates an excellent service to most towns and cities in Ireland. Irish rail also operates the suburban rail network in Dublin and DART (Dublin Area Rapid Transit) with 26 stations between Howth on the north of Dublin Bay to Bray in the south.
Tel: 01 850 366222
Web: www.irishrail.ie

Bike hire
Tracks Bikes, Botanic Road, Glasnevin.
Tel: 01 850 0252
Irish Cycling Safaris, Belfield Bike Shop, University College Dublin.
Tel: 01 260 0749

Lost property
Enquire at the nearest police station or:
Dublin Airport. Open Mon–Fri 07.00-22.30.
Tel: 01 814 5555
Dublin Bus. Open Mon–Fri 08.45–17.00.
Tel: 01 703 1321
Irish Bus. Open Mon–Fri 09.00–17.00.
Tel: 01 703 2489
Irish Rail (Connolly Station). Open Mon–Fri 09.00–17.00. **Tel: 01 703 2358**
Irish Rail (Heuston Station). Open Mon–Fri 09.00–17.00. **Tel: 01 703 2102**

Places of interest

Arbour Hill Cemetery, Arbour Hill.
The leaders of the Easter Rising are buried here.
Bank of Ireland, College Green.
Designed by Sir Edward Lovett Pearce in 1729, it was later enlarged by James Gandon and Robert Parke between 1785–1794. Originally the Parliament House, the first of a series of great public buildings erected in 18thC Dublin, it was

taken over by the Bank of Ireland in 1804. A statue of Henry Grattan, leader of the Irish parliament of 1782, stands outside on the lawn of College Green. Two huge 18thC tapestries commemorating the Siege of Londonderry and the Battle of the Boyne hang in the oak-panelled chamber of the former House of Lords.
There are guided tours of the House of Lords on Tuesdays at 10.30, 11.30, and 13.45.
Admission free. Disabled access.
Tel: 01 671 1488

Bank of Ireland Arts Centre, Foster Place.
An arts centre which presents classical concerts and recitals and houses an interactive museum. The museum illustrates the history of the adjoining College Green buildings where many of the dramatic events of Irish history were played out in the Irish parliament. The museum also reflects the role played by the Bank of Ireland in the economic and social development of Ireland.
Open Tues-Fri 9.30–16.00, Sat 10.00-16.00.
Disabled access.
Tel: 01 671 1488

Belvedere House, North Great George's Street.
One of the best 18thC mansions in Dublin. Taken over by Jesuit Belvedere College in 1841; James Joyce went to school here between 1893–1898. Not open to the public.

Casino, off Malahide Road, Marino.
A miniature 18thC neo-classical masterpiece designed by Sir William Chambers and recently restored. Casino means 'small house'. It was built as a pleasure house beside Marino House (now demolished), Lord Charlemont's country residence, for the enormous sum of £60,000. It is a compact building, remarkably containing 16 rooms, with many interesting architectural features. The interior circular hall, ringed by columns, is crowned by a coffered dome. The graceful roof urns disguise chimneys while the columns conceal drainpipes.
Open Daily (May-Oct) 10.00-17.00 (18.00 Jun-Sept); (Nov-Apr) Sat & Sun 12.00-16.00 (17.00 Apr). Closed January. Access by guided tour only. Last tour leaves 45 mins before closing. Access to interior by stairway.
Tel: 01 833 1618

City Hall, Dame Street.
Completed in 1779, this fine building was designed as The Royal Exchange. Subsequent use included a prison and corn exchange before being taken over by the city in 1852. Presently used by Dublin City Council. It features a beautiful Corinthian coffered dome and portico.

The archives include the original charter of 1171 in which Henry II granted Dublin to the citizens of Bristol.

Open Mon-Sat 10.00-17.15, Sun 14.00-17.00.
Tel: 01 222 2204
Web: www.dublincity.ie/cityhall

Custom House Visitor Centre, Custom House Quay.

The Custom House, with a magnificent long river frontage, is an architectural masterpiece designed by James Gandon and completed in 1791. Exhibits relate to James Gandon and the history of the Custom House itself, with illustrations of how the building was restored after it was gutted by fire in 1921. The building is best viewed from the south bank of the River Liffey.

Open: Wed-Fri (Nov-16 Mar) & Mon–Fri (17 Mar-Nov) 10.00–12.30, Sat & Sun 14.00–17.00. Disabled access by prior arrangement.
Tel: 01 888 2538

Drimnagh Castle, Long Mile Road.

Ireland's only castle with a flooded moat. This Norman castle has a fully restored Great Hall, medieval undercroft and 17thC style formal garden.

Open (Apr–Sept) Wed, Sat, Sun 12.00–17.00; (Oct–March) Wed, Sun 12.00–17.00. Last tour 16.15. Open at other times by appointment.
Tel: 01 450 2530
Email: drimnaghcastle@eircom.net

Dublin Castle, off Dame Street.

The Castle was originally built between 1204–1228 as part of Dublin's defensive system. The Record Tower is the principal remnant of the 13thC Anglo-Norman fortress and has walls 5 metres (16ft) thick but what remains today is largely the result of 18thC and 19thC re-building. It now contains the Garda (Police) Museum. The 15thC Bermingham Tower was once the state prison where Red Hugh O'Donnell was interned in the 16thC; it was rebuilt in the 18thC. The State Apartments, Undercroft and ornate Chapel Royal are open to the public. The State Apartments, dating from the British Administration, were once the residence of the English Viceroys and are now used for Presidential Inaugurations and state receptions. Within these apartments are the magnificent throne room and St Patrick's Hall, 25 metres (82ft) long with a high panelled and decorated ceiling. In the undercroft can be seen the remains of a Viking fortress, part of the original moat, and part of the old city wall.

The Chester Beatty Library exhibits art treasures from around the world.

Open: Mon–Fri 10.00–17.00, Sat & Sun 14.00–17.00. Access by guided tour only. Disabled access/toilets.
Tel: 01 677 7129
Web: www.dublincastle.ie
Email: info@dublincastle.ie

Dublin Experience, Trinity College.

A film about the story of Dublin which is shown every hour in the Trinity College Arts Building.

Open daily from late May to late Sept 10.00–17.00. Last showing 17.00.
Tel: 01 608 1688

Dublin Writers Museum, Parnell Square.

Tracing the history of Irish literature from its earliest times to the 20thC, this museum is a celebration of this literary heritage. Writers and playwrights including Jonathan Swift, George Bernard Shaw, Oscar Wilde, W B Yeats, James Joyce and Samuel Beckett are brought to life through personal items, portraits, their books and letters. There is also a room dedicated to children's authors. The museum is housed in a restored 18thC Georgian mansion with decorative stained-glass windows and ornate plaster-work.

Open Mon–Sat 10.00–17.00 (18.00 Jun-Aug), Sun 11.00–17.00. Disabled access to ground floor. Last entry 45 mins before closing.
Tel: 01 872 2077
Email: writers@dublintourism.ie

Dvblinia, Christ Church, St. Michael's Hill.

A multi-media recreation of Dublin life in medieval times from the Anglo-Norman arrival in 1170 to the dissolution of the monasteries in 1540. There is a scale model of the medieval city, a life size reconstruction of a merchant's house, and numerous Viking and Norman artefacts from excavations at nearby Wood Quay. The building is the old Synod Hall and is linked to Christ Church Cathedral by an ornate Victorian pedestrian bridge.

Open Mon-Fri 10.00-17.00 (Oct-Mar 11.00-16.00); Sat & Sun 10.00-16.00. Disabled access.
Tel: 01 679 4611
Web: www.dublina.ie
Email: marketing@dublinia.ie

Dublin Zoo, Phoenix Park.

The Zoo is well known for its captive-breeding programme and is committed to the conservation and protection of endangered species. The 'big cats', living in enclosures which simulate their natural habitats, include lions, tigers, jaguars and snow leopards. Attractive gardens surround two natural lakes where pelicans, flamingos, ducks and geese abound, while the islands in the lakes are home to chimps, gibbons, spider monkeys and orang-utans. A recent development 'Fringes of the

Arctic' has provided a state of the art enclosure for the polar bears and is home to wolves, arctic foxes and snowy owls. After the acquisition of more land, the zoo doubled in size in 2000 and an African Plains area has been developed providing greater space and freedom for giraffe, hippo, rhino and other African animals and birds. The city farm and pets' corner provide encounters with Irish domestic animals. Other attractions include a zoo train, discovery centre, and 'meet the keeper' programme.
Open: Mon–Sat 09.30–17.00, Sun 10.30–17.00. Last admission 16.00. Closes at dusk in winter.
Tel: 01 474 8900
Web: www.dublinzoo.ie
Email: info@dublinzoo.ie

Dunsink Observatory, Castleknock, Dublin 15.
Founded in 1783, it is one of the oldest observatories in the world and houses the astronomy section of the School of Cosmic Physics. Public open nights are held on the first and third Wednesdays of each month from October to March inclusive at 20.00. Requests for tickets for the open nights must be made by post to the Observatory.
Tel: 01 838 7911
Web: www.dunsink.dias.ie
Email: cwoods@dunsinkdias.ie

Four Courts, Inns Quay.
Originally designed by James Gandon in 1785, it was partially destroyed by a fire in 1922 in the struggle for Irish independence but restored again by 1932. The Four Courts has a 137 metre (450ft) river frontage and the building is fronted by a Corinthian portico with six columns. The square central block with circular hall is crowned by a copper-covered lantern-dome. Housed here are the Irish Law Courts and Law Library.
Tel: 01 888 6457/6460
Web: www.courts.ie
Email: schooltours@courts.ie

Fry Model Railway, Malahide Castle, Malahide.
Covering 233 square metres (2,500sq.ft) this is one of the world's largest working miniature railways and is a delight for children and adults alike. Besides the track, the railway has stations, bridges, trams, buses and barges and includes the Dublin landmarks of Heuston station and O'Connell Bridge. On display are the hand constructed models of Irish trains by Cyril Fry, draughtsman and railway engineer, who made them from the 1930s until his death in 1974. Perfectly engineered, the models represent the earliest trains to those of more modern times.

Situated in the grounds of Malahide Castle, 13km (8 miles) north of Dublin city centre.
Open (Apr-Sept) Mon-Sat 10.00-17.00, Sun & public holidays 14.00–18.00; Closed 13.00-14.00 and Oct-Mar.
Tel: 01 846 3779
Web: www.malahidecastle.com
Email: fryrailway@dublintourism.ie

GAA Museum, Croke Park.
The Gaelic Athletic Association (GAA) is Ireland's largest sporting and cultural organisation and is dedicated to promoting the games of hurling, Gaelic football, handball, rounders and camogie. The museum is at Croke Park, home of Irish hurling and football, and traces the history of Gaelic sports and their place in Irish culture right up to the present day. Interactive exhibits allow visitors the chance to try out the skills of the games for themselves. National trophies and sports equipment are also on display.
Open Mon-Sat 09.30-17.00, Sun 12.00-17.00. Last admission 1/2 hour before closing. All groups must be pre-booked.
Tel: 01 819 2323
Web: www.gaa.ie/museum
Email: gaamuseum@crokepark.ie

Heraldic Museum, Kildare Street.
Part of the National Library of Ireland, the museum illustrates the uses of heraldry with displays of coat of arms and banners and a collection of heraldic glass, seals, stamps, and coins.
Open Mon-Wed 10.00-20.30; Thurs-Fri 10.00-16.30; Sat 10.00-12.30. Admission is free.
Tel: 01 603 0311
Email: herald@nli.ie

General Post Office, O'Connell Street.
Designed by Francis Johnston and completed in 1818. A century later the GPO became the headquarters of the 1916 Easter Rising and the Proclamation of the Irish Republic was read from the steps by Patrick Pearse. Bullet marks can still be seen on the pillars. Badly damaged in 1922 in the fight for independence, it was restored in 1929. A bronze sculpture, The Death of Cúchulainn by Oliver Sheppard, stands within the building.
Tel: 01 705 7000
Email: customer.service@anpost.ie

Guinness Storehouse, St. James's Gate.
The story of Guinness is told from its beginnings in 1759, how it is made and the advertising campaigns used to make it internationally famous. Housed in St James's Gate Brewery and spread over six floors, on the highest of which can be found the bar 'Gravity',

from which a 360° view of Dublin can be enjoyed. Open July-Aug 9.30-20.00; Sept-June 9.30-17.00. Disabled access.
Tel: 01 408 4800
Web: www.guinnessstorehouse.com
Email: guinness-storehouse@guinness.com

Ha'penny Bridge, Crampton Quay.
An elegant arching narrow cast-iron pedestrian bridge spanning the Liffey; it was first opened in 1816 and the name derives from the toll once charged.

Irish Jewish Museum, Walworth Road
Opened by President Herzog of Israel in 1985, exhibits relate to the Jewish community in Ireland including synagogue fittings and the reconstruction of a typical Dublin Jewish kitchen of 100 years ago.
Open (May–Sept) Sun, Tues, Thurs 11.00–15.30; (Oct–Apr) Sun 10.30–14.30. Admission is free.
Tel: 01 490 1857

Irish Museum of Modern Art, Military Road, Kilmainham.
Opened in the 17thC Royal Hospital building and grounds in 1991, the museum is an important institution for the collection of modern and contemporary art. A wide variety of work by major established 20thC figures and that of younger contemporary artists is presented in an ever changing programme of exhibitions, drawn from the museum's own collection and from public and private collections world-wide.
Open Tues–Sat 10.00–17.15, Sun & some bank holidays 12.00–17.15. Admission is free.
Tel: 01 612 9900
Web: www.modernart.ie
Email: info@imma.ie

James Joyce Centre, North Great George's Street.
A museum in a restored Georgian town house, built in 1784, devoted to the great novelist and run by members of his family. Dennis J Maginni, dancing master in Joyce's novel Ulysses, ran his dancing school from this house. The library contains editions of Joyce's work and that of other Irish writers as well as biographical and critical writing. There is a set of biographies of real Dublin people fictionalised in Ulysses, and also the door from the house occupied by the central character of the novel, Leopold Bloom and his wife Molly. The centre hosts readings, lectures and debates on all aspects of Joyce and his literature and conducts guided city tours.
Open Tues–Sat 09.30–17.00.
Tel: 01 878 8547
Web: www.jamesjoyce.ie
Email: info@jamesjoyce.ie

James Joyce Museum, Sandycove.
The museum is housed in the Martello Tower which Joyce used as the setting for the opening chapter of Ulysses, his great work of fiction which immortalised Dublin. Joyce stayed here briefly in 1904 and the living room and view from the gun platform remains much as he described it in the novel. The museum collection includes personal possessions, letters, photographs, first editions and items that reflect the Dublin of Joyce. Situated 13km (8 miles) south of Dublin city centre, the tower was one of 15 defensive towers built along Dublin Bay in 1804 to withstand a threatened invasion from Napoleon.
Open (Mar–Oct) Mon–Sat 10.00–17.00, Sun 14.00–18.00. Closed 13.00–14.00.
Tel: 01 280 9265
Email: joycetower@dublintourism.ie

Kilmainham Gaol, Inchicore Road, Kilmainham.
Built as a gaol in 1796, Kilmainham is now dedicated to the Irish patriots imprisoned there from 1792–1924, including Emmet and his United Irishmen colleagues, the Fenians, the Invincibles and the Irish Volunteers of the Easter Rising. Patrick Pearse and James Connolly were executed in the prison yard and Eamon de Valera, later Prime Minister and then President of Ireland, was one of the last inmates. After its closure in 1924 Kilmainham re-opened as a museum in 1966. It is one of the largest unoccupied gaols in Europe with tiers of cells and overhead catwalks. Access is by guided tour only and features an exhibition and audio-visual show on the political and penal history of the gaol.
Open daily (May–Sept) 09.30–17.00; (Oct–Mar) Mon–Fri 09.30–16.00, Sun 10.00–17.00. Disabled toilets. Tours for visitors with special needs by prior arrangement.
Tel: 01 453 5984

King's Inns, Henrietta Street.
The Dublin Inns of Court is a glorious classical building, partly built to the plans of James Gandon at the end of the 19thC. The library was founded in 1787 and contains a large legal collection with about 100,000 books. The courtyard opens into Henrietta Street, where Dublin's earliest Georgian mansions remain.
Web: www.kingsinns.ie

Leinster House, Kildare Street.
Originally a handsome town mansion designed by Richard Castle for the Duke of Leinster in 1745; it has been a Parliament House since 1922. The Dáil Éireann (House of Representatives) and Seanad Éireann (Senate) sit here. The

house has two contrasting facades: an imposing formal side facing Kildare Street while from Merrion Square the building has more of the appearance of a country residence. Anybody wanting a tour of Irish Parliament must contact their respective embassy in Dublin where arrangements can be made. Advance notice is required.
Tel: 01 618 3000

Malahide Castle, Malahide.

Originally built in 1185, it was the seat of the Talbot family until 1973 when the last Lord Talbot died; the history of the family is detailed in the Great Hall alongside many family portraits. Malahide also has a large collection of Irish portrait paintings, mainly from the National Gallery, and is furnished with fine period furniture. Within the 100 hectares (250 acres) of parkland surrounding the castle is the Talbot Botanic Gardens, largely created by Lord Milo Talbot between 1948 and 1973. The grounds include walled gardens and a shrubbery with a collection of southern hemisphere plants. Malahide is situated 13km (8 miles) north of Dublin city centre.
Open Mon-Sat 10.00-17.00; Sundays & Bank Holidays 11.00-17.00 (18.00 Apr-Oct); Closed 13.00-14.00. Combined tickets with Fry Model Railway are available.
Tel: 01 846 2184
Web: www.malahidecastle.com
Email: malahidecastle@dublintourism.ie

Mansion House, Dawson Street.

Built in 1705, this Queen Anne style house has been the official residence of the Lord Mayor of Dublin since 1715. The first Irish parliament assembled here in 1919 to adopt Ireland's declaration of Independence and ratify the 1916 proclamation of the Irish Republic. Not open to the public.

National Museum of Ireland, Archaeology and History, Kildare Street.

Houses a fabulous collection of national antiquities including prehistoric gold ornaments, and outstanding examples of Celtic and medieval art. The 8thC Ardagh Chalice and Tara Brooch are amongst the treasures. The entire history of Ireland is reflected in the museum with 'The Road to Independence Exhibition' illustrating Irish history from 1916–1921. Additionally, there is an Ancient Egypt exhibition.
Open Tues–Sat 10.00–17.00, Sun 14.00–17.00. Admission is free. A Museumlink bus linking the 3 sites of the National Museum operates regularly throughout the day.
Tel: 01 677 7444
Web: www.museum.ie

National Museum of Ireland, Decorative Arts and History (Collins Barracks), Benburb Street.

Ireland's museum of decorative arts and economic, social, political and military history, based in the oldest military barracks in Europe. Major collections include Irish silver, Irish country furniture, and costume jewellery and accessories. The work of museum restoration and conservation is explained and the Out of Storage gallery provides visitors with a view of artefacts in storage.
Open Tues–Sat 10.00–17.00; Sun 14.00–17.00. Admission is free. Full disabled access. A Museumlink bus linking the 3 sites of the National Museum operates regularly throughout the day.
Tel: 01 677 7444
Web: www.museum.ie

National Museum of Ireland, Natural History, Merrion Street.

First opened in 1857 and hardly changed since then, the museum houses a large collection of stuffed animals and the skeletons of mammals and birds from both Ireland and the rest of the world. The exhibits include three examples of the Irish Great Elk which became extinct over 10,000 years ago and the skeleton of a Basking Shark. Fascinating glass reproductions of marine specimens, known as the Blaschka Collection, are found on the upper gallery.
Open Tues–Sat 10.00–17.00; Sun 14.00–17.00. Admission is free. A Museumlink bus linking the 3 sites of the National Museum operates regularly throughout the day.
Tel: 01 677 7444
Web: www.museum.ie

National Print Museum, Haddington Road.

Situated in the former Garrison Chapel in Beggars Bush Barracks, the museum illustrates the development of printing from the advent of printing to the use of computer technology with a unique collection of implements and machines from Ireland's printing industry.
Open Mon–Fri 09.00–17.00, Sat & Sun and Bank Holidays 14.00–17.00.
Tel: 01 660 3770

National Sea Life Centre, Bray.

Features marine life from the seas around Ireland including stingrays, conger eels, and sharks; also freshwater fish from Irish rivers and streams. A touch pool gives children the opportunity to pick up small creatures such as starfish, crabs and sea anemones. By way of contrast is the fascinating 'Danger in the Depths' tank with many sea creatures from around the world which have proved harmful or fatal to humans.

Open (May-Sept) Mon-Fri 10.00-18.00, Sat & Sun 10.00-18.30; (Oct-Apr) Mon-Fri 11.00-17.00, Sat & Sun 11.00-18.00.

Tel: 01 286 6939

National Transport Museum, Howth.

A collection of buses, trams, trucks, tractors and fire engines, some dating back to 1880, along with other memorabilia from the transport industry.

Open (Jun–Aug) Mon–Fri 10.00–17.00, Sat & Sun 14.00–17.00; (Sept-May) Sat & Sun only 14.00–17.00. Bank holidays 14.00–17.00.

Tel: 01 848 0831

Web: www.nationaltransportmuseum.org

Email: info@nationaltransportmuseum.org

National Wax Museum, Granby Row.

Over 300 life-size wax figures of well-known people and personalities from the past and present ranging from Eamon De Valera to Elvis Presley. Also a dimly lit Chamber of Horrors.

Open: Mon–Sat 10.00–17.30, Sun 12.00–17.30.

Tel: 01 872 6340

Newbridge House, Donabate.

Built in 1737 for Archbishop Charles Cobbe, and still the residence of his descendants, Newbridge has one of the most beautiful period manor house interiors in Ireland and is set within 142 hectares (350 acres) of parkland. A fully restored 18thC farm lies on the estate together with dairy, forge, tack room, and estate worker's house. Situated 19km (12 miles) north of Dublin.

Open (Apr–Sept) Tues–Sat 10.00–17.00, Sun & bank holidays 14.00–18.00; (Oct–Mar) Sat, Sun & bank holidays 14.00–17.00.

Tel: 01 843 6534

Newman House, St Stephen's Green.

Newman House is made up of two splendid Georgian mansions, No 85 and No 86, which were once part of the buildings of the Catholic University of Ireland and named after Cardinal Newman, the first rector of the university. They are now owned by University College Dublin. No 86 was built in 1765 for Richard Whaley MP with marvellous stucco by Robert West, the house has also been owned by the celebrated gambler Buck Whaley. The smaller house, No 85, was designed by Richard Castle in 1739 with beautiful plasterwork by the Swiss La Franchini brothers and includes the Apollo Room with a figure of the god above the mantle. Gerald Manley Hopkins was Professor of Classics here at the end of the 19thC and his study is on view. Also open to the public is a classroom furnished as it would have been when James Joyce was a

pupil here from 1899–1902. A guided tour explains the history and heritage of the house and how it was restored.

Open (Jun, Jul, Aug) Tues–Fri 12.00–17.00.

Tel: 01 716 7422

Number 29, Lower Fitzwilliam Street.

This elegant four-storey house has been restored and furnished exactly as it would have been between 1790–1820 by any well-to-do middle class family. Everything in the house is authentic with period items from the National Museum. The wallpaper was hand-made for Number 29 using 18thC methods. Among the rooms in the house are a kitchen, pantry, governess' room, nursery and boudoir.

Open Tues–Sat 10.00–17.00, Sun 14.00–17.00. Closed for about 2 weeks preceding Christmas.

Tel: 01 702 6165

Old Jameson Distillery, Bow Street, Smithfield Village.

The art of Irish Whiskey making shown through an audio-visual presentation, working models of the distilling process, and guided tour of the old distillery which was in use between 1780–1971.

Open daily 09.00–17.30 (tours only). Disabled access.

Tel: 01 807 2355

Pearse Museum, St. Enda's Park, Grange Road, Rathfarnham.

Housed in the former school run by nationalist Patrick Pearse from 1910–1916, it includes an audio-visual presentation and a nature study room with displays on Irish flora and fauna. Pearse was executed in 1916 for his part in the Easter Rising.

Open (Feb-Apr) 10.00-17.00; (May-Aug) 10.00-17.30; (Sept-Oct) 10.00-17.00; (Nov-Jan) 10.00-16.00; closed 13.00-14.00. Admission is free. Disabled access to ground floor/toilet.

Tel: 01 493 4208

Powerscourt Centre, South William Street.

A lively three storey centre of craft shops, galleries, boutiques and cafés, converted from Powerscourt Townhouse, a classical style mansion designed by Robert Mack and built between 1771–74. It features the original grand wooden staircase and finely detailed plasterwork.

Web: www.powerscourtcentre.com

Powerscourt House & Gardens,
County Wicklow.

First laid out in the 1740s, the 18 hectare (45 acre) gardens, perhaps the finest in Ireland, include sweeping terraces cut into a steep hillside, statues and ornamental lakes. A

spectacular Italian style stairway leading down to the main lake was added in 1874. Secluded Japanese gardens with bamboo and walled gardens are also notable and there is a huge variety of trees and shrubs. The house suffered a serious fire in 1974 and is no longer lived in. Visitors may walk through the old ballroom, and an exhibition area illustrates the history of the construction of the house and there are models of some of the rooms as they would have been before the fire. The house dates back to the 18thC when in 1731 architect Richard Castle was commissioned by Richard Wingfield to transform the medieval Powerscourt Castle into a grand Pallladian style mansion; the castle walls were used to form the main structure and the central courtyard was converted into an entrance hall. Powerscourt is in the foothills of the Wicklow mountains, 19km (12 miles) south of Dublin.
Open daily 09.30–17.30.
Tel: 01 204 6000
Web: www.powerscourt.ie

Phoenix Park Visitor Centre, Phoenix Park.
The visitor centre illustrates the history and wildlife of the park with an audio-visual display, a variety of fascinating exhibits and temporary exhibitions. Adjoining the centre is a restored medieval tower house, Ashtown Castle. On Saturdays there are free guided tours to the Irish President's House which is situated in the Park.
Open: (Jun-Sept) 10.00-18.00; (Apr-May) 09.30-17.30; (Nov-Mar) Sat & Sun only 09.30-16.30. Last admission 45 minutes before closing. Toilet for people with disabilities.
Tel: 01 677 0095

Rathfarnham Castle, Rathfarnham.
Dating from around 1583, this castle has 18thC interiors by Sir William Chambers and James Stuart and is presented to visitors as a castle undergoing conservation. There is a toilet for people with disabilities but restricted access to the castle.
Open daily from May–Oct 09.30–17.00 (last tour 16.30).
Tel: 01 493 9462

Royal Hospital, Military Road, Kilmainham.
The Royal Hospital was built as a home for army pensioners and invalids by Charles I, and continued in use for almost 250 years. Designed by Sir William Robinson in 1684, it has a formal facade and large courtyard and bears similarities to Les Invalides in Paris and The Royal Hospital in Chelsea. The restored building has one of Dublin's finest interiors and houses

the Irish Museum of Modern Art in which there is an audio-visual presentation "The Story of the Royal Hospital Kilmainham". The grounds, including a formal garden, are open to the public.
Tel: 01 612 9900

Shaw Birthplace, Synge Street.
This delightful Victorian terrace home was the birthplace of one of Ireland's four Nobel prize-winners for literature, George Bernard Shaw. Restored to give the feeling that the Shaw family is still in residence, the home provides an insight into the domestic life of Victorian Dubliners.
Open (May–Sept) Mon–Fri 10.00–17.00, Sat & Sun 14.00–17.00. Closed 13.00–14.00.
Tel: 01 872 2077
Email: shawhouse@dublintourism.ie

Tara's Palace – Dolls House, Malahide.
The centrepiece of this museum is the one-twelfth size scale model house reflecting the splendour of 18thC Irish mansions. Conceived by Ronald and Doreen McDonnell in 1980, it was ten years in the making. Irish craftsmen paid meticulous attention to detail, with unique miniature furniture and paintings adorning the walls. The museum also has rare pieces of porcelain, miniature glass and silver. Dolls houses of the 18thC and 19thC are displayed, together with dolls and antique toys.
Open (Apr–Sept) Mon–Sat 10.00–17.00, Sun and bank holidays 14.00–18.00; (Oct–Mar) Sat, Sun and bank holidays 14.00–17.00. Closed all year 13.00–14.00.
Tel: 01 846 3779

Temple Bar
Named after a 17thC landowner, Sir William Temple, this charming neighbourhood is Dublin's cultural quarter. With its narrow cobbled streets running close to the Liffey, Temple Bar is full of character and home to many artists and musicians. The area has been regenerated in recent years and boasts a wide variety of cultural venues and events and an eclectic mix of studios, galleries, shops, markets and eating-places. Modern architecture now blends with the historic. Many free open-air events take place in summer at Meeting House Square and Temple Bar Square, including circus acts, concerts and the outdoor screening of films. Temple Bar is bounded by the south quays of the Liffey, Dame Street, Westmoreland Street and Fishamble Street.
Temple Bar Information Centre, 12 Essex Street East.
Tel: 01 677 2255
Web: www.temple–bar.ie
Email: info@templebar.ie

The Chimney, Smithfield Village.

Originally built in 1895, this 53 metre (175ft) chimney which belonged to the Jameson Whiskey Distillery now provides a 360 degree panoramic viewpoint over the city. A glass walled lift takes visitors up the side of the chimney to two viewing galleries at the top.
Open daily 10.00–17.30.
Tel: 01 817 3800

Trinity College, College Green.

The original Elizabethan college was founded in 1592 but the present building was largely built between 1755–1759. The cruciform complex surrounding cobbled quadrangles and peaceful gardens has an impressive 91 metre (300ft) Palladian facade designed by Henry Keene and John Sanderford. One of the most notable features within the main college square is the 30 metre (98ft) Campanile or bell tower built in 1853 by Sir Charles Lanyon. The oldest surviving part of the college is the red brick apartment building from 1700 known as The Rubrics. Originally a Protestant College, Catholics did not start entering Trinity until the 1970s. The Library has over a million books and a magnificent collection of early illuminated manuscripts, including the famous Book of Kells; areas open to the public include the Colonnades, the Treasury, and the Long Room Library. Edmund Burke, Oliver Goldsmith and Samuel Beckett are among famous former Trinity College students.
Web: www.tcd.ie

Waterways Visitor Centre, Grand Canal Quay.

A modern centre built on piers over the Grand Canal, housing an exhibition about Ireland's inland waterways. Working models of various engineering features are displayed and there is an interactive multimedia presentation.
Open (Jun–Sept) daily 09.30–17.00; (Oct–May) Wed–Sun 12.30–17.00. Last admission 45 minutes before closing. Access to ground floor for people with disabilities.
Tel: 01 677 7510

Cathedrals and churches

Augustinian Church, Thomas Street.

Designed by E W Pugin and G C Ashlin in 1862, it has a mountainous exterior with lofty side aisles to the nave and a 49 metre (160ft) high tower crowned by a spire.

Christ Church Cathedral, Christchurch Place.

The Cathedral was established by Strongbow and Archbishop Laurence O'Toole in 1173 on the site of the cathedral founded around 1030 by the Norse King Sitric Silkenbeard. Lambert Simnel, pretender to the English throne, was crowned here as Edward VI in 1487. It was extensively restored between 1871–78 by George Edmund Street and is one of the best examples in Ireland of early Gothic architecture. The medieval crypt is one of the oldest and largest in Ireland.
Open Mon–Fri 09.45-17.00, Sat & Sun 10.00-17.00.
Tel: 01 677 8099
Web: www.cccdub.ie
Email: welcome@cccdub.ie

Franciscan Church, (Adam and Eve's) Merchants Quay.

Designed by Patrick Byrne in 1830.

St. Ann's Church, Dawson Street.

Designed by Isaac Wells in 1720 with a Romanesque-style facade added by Sir Thomas Deane in 1868. Much of the colourful stained glass dates back to the mid 19thC. Wooden shelves behind the altar were once used to take bread for distribution to the poor. Music recitals are held in the church.
Tel: 01 676 7727

St. Audoen's Church, High Street.

Dublin's only surviving medieval parish church, with a 12thC font and portal. The bell tower, restored in the 19thC, has three 15thC bells. The guild chapel has an exhibition on the importance of the church in the life of the medieval city. Dublin's only surviving city gate, known as St. Audoen's Arch, stands nearby.
Open Jun–Sept 09.30 (10.15 on Sun)–16.45. Toilet for people with disabilities and church partly accessible.
Tel: 01 677 0088

St. Audoen's RC Church, High Street.

Designed by Patrick Byrne in 1841–47, it has a monumental, cliff-like exterior with a huge Corinthian portico added by Stephen Ashlin in 1898.

St. George's, Temple Street.

This neo-classical church was designed by Francis Johnston in 1802 and has a 61 metre (200ft) high steeple modelled on St. Martin-in-the-Fields, London.

St. Mary's Church, Mary Street.

A handsome galleried church designed by Thomas Burgh in 1627. Wolfe Tone, leader of the United Irishmen, was baptised here in 1763 and Sean O'Casey in 1880.

St. Mary's Abbey, Meetinghouse Lane.

Established originally as a Benedictine foundation in 1139, it became Cistercian eight years later. Until the 16thC it was one of the largest and most important monasteries in

Ireland. The remains include a fine vaulted Chapter House of 1190 and there is an interesting exhibition about the history of the abbey.
Open mid June–mid Sept, Wed and Sun 10.00–17.00. Last admission 45 minutes before closing.
Tel: 01 872 1490

St. Mary's Pro-Cathedral, Marlborough Street.
A Greek Doric style building with the interior modelled on the Church of St. Philippe de Roule in Paris, designed by John Sweetman and built between 1815–1825. St. Mary's is Dublin's most important Catholic Church and is used on State occasions. Tenor John McCormack was once a member of the Palestrina choir that sings a Latin mass every Sunday at 11.00.
Open Mon-Fri 07.30-18.45, Sat 07.30-19.15, Sun 09.00-13.45 and 17.30-19.45.
Tel: 01 874 5441
Web: www.procathedral.ie

St. Michan's Church, Church Street.
Founded in 1095 as a Viking parish church, largely rebuilt in 1685 and restored in 1828. Famous for the 17thC mummified bodies in the crypt which are preserved with skin and hair because of the dry atmosphere created by the limestone walls. Handel is thought to have played on the organ which dates from 1724.
Open (March/April–Oct) Mon–Fri 10.00–12.45 and 14.00-16.45; (Nov–March) Mon–Fri 12.30–15.30; all Saturdays 10.00–12.45. Vaults closed on Sundays.
Tel: 01 872 4154

St. Patrick's Cathedral, St. Patrick's Close.
The National Cathedral of the Church of Ireland, it was built in the late 12thC on the site of the pre-Norman parish church of St. Patrick. It gained and lost cathedral status more than once in its chequered history and Cromwellian soldiers stabled horses here in the Civil War. Architect John Semple added a spire in 1749 and St. Patrick's was fully restored in the 19thC with finance from the Guinness family. The massive west tower houses the largest ringing peel of bells in Ireland. The cathedral is full of memorial brasses, busts and monuments to famous Irishmen. Jonathan Swift was Dean here from 1713–1745; there are memorials to Swift and his beloved Stella (Esther Johnson) and Swift's pulpit contains his writing table and chair, and portrait.
Usually open daily 09.00–17.00. Wheelchair access by arrangement.
Tel: 01 453 9472
Web: www.stpatrickscathedral.ie
Email: admin@stpatrickscathedral.ie

St. Saviour's, Dominick Street.
Designed by J J McCarthy in 1858, this extravagant French style Gothic edifice has a bold west door under a triangular hood, crowned by a large rose window.

St. Stephen's (Pepper Canister), Mount Street Crescent.
This handsome neo-classical church, designed by John Bowden in 1824, has a Greek style portico.

St. Werburgh's Church, Werburgh Street.
Originally the site of an Anglo-Norman foundation, the present church was built in 1715–19 and rebuilt in 1759 following a fire. St. Werburgh's was the Chapel Royal until 1790. Lord Edward Fitzgerald, one of the leaders of the 1798 rebellion, is buried in the vaults.

Whitefriar Street Carmelite Church, Aungier Street.
19thC church standing on the site of a 16thC Carmelite Priory. The remains of Saint Valentine are buried here and there is a 15thC oak statue of the Virgin and Child, thought to be the only surviving Pre-reformation statue of its kind.
Tel: 01 475 8821

Libraries

Central Catholic Library, Merrion Square.
Of religious and general interest, with a large Irish section.
Open Mon–Fri 11.00–18.00, Sat 11.00–17.30.
Tel: 01 676 1264
Web: www.catholiclibrary.ie

Central Library, Ilac Centre.
Tel: 01 873 4333.
Enquiries about other Dublin City Public Libraries (lending, reference and special collections).
Tel: 01 674 4800
Web: www.iol.ie/dublincitylibrary
Email: dublinpubliclibraries@dublincity.ie

Chester Beatty Library, Dublin Castle, Dame Street.
Reopened in 2000 in a purpose designed home in the Clock Tower building of Dublin Castle, the library is a treasure of manuscripts, books, prints and textiles collected by American scholar Sir Alfred Chester Beatty. It has some of the rarest original manuscripts still in existence. The collection reflects the art of manuscript production and printing from many parts of the world and from early to modern times with picture scrolls, jade books and woodblock prints from the Far East, around 4,000 Islamic manuscripts, and fine books, bindings and

manuscripts from Western Europe. With many Early Christian papyri, the library is a major resource for the study of the Old and New Testaments.
Open Mon-Fri 10.00–17.00, Sat 11.00–17.00, Sun 13.00–17.00.   Oct-Apr   closed   Mondays. Admission is free.
Tel: 01 407 0750
Web: www.cbl.ie
Email: info@cbl.ie

Genealogical Office, Kildare Street.
Part of the National Library, the genealogical office offers a service to assist in the task of tracing family history, familiarising people with the relevant records and procedures.
Open Mon–Fri 10.00–17.00, Sat 10.00–12.30.
Tel: 01 603 0200

Gilbert Library, Pearse Street.
Books and manuscripts relating to Dublin which were accumulated by 19thC Dublin historian Sir John T Gilbert and now in the care of Dublin Corporation. The collection includes rare early Dublin newspapers, 18thC bindings, Irish Almanacs, manuscripts of the municipal records of the City of Dublin and the records of the Dublin guilds.
Tel: 01 674 4800

Goethe Institute Library, Merrion Square.
German cultural information centre and library.
Open Tues-Thurs 12.00–20.00, Fri 10.00-14.30, Sat 10.00-13.30.
Tel: 01 661 1155

Irish Architectural Archive, Merrion Square.
Open Tues–Fri 10.00-17.00.
Tel: 01 663 3040

Marsh's Library, St Patrick's Close.
Given to the city by Archbishop Narcissus Marsh and opened in 1701, this is Ireland's oldest public library containing many rare books still in their original carved bookcases. The building was designed by Sir William Robinson who was also the architect of the Royal Hospital, Kilmainham. To prevent the theft of rare books readers were locked in wire cages and three of these cages survive.
Open Mon-Fri 10.00-17.00 (closed 13.00-14.00); Sat 10.30-13.00; closed Tuesdays.
Tel: 01 454 3511
Web: www.marshlibrary.ie
Email: keeper@marshlibrary.ie

National Library of Ireland, Kildare Street.
Offers over half a million books, a vast collection of maps, prints and manuscripts and an invaluable collection of Irish newspapers and periodicals. The impressive Victorian building has been home to the Library since 1890, and there is a large domed reading room. Holds temporary exhibitions on Irish writers and books.
Open: Mon–Wed   10.00–21.00,   Thurs–Fri 10.00–17.00, Sat 10.00–13.00.
Tel: 01 603 0200
Web: www.nli.ie
Email: info@nli.ie

National Photographic Archive,
Meeting House Square.
Only established in 1998, it has over 600,000 photographs recording people, political events, and   scenes   of   Irish   cities,   towns   and countryside.   Images from the collection are always on view. There is also a reading room and darkrooms.
Open: Mon–Fri 10.00–17.00. Sat 10.00-14.00 (exhibition only) Admission is free.   Disabled access/toilet.
Tel: 01 603 0374
Web: www.nli.ie/fr_arch.htm
Email: photoarchive@nli.ie

Royal Irish Academy Library, Dawson Street.
One of the largest collections of ancient Irish manuscripts in the country with one usually on display together with a small exhibition. Access may be restricted depending on Royal Academy meetings and large groups need to make a prior arrangement to visit.
Open Mon–Fri 10.00–17.00. Admission is free.
Tel: 01 676 2570

Trinity College Library, College Green.
The oldest and most famous of Dublin's libraries dating from the late 16thC. Entitled to receive a copy of every book published in Ireland, the library also contains an extensive collection of Irish manuscripts including the Book of Kells, a beautifully illuminated copy of the gospels written on vellum in Latin around the year AD800. The Book of Kells is now bound in four volumes and two are always on display in the Treasury, one open at a major ornamental page and the other to show two pages of script. An exhibition explains how the Book of Kells and other manuscripts such as the Book of Durrow (AD675) and Book of Armagh (AD807) were created and illustrates monastic life in the 8thC. The impressive Old Library or Long Room Library is lined with marble busts of scholars and is nearly 64 metres (210ft) long. It rises two storeys with a high barrel vaulted ceiling and contains over 200,000 of the college's books.

Open Mon–Sat 09.30–17.00; Sun 09.30–16.30 (Jun–Sept), Sun 12.00–16.30 (May–Oct). Last admission 30 minutes before closing.
Tel: 01 608 2308
Web:www.tcd.ie

Arts centres, galleries and concert halls

Douglas Hyde Gallery, Trinity College.
Showing mainly temporary exhibitions of contemporary art.
Tel: 01 608 1116
Web: www.douglashydegallery.com
Email: dhgallery@tcd.ie

Gallery of Photography, Meeting House Square.
Exhibitions of contemporary photography. Roof terrace has views over the square.
Tel: 01 671 4654
Web: www.irish-photography.com
Email: gallery@irish–photography.com

Hugh Lane Municipal Gallery of Modern Art, Parnell Square North.
19thC and 20thC paintings, mainly Impressionist works, bequeathed by Sir Hugh Lane who was drowned in the Lusitania in 1915, form the nucleus of this collection. The Lane Collection is split with the Tate Gallery in London; each half is alternated between the galleries every 5 years. There is an extensive range of Irish and international paintings, sculpture and stained glass and the acquisition of contemporary work is ongoing. Included is the London studio of Dublin-born artist Francis Bacon, which was carefully dismantled and reconstructed here. Regular 'Sundays at Noon' Concerts are held at the gallery (apart from July and August) with everything from early music to commissioned new works; the music is often arranged to complement one of the temporary exhibitions. The classical building which houses the gallery, Charlemont House, was designed by William Chambers in 1763 for James Caulfield, later 1st Earl Charlemont. It was reconstructed in 1929 to house the Lane Collection and opened in 1933.
Open Tues–Thurs 09.30–18.00, Fri & Sat 09.30–17.00, Sun 11.00–17.00. Admission free except for special exhibitions. Disabled access.
Tel: 01 874 1903
Web: www.hughlane.ie
Email: info@hughlane.ie

National Concert Hall, Earlsfort Terrace.
Home of the National Symphony Orchestra of Ireland, but also a venue for international artists and orchestras, jazz, contemporary and traditional Irish music. The classical building was designed for the Great Exhibition of 1865, then became the centrepiece of University College Dublin before opening as Ireland's National Concert Hall in 1981.
Booking office open Mon–Sat 10.00–19.00. Disabled access/toilet.
Tel: 01 417 0000
Web: www.nch.ie (online booking)
Email:info@nch.ie

National Gallery of Ireland, Merrion Square.
Paintings by illustrious 20thC European artists such as Morrisot, Bonnard, Picasso and Monet hang in the National Gallery as well as the work of Old Masters including Titian, Caravaggio, Rembrandt and Vermeer. There is the National Collection of Irish art, a room dedicated to the work of Jack B Yeats, English paintings, and over 250 sculptures. William Dargan organised the 1853 Dublin Exhibition on this site and used the proceeds to found the collection; his statue stands on the lawn.
Open Mon–Sat 09.30–17.30, Thurs 09.30–20.30, Sun 12.00–17.30. Admission free. Disabled access/toilet.
Tel: 01 661 5133
Web: www.nationalgallery.ie
Email: info@ngi.ie

Royal Dublin Society, Ballsbridge.
Venue for large events including craft and antiques fairs and Ideal Homes exhibitions.
Tel: 01 668 0866
Web: www.rds.ie

Royal Hibernian Academy Gallagher Gallery, Ely Place.
Showing both traditional and innovative work from both Irish and international artists.
Tel: 01 661 2558
Web: www.royalhibernianacademy.com
Email: www.rhagallery@eircom.net

Solomon Gallery, Powerscourt Centre.
One of Ireland's leading contemporary art galleries, situated in an 18thC Georgian townhouse.
Open Mon–Sat 10.00–17.30. Admission free.
Tel: 01 679 4237
Web: www.solomongallery.com
Email: info@solomongallery.com

Temple Bar Gallery and Studios, Temple Bar.
A large complex with studios and exhibition spaces.
Tel: 01 671 0073
Web: www.templebargallery.com
Email: info@templebargallery.com

Temple Bar Music Centre, Curved Street.
Live music venue with recording and rehearsal studios.
Tel: 01 677 0647
Web: www.tbmc.ie
Email: info@tbmc.ie

Taylor Galleries, Kildare Street.
Contemporary art gallery, mainly Irish, with the emphasis on painting and sculpture.
Tel: 01 676 6055

The Ark, Eustace Street.
A cultural centre for children with a child-size theatre.
Tel: 01 670 7788
Web: www.ark.ie
Email: boxoffice@ark.ie

Parks and gardens

Garden of Remembrance, Parnell
Square East.
The Garden of Remembrance, opened in 1966, is dedicated to all those who died in the cause of Irish Freedom. There is a sculpture by Oisín Kelly representing the Irish legend, "Children of Lir".
Open (Oct-Mar) 09.30-1600, (Apr-Sept) 08.30-18.00.
Tel: 01 874 3074 (garden) or 01 647 2498 (head office)

Iveagh Gardens, Clonmel Street.
Designed by Ninian Niven in 1863, this is one of the least known and most tranquil of Dublin's parks. Features include a rustic grotto, cascade, fountains, maze, archery grounds, wilderness and woodlands.
Opening according to daylight hours.
Tel: 01 475 7816

Marlay Park, Rathfarnham.
This large park situated at the foot of the Dublin Mountains contains areas of woodland, a large pond, nature trail and model railway.

National Botanic Gardens, Glasnevin.
Established in 1795, these magnificent gardens occupy an area of 20 hectares (49 acres) and contain a fabulous collection of plants, shrubs and trees. Many of the plants come from tropical Africa and South America and are housed in large Victorian glasshouses. Features include a rose garden, rockery and wall plants, herbaceous borders, vegetable garden and arboretum.
Open Summer Mon-Sat 09.00-18.00, Sun 10.00-18.00; Winter Mon-Sat 10.00-16.30, Sun 10.00-16.30. Shorter opening hours for glasshouses. Admission is free. Toilet for people with disabilities, and gardens largely accessible.
Tel: 01 857 0909

Phoenix Park
Phoenix Park, covering over 712 hectares (1,760 acres), is Europe's largest enclosed city park. Its name is thought to derive from the Irish meaning "clear water" and a spring does rise in the park. Enclosed by an 11km (7 mile) long stone wall, the park was laid out in the mid 18thC and was the scene of the Phoenix Park murders in 1882, when the Chief Secretary and the Under-Secretary for Ireland were assassinated. A more recent event was when the Pope celebrated mass in the park in front of 1 million people; a 27 metre (90ft) steel cross marks the spot. The park includes a number of buildings, the most important of which is Áras an Uachtaráin; the Viceroy's Lodge built in 1751 but later becoming the official house of the President of Ireland when Dr Douglas Hyde moved there in 1938. Other important buildings are the American ambassador's residence and the Ordnance Survey Office. A 60 metre (205 ft) high obelisk, erected in 1817, is a memorial to the Dublin-born Duke of Wellington. The People's Garden by the main entrance on Parkgate Street is laid out with ornamental planting in ribbon borders, much as it would have been in Victorian times. Dublin Zoo is in the south-east corner. The open space covered by playing fields and paths, known as Fifteen Acres but actually covering more than 200, was used in the 18thC as a duelling ground. Phoenix Park is open to the public at all times but the People's Gardens usually close at sunset.

St. Anne's Park, Dollymount.
Once part of the Guinness family estate, the park covers over 110 hectares (270 acres) and is wooded with oak, pine, beech, chestnut and lime. There is a lovely rose garden, opened in 1975.

St. Enda's Park, Grange Road,
Rathfarnham.
The park surrounds the Pearse Museum and includes a walled garden, riverside walks and waterfall. Open daily from 10.00, closing time varies according to daylight hours. Limited access for people with disabilities.

St. Stephen's Green
In the heart of the city, St Stephen's Green was originally an open common but was enclosed in 1663. Opened to the general public in 1877, it is laid out as a public park with flowerbeds, an ornamental pond and several sculptures. There is a garden for the visually impaired and there are summer lunchtime concerts.
Open daily 08.00 (Sun & bank Holidays 10.00); closes according to daylight hours.
Tel: 01 475 7816

War Memorial Garden, South Circular Road, Islandbridge.
Dedicated to the memory of the Irish soldiers who died in the First World War, these gardens include a sunken rose garden and herbaceous borders. They were designed by Sir Edward Lutyens. The names of the 49,400 soldiers who died between 1914–1918 are contained in the granite bookrooms in the gardens, access to which is only by arrangement with the management.
Open Mon–Fri 08.00, Sat & Sun 10.00; closes according to daylight hours.
Tel: 01 677 0236 (gardens)
Tel: 01 647 2498 (head office)

Theatres

Abbey Theatre, Lower Abbey Street.
Ireland's National Theatre, founded by Lady Gregory and W B Yeats in 1904. The Abbey quickly became world renowned, staging plays by J M Synge and Sean O'Casey, and played a significant role in the renaissance of Irish culture. It also provoked controversy in Dublin and even riots. The present theatre was built in 1966 to replace the previous building which had been destroyed by fire. The Abbey stages classic Irish plays, while the Peacock theatre downstairs presents new and experimental drama.
Tel: 01 878 7222
Web: www.abbeytheatre.ie

Andrews Lane Theatre and Studio,
Andrews Lane.
A wide variety of works shown both in the theatre and studio.
Tel: 01 679 5720
Web: www.andrewslane.com

Civic Theatre, Tallaght.
New theatre staging everything from drama to variety shows
Tel: 01 462 7477
Web: www.civictheatre.ie

Focus Theatre, Pembroke Place, Pembroke Street.
Small theatre presenting the classics and new writing.
Tel: 01 676 3071

Gaiety Theatre, South King Street.
Restored Victorian building and Dublin's oldest theatre, founded in 1837. Drama, opera (Opera Ireland have two seasons a year), ballet, musicals, pantomime, comedy.
Tel: 01 677 1717
Web: www.gaietytheatre.net

Gate Theatre, Cavendish Row.
Modern Irish and classical drama, also international plays. Founded in 1928.
Tel: 01 874 4045
Web: www.gate-theatre.ie

Lambert Puppet Theatre, Clifton Lane, Monkstown.
Tel: 01 280 0974
Web: www.lambertpuppettheatre.com

Olympia Theatre, Dame Street.
Comedy, drama, pantomime, musicals, concerts.
Tel: 0818 719330

Peacock Theatre, Lower Abbey Street.
New and experimental work.
Tel: 01 878 7222

Project Arts Centre, 39 East Essex Street.
Moved in 2000 into new custom designed building with performance and gallery space; generally innovative new work and everything from drama and visual arts to talks and events.
Tel: 01 881 9613
Web: www.project.ie
Email: info@project.ie

Samuel Beckett Theatre, Trinity College.
Trinity College School of Drama theatre with a variety of student productions during term and touring companies at other times. Venue for Festival Fringe events.
Tel: 01 608 2461

The Point, North Wall Quay.
Theatre and concert venue including ballet.
Tel: 01 836 3633

Sugar Club, Lower Leeson Street.
Multimedia theatre with wide range of entertainment; drama, film, cabaret, comedy, music, events.
Tel: 01 678 7188
Web: www.thesugarclub.com

The Dublin Theatre Festival, held at many venues throughout the city, runs for two weeks every October.
Tel: 01 677 8439, Box office 01 677 8899
Web: www.dublintheatrefestival.com

The Fringe Festival which presents theatre, dance and the visual arts is held for three weeks, commencing in September.
Tel: 01 872 9433
Web: www.fringefest.com

Cinemas

Most cinemas offer cheaper seats before 5pm.
IMC, Dún Laoghaire,
Tel: 01 280 7777. 12 screens.

Irish Film Institute, Eustace Street,
Art house with 2 screens and restaurant converted from old Quaker meeting house. New Irish films and film seasons. The Irish Film Archive, library and special events.
Tel: 01 679 3477.
Web: www.irishfilm.ie
Email: info@irishfilm.ie

Omniplex, Santry, **Tel: 01 842 8844**. 11 screens.

Ormonde Cinema, Stillorgan,
Tel: 01 278 0000. 7 screens.

Savoy Cinema, O'Connell Street Upper,
Tel: 01 874 6000. 6 screens.

Screen Cinema, D'Olier Street,
Tel: 01 672 5500. 3 screens.

Ster Century, Liffey Valley Shopping Centre, Fonthill Road
Tel: 01 605 5700. 14 screens.

UCI Cinema, Blanchardstown,
Tel: 01 8222 624. 9 screens.

UCI Cinema, Coolock,
Tel: 01 848 5122. 10 screens.

UCI Cinema, Tallaght,
Tel: 01 459 8400. 12 screens.

UGC Cinemas, Parnell Street,
Tel: 01 872 8444. 17 screens.
The largest cinema in Ireland.

Shopping

Opening hours are generally 09.00–18.00 Mon–Sat. Many city centre shops and shopping centres remain open until 20.00 or 21.00 on Thursdays and Fridays and open 12.00–18.00 on Sundays.
The main city centre shopping areas are around Grafton Street and Nassau Street to the south of the Liffey and around Henry Street (off O'Connell Street) to the north of the river. Both Grafton Street and Henry Street are pedestrianised. Many up-market and international designer stores can be found in Grafton Street, while shops around Henry Street are generally less expensive. The Temple Bar area has a number of craft and specialist shops.

Department stores

Arnotts, Henry Street, **Tel: 01 872 1111.**

Brown Thomas, Grafton Street,
Tel: 01 605 6666.

Clery and Co, O'Connell Street Lower,
Tel: 01 878 6000.

Debenhams, Jervis Centre, **Tel: 01 878 1222.**

Dunnes Stores, Henry Street, **Tel: 01 671 4629.**

Guiney & Co, Talbot Street, **Tel: 01 878 8835.**

Marks & Spencers, Grafton Street,
Tel: 01 679 7855.

Penneys Stores, Mary Street, **Tel: 01 872 7788.**

Roches Stores, Henry Street, **Tel:01 873 0044.**

Shopping centres

Dún Laoghaire Shopping Centre, Marine Road,
Tel: 01 280 2981.

Ilac Centre, Henry Street, **Tel: 01 704 1460.**

Irish Life Shopping Mall, Abbey Street,
Tel: 01 704 1452.

Jervis Shopping Centre, Jervis Street,
Tel: 01 878 1323.

Powerscourt Centre, South William Street,
Tel: 01 679 4144.

St. Stephen's Green Centre, **Tel: 01 478 0888.**
There are also shopping centres at Clondalkin (Liffey Valley), Blanchardstown, and Tallaght on the outskirts of Dublin.

Markets

Blackrock, Sat, Sun & bank holidays 11.00–17.30 (bric-a-brac, china and antiques).
Tel: 01 283 3522

George's Street Market Arcade (second hand clothes, jewellery, records).
Tel: 01 280 8683

Liberty Market (clothes, fabrics, household goods), Meath Street.
Tel: 01 280 8683

Moore Street Market, Mon–Sat (flower, fruit and vegetables), off Henry Street.

St. Michan's Street Vegetable Market (fruit, vegetables, fish and flowers).

Temple Bar Square. Food market is open every Saturday from 09.30–18.00 selling organic fruit and vegetables, bread, cheeses, oysters, and smoked fish. Book Market is open on Saturdays from 09.30.
Tel: 01 677 2255

Sport and leisure

International sports venues:
Athletics – Croke Park.
Tel: 01 836 3222

Gaelic Football and Hurling – Croke Park.
Tel 01 836 3222

Rugby and Soccer – Lansdowne Road, Ballsbridge.
Tel: 01 668 4601

Golf (18-hole golf clubs):
Balcarrick Golf Club, Donabate, 16km (10m) north of city centre.
Tel: 01 843 6957

Ballinascorney, 13km (8m) south west of city centre.
Tel: 01 451 6430

Beaverstown Golf Club, Donabate, 16km (10m) north of city centre.
Tel: 01 843 6439

Blanchardstown Golf Centre, Mulhuddart, 13km (8m) north west of city centre.
Tel: 01 821 2054

Castle Golf Club, Rathfarnham, 6km (4m) south of city centre.
Tel: 01 490 4207

Citywest Golf Resort, Saggart, 16km (10m) south west of city centre.
Tel: 01 401 0500

Corballis Golf Links, Donabate,16km (10m) north of city centre.
Tel: 01 843 6583
Web: www.golfdublin.com
Email: corballislinks@golfdublin.com

Deerpark Hotel and Golf Courses, Howth, 14km (9 m) north east of city centre.
Tel: 01 832 2624
Web: www.deerpark–hotel.ie
Email: sales@deerpark.iol.ie

Druids Glen, Newmountkennedy, 32km (2m) south east of city centre.
Tel: 01 287 3600
Web: www.druidsglen.ie
Email: info@druidsglen.ie

Edmondstown, Rathfarnham, 11km (7m) south of city centre.
Tel: 01 493 1082
Email: info@edmondstowngolfclub.ie

Elmgreen Golf Centre, Castleknock, 8km (5m) north west of city centre.
Tel: 01 820 0797
Web: www.golfdublin.com
Email: elmgreen@golfdublin.com

Elm Park, Donnybrook, 5km(3m) south of city centre.
Tel: 01 269 3438
Email: office@elmparkgolfclub.ie

Forrest Little Golf Club, Cloghean, 9km (6m) north of city centre, near to airport.
Tel: 01 840 1183

Grange Castle, Clondalkin, 8km (5m) south west of city centre.
Tel: 01 464 1043
Web: www.grange-castle.com

Grange Golf Club, Rathfarnham, 6km (4m) south of city centre.
Tel: 01 493 2889

Hermitage Golf Club, Lucan, 11km (7m) west of city centre.
Tel: 01 626 8491

Howth Golf Club, Sutton, 14km (9m) north east of city centre.
Tel: 01 832 3055
Web: www.howthgolfclub.ie
Email: manager@howthgolfclub.ie

Island, Corballis, Donabate, 14km (9m) north of city centre.
Tel: 01 843 6462
Web: www.theislandgolfclub.com
Email: info@theislandgolfclub.com

Luttrellstown Castle, Castleknock, 10 km (6 m) west of city centre.
Tel: 01 808 9988
Email: golf@luttrellstown.ie

Malahide Golf Club, 13km (8m) north of city centre. **Tel: 01 846 1611**
Web: www.malahidegolfclub.ie
Email: malgc@clubi.ie

Portmarnock Golf Club, 11km (7m) north east of city centre.
Tel: 01 846 2968
Web: www.portmarnockgolfclub.ie
Email: emer@portmarnockgolfclub.ie

Portmarnock Hotel and Golf Links, 11km (7m) north east of city centre.
Tel: 01 846 1800
Email: golfres@portmarnock.com

Royal Dublin Golf Club, Dollymount, 5km (3m) north east of city centre.
Tel: 01 833 6346
Web: www.theroyaldublingolfclub.com
Email: info@theroyaldublingolfclub.com

St. Anne's Golf Club, Dollymount, 5km (3m) north east of city centre.
Tel: 01 833 6471
Web: www.stanneslinksgolf.com
Email: info@stanneslinksgolf.com

St. Margaret's Golf Club, 11km (7m) north of city centre.
Tel: 01 864 0400
Web: www.stmargaretsgolf.com
Email: info@stmargaretsgolf.com

Swords Open Golf Course, 13km (8m) north of city centre.
Tel: 01 840 9819/890 1030

Greyhound racing
Greyhound racing is one of Ireland's leading spectator sports. Meetings are held at:

Shelbourne Park Stadium, Ringsend, (Wed, Thurs, Sat at 20.00).
Tel: 01 668 3502
Web: www.shelbournepark.com

Harold's Cross Stadium, (Mon, Tues & Fri at 20.00).
Tel: 01 497 1081

Horse racing

There are two racecourses on the outskirts of Dublin:

Leopardstown.
10km (6 miles) south of Dublin. National Hunt and Flat racing with 22 meetings including 4 day Christmas National Hunt Festival.
Tel: 01 289 3607
Web: www.leopardstown.com
Email: info@leopardstown.com

Fairyhouse.
19km (12 miles) north west of Dublin. Home of the Irish Grand National.
Tel: 01 825 6167
Web: www.fairyhouseracecourse.ie
Email: info@fairyhouseracecourse.ie

Sailing

The Irish Sailing Association, Dún Laoghaire, for information on sailing, windsurfing and powerboating in the Dublin area and elsewhere in Ireland.
Tel: 01 280 0239
Web: www.sailing.ie

Sports centres
Aughrim Street, **Tel: 01 838 8085**
Glin Road, Coolock, **Tel: 01 847 8177**

Swimming pools
Ballymun, Town Centre, **Tel: 01 842 1368**
Coolock, Northside Shopping Centre,
Tel: 01 847 7743
Crumlin, Windmill Road, **Tel: 01 455 5792**
Finglas, Mellowes Road, **Tel: 01 864 2584**
Markievicz Pool, Townsend Street,
Tel: 01 672 9121
Rathmines, Lower Rathmines Road,
Tel: 01 496 1275
Sean, McDermott Street, **Tel: 01 872 0752**

Help and advice

Embassies
Apostolic Nunciature, Navan Road.
Tel: 01 838 0577
Argentina, Ailesbury Drive. Tel: 01 269 1546
Australia, Fitzwilton House, Wilton Terrace.
Tel: 01 676 1517
Austria, Ailesbury Road. Tel: 01 269 4577
Belgium, Shrewsbury Road. Tel: 01 269 2082
Brazil, Harcourt Street. Tel: 01 475 6000
Britain, Merrion Road. Tel: 01 205 3700
Bulgaria, Burlington Road. Tel: 01 660 3293
Canada, St. Stephen's Green. Tel: 01 478 1988
China, Ailesbury Road. Tel: 01 269 1707

Czech Republic, Northumberland Road.
Tel: 01 668 1135
Denmark, St. Stephen's Green.
Tel: 01 475 6404
Egypt, Clyde Road. Tel: 01 660 6566
Finland, St. Stephen's Green. Tel: 01 478 1344
France, Ailesbury Road. Tel: 01 260 1666
Germany, Trimleston Avenue. Tel: 01 269 3011
Greece, Pembroke Street Upper.
Tel: 01 676 7254
Hungary, Fitzwilliam Place. Tel: 01 661 2902
India, Leeson Park. Tel: 01 497 0843
Iran, Mount Merrion Avenue. Tel: 01 288 0252
Israel, Pembroke Road. Tel: 01 668 0303
Italy, Northumberland Road. Tel: 01 660 1744
Japan, Merrion Centre. Tel: 01 202 8300
Korea, Clyde Road. Tel: 01 660 8800
Mexico, Ailesbury Road. Tel: 01 260 0699
Morocco, Raglan Road. Tel: 01 660 9449
Netherlands, Merrion Road. Tel: 01 269 3444
Nigeria, Leeson Park. Tel: 01 660 4366
Norway, Molesworth Street. Tel: 01 662 1800
Poland, Ailesbury Road. Tel: 01 283 0855
Portugal, Knocksinna Road. Tel: 01 289 4416
Romania, Ailesbury Road. Tel: 01 269 2852
Russian Federation, Orwell Road.
Tel: 01 492 3492
Slovakia, Clyde Road. Tel: 01 660 0008
South Africa, Earlsfort Terrace.
Tel: 01 661 5553
Spain, Merlyn Park. Tel: 01 269 1640
Sweden, Dawson Street. Tel: 01 671 5822
Switzerland, Ailesbury Road. Tel: 01 269 2515
Turkey, Clyde Road. Tel: 01 668 5240
USA, Elgin Road. Tel: 01 668 8777

Health centres and pharmacies
Grafton Street Centre, Open Mon, Tues & Thurs 08.30-18.15, Wed 09.30-18.15, Fri 08.30-17.45.
Tel: 01 671 2122

Mercer's Medical Centre, Stephen Street Lower, Open: Mon–Thurs 09.00–17.30, Fri 09.00–16.30.
Tel: 01 402 2300

O'Connell's Late Night Pharmacy, O'Connell Street Lower, Open daily Mon-Fri 07.30-22.00, Sat 08.00-22.00, Sun 10.00–22.00.
Tel: 01 873 0427

Garda Síochána (Police)
City centre Garda stations:
Pearse Street station, Tel: 01 666 9000
Store Street station, Tel: 01 666 8000

Dublin Metropolitan Area Headquarters, Harcourt Square,
Tel: 01 666 6666

Greater Dublin Area Headquarters, Phoenix Park,
Tel: 01 666 0000

Dún Laoghaire station, Tel: 01 666 5000
Web: www.garda.ie

Post Offices
General Post Office, O'Connell Street. Open Mon–Sat 08.00-20.00.
Tel: 01 705 8833
Web: www.anpost.ie

Post offices are usually open Mon–Fri 09.00–17.30 (closed 13.00–14.15) and from 09.00–13.00 on Saturdays.

Welfare organisations
Citizens Information Centre (Comhairle), 13a O'Connell Street Upper.
Tel: 01 809 0633

Samaritans, 112 Marlborough Street.
Tel: 01 872 7700 or callsave 1850 609 090
Web: www.samaritans.org

Social Welfare Services, Store Street.
Tel: 01 874 8444

Tourist Victim Support Service, Garda Headquarters, Harcourt Square.
All referrals must go through the Garda.
Open: Mon–Sat 10.00–18.00, Sun 12.00–18.00.
Tel: 01 478 5295
Web: www.victimsupport.ie/tourist.html
Email: info@touristvictimsupport.ie

Hospitals

Baggot Street Community Hospital, Upper Baggot Street. **Tel: 01 668 1577**

Beaumont, Beaumont Road. **Tel: 01 809 3000**

Blackrock Clinic (private), Rock Road.
Tel: 01 283 2222

Bon Secours Private Hospital, Glasnevin.
Tel: 01 837 5111

Cappagh National Orthopaedic, Cappagh Road.
Tel: 01 834 1211

Central Mental Hospital, Dundrum.
Tel: 01 298 9266

Clonskeagh Hospital, Clonskeagh.
Tel: 01 268 0500

Coombe Women's Hospital, Dolphin's Barn Street. **Tel: 01 408 5200**

Dental Hospital, Lincoln Place, **Tel: 01 612 7200**

James Connolly Memorial Hospital, Blanchardstown. **Tel: 01 646 5000**

Mater Misericordiae, Eccles Street.
Tel: 01 803 2000

Mater Private, Eccles Street. **Tel: 01 885 8888**

Mount Carmel, Braemor Park. **Tel: 01 492 2211**

National Maternity, Holles Street.
Tel: 01 661 0277

Orthopaedic Hospital of Ireland, Clontarf.
Tel: 01 833 8167

Our Lady's Hospital for Sick Children, Crumlin.
Tel: 01 409 6100

Rotunda Hospital, Parnell Square.
Tel: 01 873 0700

Royal Hospital, Donnybrook. **Tel: 01 406 6600**

Royal Victoria Eye and Ear, Adelaide Road.
Tel: 01 678 5500

St. Brendan's, Rathdown Road. **Tel: 01 838 5844**

St. James's, James's Street, **Tel: 01 410 3000**

St. Luke's, Rathgar. **Tel: 01 406 5000**

St. Mary's Hospital, Phoenix Park.
Tel: 01 677 8132

St. Michael's, George's Street Lower,
Dún Laoghaire. **Tel: 01 280 6901**

St. Patrick's, James's Street.
Tel: 01 249 3200

St. Vincent's, Convent Avenue, Richmond Road.
Tel: 01 884 2400

St. Vincent's (private), Herbert Avenue.
Tel: 01 260 9200

St. Vincent's University Hospital, Elm Park.
Tel: 01 269 4533

Skin and Cancer Hospital, Hume Street.
Tel: 01 676 6935

Artane	14 B3	Donnybrook	45 C2	Irishtown	37 D3	Rathmines	44 A2
Ashtown	9 C3	Drimnagh	41 D1	Islandbridge	34 A1	Ringsend	37 D2
Ballsbridge	45 D1	Drumcondra	28 A1	Kilbarrack	17 C2	Rossmore	49 D2
Ballyfermot	32 B2	Dundrum	53 C3	Kildonan	10 A1	Sandymount	38 A3
Ballymount	40 A2	Dún Laoghaire		Killester	14 B3	Shielmartin	22 B2
Beaumont	13 C1	(Dunleary)	57 C3	Kilmainham	34 A2	Stillorgan	54 B3
Blackrock	55 D1	Dunleary		Kimmage	42 B3	Stradbrook	56 A3
Bluebell	40 B1	(Dún Laoghaire)	57 C3	Marino	29 C2	Sutton	18 A1
Booterstown	54 B1	Finglas	11 C2	Merrion	46 A3	Templeogue	50 A2
Cabra	27 C2	Finglas East	10 B1	Milltown	44 B3	Terenure	51 C1
Chapelizod	32 B1	Glasnevin	12 A3	Monkstown	56 B3	Wainsfort	50 A1
Churchtown	52 A2	Glasnevin North	11 D1	Mount Merrion	54 A2	Walkinstown	40 B2
Clonskeagh	45 C3	Goatstown	53 C3	Pelletstown	9 D3	Whitehall	12 B3
Clontarf	30 A2	Goldenbridge	33 D3	Phibsborough	27 D2	Willbrook	50 B3
Coolock	14 B1	Greenhills	48 B1	Raheny	16 A3	Williamstown	55 D1
Crumlin	41 D2	Harold's Cross	43 C1	Ranelagh	44 B1	Windy Arbour	53 C2
Dollymount	31 D2	Howth	20 B2	Rathfarnham	51 C2		
Dolphin's Barn	35 C3	Inchicore	33 D2	Rathgar	43 D3		

Index to street names

General abbreviations

All	Alley	Dr	Drive	Junct	Junction	S	South
Av	Avenue	Dws	Dwellings	La	Lane	Sch	School
Ave	Avenue	E	East	Lo	Lodge	Sq	Square
Bk	Bank	Ex	Exchange	Lwr	Lower	St.	Saint
Bldgs	Buildings	Ext	Extension	Mans	Mansions	St	Street
Boul	Boulevard	Fld	Field	Mkt\	Market	Sta	Station
Br	Bridge	Flds	Fields	Ms	Mews	Ter	Terrace
Bri	Bridge	Fm	Farm	Mt	Mount	Vil	Villa, Villas
Cem	Cemetery	Gdn	Garden	N	North	Vw	View
Cen	Central,	Gdns	Gardens	No	Numbers	W	West
	Centre	Gra	Grange	Par	Parade	Wd	Wood
Cl	Close	Grd	Ground	Pas	Passage	Wds	Woods
Clo	Close	Grn	Green	Pk	Park	Wk	Walk
Coll	College	Gro	Grove	Pl	Place	Yd	Yard
Cotts	Cottages	Ho	House	Prom	Promenade		
Cres	Crescent	Hosp	Hospital	Rd	Road		
Ct	Court	Hts	Heights	Ri	Rise		

District abbreviations

Abb.	Abberley	Clond.	Clondalkin	Grey.	Greystones	Manor.	Manorfields
B'brack	Ballybrack	Clons.	Clonsilla	Jobs.	Jobstown	Mulh.	Mulhuddart
B'mun	Ballymun	Collins.	Collinstown	Kill.	Killiney	Palm.	Palmerston
Bald.	Baldoyle	Cool.	Coolmine	Kilsh.	Kilshane	Port.	Portmarnock
Balg.	Balgriffin	Corn.	Cornelscourt	Kilt.	Kiltipper	Sally.	Sallynoggin
Black.	Blackrock	D.L.	Dún Laoghaire	Kins.	Kinsaley	Sandy.	Sandyford
Boot.	Booterstown	Deans Gra	Deans Grange	Leix.	Leixlip	Shank.	Shankill
Cabin.	Cabinteely	Dunb.	Dunboyne	Leo.	Leopardstown	Still.	Stillorgan
Carp.	Carpenterstown	Fox.	Foxrock	Lou.V.	Louisa Valley	Will.	Willbrook
Carrick.	Carrickmines	G'geary	Glenageary	Lough.	Loughlinstown		
Castle.	Castleknock	Gra M.	Grange Manor	Mala.	Malahide		

Some streets are not named on the map due to insufficient space. In some of these cases the nearest street that does appear on the map is listed in *italics*. In other cases they are indicated on the map by a number which is listed here in **bold**.

A

Abbey Cotts 1
  off Abbey St Upr 58 C2
Abbey Ct 5 14 B3
Abbeyfield 5 14 B3
Abbeyfield 6 44 B3
Abbey Pk 5 14 A3
Abbey Pk 13 17 C1
Abbey St 13 21 C2
Abbey St Lwr 1 59 D2
Abbey St Mid 1 59 D2
Abbey St Old 1 59 E2
Abbey St Sta 1 59 D2
Abbey St Upr 1 58 C2
Abbotstown Av
  (Ascal Bhaile An
  Abba) 11 9 D1
Abbotstown Dr 11 9 D1
Abbotstown Rd 11 10 A1
Abercorn Rd 3 37 C1
Abercorn Sq 8 33 D2
Abercorn Ter 7 27 C3
Abercorn Ter 8 33 D2
Aberdeen St 7 34 B1
Achill Rd 9 28 B1
Acres Rd 8 25 D3
Adair 4 45 D1
Adam Ct 2
  off Grafton St 59 D4
Adare Av 17 14 A1
Adare Dr 17 14 A1
Adare Grn 17 14 B1
Adare Pk 17 14 B1
Addison Rd 3 28 A1
Addison Rd 3 29 C2
Addison Ter 9 28 A1
Adelaide Ms 4 46 B2
Adelaide Rd 2 36 A3
Adelaide St D.L. 57 D3
Adelaide Ter 8
  off Brookfield St 34 B2
Adrian Av 6W 43 C2
Aideen Av 6W 42 B3
Aideen Dr 6W 42 B3
Aideen Pl 6W 42 B3
Aikenhead Ter 4 37 D2
Ailesbury 9 12 B1
Ailesbury Cl 4 45 D2
Ailesbury Dr 4 45 D2
Ailesbury Gdns 4 46 A2
Ailesbury Ms 4 46 B2
Ailesbury Pk 4 46 A2
Ailesbury Rd 4 45 D2
Airfield Ct 4 45 D3
Airfield Manor 4 45 D3
Airfield Pk 4 45 D3
Airfield Rd 6 43 D3
Airfield Ter 4 45 D3
Airton Cl 24 46 B3
Albany Av Black. 56 B3
Albany Rd 6 44 B2
Albert Coll Av 9 12 A2
Albert Coll Cres 9 12 A2
Albert Coll Dr 9 12 A2
Albert Coll Lawn 9 12 A2
Albert Coll Pk 9 12 A2
Albert Coll Ter 9 12 A2
Albert Ct E 2 37 C2
Albert Pl 8
  off Inchicore Rd 34 A2
Albert Pl E 2 37 C2
Albert Pl W 2 36 A3
Albert Ter 8
  off Albert Pl W 36 A3
Albion Ter 8
  off Inchicore Rd 34 A2
Aldborough Par 1 29 C3
Aldborough Pl 1 28 B3
Aldborough Sq 1 28 B3
Alden Dr 13 16 B1
Alden Pk 13 17 C1
Alden Rd 13 16 B1
Alders, The D.L. 57 C3
Aldrin Wk 5 14 A1
Alexander Ter 1 37 C1
Alexander Ter 8 35 D3
Alexandra Quay 1 38 A1
Alexandra Rd 1 37 D1
Alexandra Rd
  Extension 1 39 C1

Alexandra Ter 3
  off Clontarf Rd 31 C3
Alexandra Ter 6 43 D3
Alexandra Ter
  (Dundrum) 14 52 B3
Alfie Byrne Rd 3 29 D3
All Hallows La 9
  off Drumcondra
  Rd Upr 28 B1
Allied Ind Est 10 32 B3
Allingham St 8 35 C2
All Saints Dr 5 15 D3
All Saints Pk 5 15 D3
All Saints Rd 5 15 C3
Alma Pl Black. 56 B3
Alma Rd Black. 56 A2
Almeida Av 8
  off Brookfield St 34 B2
Almeida Ter 8
  off Brookfield St 34 B2
Alone Wk 5 14 B3
Altona Ter 7 27 C3
Alverno 3 30 A2
Amiens St 1 59 F1
Anglesea Av Black. 55 D2
Anglesea Br 4 45 C1
Anglesea Fruit Mkt 7
  off Green St Little 58 B2
Anglesea La D.L. 57 D3
Anglesea Rd 4 45 D2
Anglesea Row 7 58 B2
Anglesea St 2 59 D3
Annadale Av 3 29 C2
Annadale Cres 9 29 C1
Annadale Dr 9 29 C1
Annaly Rd 7 27 C2
Annamoe Dr 7 27 C2
Annamoe Par 7 27 C3
Annamoe Pk 7 27 C3
Annamoe Rd 7 27 C2
Annamoe Ter 7 27 C3
Anna Vil 6 44 B2
Annaville Gro 14 53 C2
Annaville Ter 14
  off Annaville Gro 53 C2
Anne Devlin Av 14 50 B3
Anne Devlin Dr 14 50 B3
Anne Devlin Pk 14 50 B3
Anne Devlin Rd 14 50 B3
Anner Rd 8 34 A2
Annes La 2 59 D4
Annesley Av 3 29 C3
Annesley Br 3 29 C2
Annesley Br Rd 3 29 C2
Annesley Pk 6 44 B2
Annesley Pl 3 29 C2
Anne St N 7 58 B1
Anne St S 2 59 D4
Annsbrook 14 53 C1
Appian Way, The 6 44 B1
Aranleigh Ct 14 51 D3
Aranleigh Gdns 14 51 D3
Aranleigh Mt 14 51 D3
Aranleigh Pk 14 51 D3
Aranleigh Vale 14 51 D3
Arbour Hill 7 35 C1
Arbour Pl 7 35 C1
Arbour Ter 7 35 C1
Arbutus Av 12 43 C1
Arbutus Pl 8 35 D3
Arcade 1 59 D2
Ardagh Rd 12 42 B1
Ardbeg Cres 5 14 B2
Ardbeg Dr 5 14 B2
Ardbeg Pk 5 14 B2
Ardbeg Rd 5 14 B2
Ardcollum Av 5 14 A2
Ardee Gro 6 44 A1
Ardee Rd 6 44 A1
Ardee Row 8 58 A4
Ardee St 8 58 A4
Ardenza Pk Black.
  off Seapoint Av 56 A2
Ardenza Ter Black. 56 A2
Ardilaun Rd 3 28 B3
Ardilea Downs 14 53 D2
Ardlea Rd 5 14 A2
Ardmore Av 7 27 C3
Ardmore Cl 5 13 D2
Ardmore Cres 5 14 A2
Ardmore Dr 5 13 D2
Ardmore Gro 5 13 D2
Ardmore Pk 5 14 A2

Ardpatrick Rd 7 26 A2
Ard Ri Pl 7
  off Ard Ri Rd 35 C1
Ard Ri Rd 7 35 C1
Ardtona Av 14 52 B2
Argyle Rd 4 45 C1
Arklow St 7 27 C3
Armagh Rd 12 42 A2
Armstrong St 6
  off Harolds Cross Rd 43 D1
Arnott St 8 35 D3
Arranmore Av 7 28 A2
Arranmore Rd 4 45 C1
Arran Quay 7 58 A2
Arran Quay Ter 7 58 A2
Arran Rd 9 28 B1
Arran St E 7 58 B2
Arran St W 7 58 A2
Arundel Black. 56 B3
Ascal An Charrain Chno
  (Nutgrove Av) 14 51 D3
Ascal Bhaile An Abba
  (Abbotstown Av) 11 9 D1
Ascal Bhaile Thuaidh
  (Ballyhoy Av) 5 15 D3
Ascal Dun Eanna
  (Ennafort Av) 5 15 C3
Ascal Measc
  (Mask Av) 5 14 B2
Ascal Phairc An Bhailtini
  (Villa Pk Av) 7 26 A2
Ascal Ratabhachta
  (Ratoath Av) 11 9 D2
Asgard Rd 13 21 C2
Asgard Rd 13 21 C2
Ash, The 15 8 A3
Ashbrook 3 30 A1
Ashbrook 7 25 C1
Ashcroft 5 15 D2
Ashdale Av 6W 43 C3
Ashdale Gdns 6W 43 C3
Ashdale Pk 6W 43 C3
Ashdale Rd 6W 43 C3
Ashfield
  (Templeogue) 6W 50 A2
Ashfield Av 6 44 B2
Ashfield Cl 6W
  off Ashfield 50 A2
Ashfield Pk
  (Templeogue) 6W
  off Ashfield 50 A2
Ashfield Pk
  (Terenure) 6W 43 C3
Ashfield Pk Boot. 54 A1
Ashfield Rd
  (Ranelagh) 6 44 B2
Ashford Cotts 7
  off Ashford St 27 C3
Ashford Pl 7
  off Ashford St 27 C3
Ashford St 7 27 C3
Ashgrove Ter 1 16 53 C3
Ashington Av 7 26 A1
Ashington Cl 7 9 D3
Ashington Ct 7 26 A1
Ashington Dale 7 10 A3
Ashington Gdns 7 26 A1
Ashington Grn 7 26 A1
Ashington Ms 7 10 A3
Ashington Pk 7 25 D1
Ashington Ri 7 9 D3
Ashleaf Shop Cen 12 41 D3
Ashling Cl 12 42 B1
Ash St 8 58 A4
Ashton Pk Black. 56 B3
Ashtown Gate Rd 8 25 C1
Ashtown Gro 7 25 D1
Ashtown Rd 15 9 C3
Ashtown Sta 15 9 C3
Aston Pl 2 59 D2
Aston Quay 2 59 D2
Athlumney Vil 6 44 A1
Auburn Av 4 45 C2
Auburn Av 15 24 A1
Auburn Cl 15
  off Auburn Dr 8 A3
Auburn Dr 15 8 A3
Auburn Grn 15
  off Auburn Dr 8 A3
Auburn Rd 4
  off Auburn Av 45 C2
Auburn St 7 27 D3
Auburn Vil 6 43 D3

Auburn Wk 7 27 C3
Aughavanagh Rd 12 43 C1
Aughrim La 7 27 C3
Aughrim Pl 7 27 C3
Aughrim St 7 27 C3
Aughrim Vil 7
  off Aughrim St 27 C3
Aungier Pl 2 58 C4
Aungier St 2 58 C4
Austins Cotts 3
  off Annesley Pl 29 C2
Ave Maria Rd 8 35 C3
Avenue, The 6W 50 A2
Avenue Rd 8 35 D3
Avila Pl 9 9 D1
Avoca Av Black. 55 C1
Avoca Pk Black. 55 C1
Avoca Pl Black. 55 D2
Avoca Rd Black. 55 C3
Avonbeg Ind Est 12 40 B1
Avondale Av 7 27 D3
Avondale Business Pk
  Black. 55 D2
Avondale Lawn Black. 55 D3
Avondale Lawn Extension
  Black. 55 D3
Avondale Pk 5 16 A3
Avondale Rd 7 27 D3
Avondale Ter 12 41 D3
Ayrefield Av 13 15 C1
Ayrefield Ct 13 15 C1
Ayrefield Dr 13 15 C1
Ayrefield Gro 13 15 C1
Ayrefield Pl 13 15 C1

B

Bachelors Wk 1 59 D2
Back La 8 58 B3
Baggot Ct 2
  off Baggot St Lwr 36 B3
Baggot Ct 2 36 B3
Baggot La 4 37 C3
Baggot Rd 7 25 D2
Baggot St Lwr 2 36 B3
Baggot St Upr 4 37 C3
Baggot Ter 7
  off Blackhorse Av 25 D2
Bailey Grn Rd 13 23 D2
Baldoyle Ind Est 13 17 C1
Baldoyle Rd 13 18 A1
Balfe Av 12 41 D2
Balfe Rd 12 41 D2
Balfe Rd E 12 41 D2
Balfe St 2
  off Chatham St 59 D4
Balglass Est 13 20 B2
Balglass Rd 13 21 C2
Balkill Pk 13 20 B2
Balkill Rd 13 21 C3
Ball's Br 4 45 D1
Ballsbridge Av 4
  off Ballsbridge Av 45 D1
Ballsbridge Pk 4 45 D1
Ballsbridge Ter 4
  off Ballsbridge Av 45 D1
Ballsbridge Wd 4 37 D3
Ballyboden Ind Est 11 10 A3
Ballyboggan Rd 11 10 B3
Ballybough Av 3
  off Spring Gdn St 29 C3
Ballybough Br 3 29 C2
Ballybough Ct 3
  off Spring Gdn St 29 C3
Ballybough Rd 3 28 B3
Ballyfermot Av 10 32 B2
Ballyfermot Cres 10 32 B2
Ballyfermot Dr 10 32 A2
Ballyfermot Par 10 32 A2
Ballyfermot Rd (Bothar
  Baile Thormod) 10 32 A2
Ballygall Av 11 11 C1
Ballygall Cres 11 10 B2
Ballygall Par 11 10 B2
Ballygall Pl 11 11 C2
Ballygall Rd E 11 11 D2
Ballygall Rd W 11 10 B2
Ballyhoy Av (Ascal
  Bhaile Thuaidh) 5 15 D3

Ballymace Grn 14   50 A3
Ballymount Av 12   48 B1
Ballymount Av 24   48 B1
Ballymount Cross 24   40 A3
Ballymount Dr 12   40 B3
Ballymount Ind Est 12   40 B3
Ballymount Lwr Rd 12   40 A3
Ballymount Rd
   Ind Est 12   40 B2
Ballymount Rd Upr 24   40 A3
Ballymount Trd Est 12   41 C3
Ballymun Rd 9   12 A3
Ballyneety Rd 10   33 C2
Ballyroan Ct **1** 16   50 A3
Ballyroan Cres 16   50 B3
Ballyroan Pk 16   50 A3
Ballyroan Rd 16   50 A3
Ballyshannon Av 5   13 D1
Ballyshannon Rd 5   13 D1
Ballytore Rd 14   51 D1
Balnagowan 6   44 B3
Balrothery Cotts 24   49 C3
Balrothery Est 24   48 B3
Balscadden Rd 13   21 C2
Bancroft Av 24   48 A3
Bancroft Cl 24   48 B3
Bancroft Gro 24   48 B3
Bancroft Pk 24   48 A3
Bancroft Rd 24   48 B3
Bangor Dr 12   42 B1
Bangor Rd 12   42 B1
Bankside Cotts 14   52 B1
Bannow Rd 7   26 B1
Bann Rd 11   10 B3
Bantry Rd 9   12 A3
Banville Av 10   32 A3
Barclay Ct Black.   55 D2
Bargy Rd 3   29 D3
Barnamore Cres 11
   off Barnamore Gro
Barnamore Gro 11   10 B3
Barnamore Pk 11   10 B3
Barrett St D.L.   57 C3
Barrow Rd 11   27 C1
Barrow Sta 4   37 C2
Barrow St 4   37 C2
Barry Grn 11   10 A1
Barry Pk 11   10 A1
Barry Rd 11   10 A1
Barryscourt Rd 17   14 A1
Barton Av 14   51 C3
Barton Dr 14   51 C3
Basin St Lwr 8   35 C2
Basin St Upr 8   35 C2
Basin Vw Ter 7   27 D3
Bass Pl 2   59 F4
Bath Av 4   37 D3
Bath Av Gdns 4   37 D3
Bath Av Pl 4   37 D3
Bath La 1   28 A3
Bath Pl Black.   55 D2
Bath St 4   37 D2
Baymount Pk 3   31 D1
Bayside Boul N 13   17 C1
Bayside Boul S 13   17 C1
Bayside Pk 13   17 C1
Bayside Sq E 13   17 C1
Bayside Sq N 13   17 C1
Bayside Sq S 13   17 C1
Bayside Sq W 13   17 C1
Bayside Sta 13   17 D1
Bayside Wk 13   17 C1
Bayview 4
   off Pembroke St
Bayview Av 3   37 D2
Beach Av 4   29 C3
Beach Dr 4   38 A3
Beach Rd 4   38 A3
Beach Vw 13   38 A3
Beaconsfield Ct 8   17 C2
   off The Belfry
Beattys Av 4   34 A2
Beaufield Manor Still.   45 D1
Beaufield Pk Still.   54 B3
Beaufort Downs 14   54 B3
Beaumont Av 14   51 C3
Beaumont Cl 14   52 A3
    52 A3

Beaumont Cres 9   13 D2
Beaumont Dr 14   52 B3
Beaumont Gdns Black.   55 C2
Beaumont Gro 9   13 C2
Beaumont Rd 9   13 C2
Beauvale Pk 5   14 A2
Beaver Row 4   45 C3
Beaver St 1   28 B3
Bedford Row 2
   off Temple Bar   59 D3
Beechdale Ms 6   44 A2
Beeches, The 13   16 A1
Beeches, The 6 14   51 C3
Beeches, The Black.   56 B3
Beechfield Av 12   41 D3
Beechfield Cl 12   41 D3
Beechfield Rd 12   41 D3
Beech Gro Boot.   54 B1
Beech Hill 4
   off Beech Hill Rd   45 C3
Beech Hill Av 4   45 D2
Beech Hill Cres 4   45 D3
Beech Hill Dr 4   45 D2
Beech Hill Rd 4   45 C3
Beech Hill Ter 4   45 D3
Beech Hill Vil 4
   off Beech Hill Ter   45 D3
Beechlawn Boot.   54 B2
Beechlawn Ind
   Complex 12   41 C3
Beechmount Dr 14   53 C1
Beech Pk 15   8 A3
Beech Pk Av 5   14 B1
Beech Pk Av 15   8 A3
Beechpark Ct 5   14 B1
Beech Pk Cres 15   8 A3
Beech Pk Lawn 15   8 A3
Beech Rd 12   40 A2
Beechwood Av Lwr 6   44 B2
Beechwood Av Upr 6   44 B2
Beechwood Pk 6   44 B2
Beechwood Rd 6   44 B2
Beechwood Sta 6   44 B2
Belfield Cl 14   53 C1
Belfield Ct 4   45 D3
Belfield Downs 14   53 C2
Belfield Office Pk 4   45 C3
Belfry, The 8   34 A2
Belgrave Av 6   44 A2
Belgrave Pl 6   44 A2
Belgrave Rd 6   44 A2
Belgrave Rd Black.   56 A2
Belgrave Sq E 6   44 A2
Belgrave Sq E Black.   56 B3
Belgrave Sq N 6   44 A2
Belgrave Sq N Black.   56 A2
Belgrave Sq S 6   44 A2
Belgrave Sq S Black.   56 A2
Belgrave Sq W 6   44 A2
Belgrave Sq W Black.   56 A2
Belgrave Ter Black.
   off Belgrave Rd
Belgrove Lawn 20   24 B3
Belgrove Pk 20   32 B1
Belgrove Rd 3   30 B2
Bella Av 1
   off Bella St   28 B3
Bella St 1   28 B3
Belle St 6   35 C2
Belleville Av 6   43 D3
Bellevue 8   35 C2
Bellevue Av Boot.   46 B3
Bellevue Copse Boot.   46 B3
Bellevue Ct Boot.   46 B3
Bellevue Pk Boot.   46 A3
Bellevue Pk Av Boot.   46 B3
Bellmans Wk 1
   off Ferrymans
   Crossing   37 C1
Belmont Av 4   45 C2
Belmont Ct 4
   off Belmont Av   45 C2
Belmont Gdns 4   45 C2
Belmont Pk 4   45 C2
Belmont Pk 5   16 A2
Belmont Vil 4   45 C2
Belton Pk Av 9   13 D3
Belton Pk Gdns 9   13 D3
Belton Pk Rd 9   13 D3
Belton Pk Vil 9   13 D3
Belvidere Av 1   28 A3
Belvidere Ct 1   28 A3
Belvidere Pl 1   28 A3

Belvidere Rd 1   28 A2
Belview Bldgs 8
   off School St   35 C2
Benbulbin Av 12   42 A1
Benbulbin Rd 12   34 A3
Benburb St 7   35 C1
Beneavin Ct 11   11 C2
Beneavin Dr 11   11 D2
Beneavin Pk 11   11 C1
Beneavin Rd 11   11 C1
Ben Edar Rd 7   27 C3
Bengal Ter 9   27 D1
Ben Inagh Pk Boot.   55 C1
Benmadigan Rd 12   34 A3
Benson St 2   37 D2
Benson St Enterprise
   Cen 2   37 C2
Beresford 9   28 B1
Beresford Av 9   28 B1
Beresford La 1   59 E1
Beresford La 9   28 B1
Beresford Pl 1   59 E2
Beresford St 7   58 B1
Berkeley Rd 7   27 D2
Berkeley St 7   28 A3
Berkeley Ter 4   37 C3
Berryfield Cres 11   10 A2
Berryfield Dr 11   10 A2
Berryfield Rd 11   10 A2
Berwick 14   51 D3
Berwick Hall 14   51 D3
Berystede 6
   off Leeson Pk   44 B1
Bessborough Av 3   29 C3
Bessborough Par 6   44 A1
Bethesda Pl 1
   off Dorset St Upr   28 A3
Bettyglen 5   16 B3
Bettystown Av 5   15 D3
Big Br 6W   51 C1
Bigger Rd 12   41 D2
Binn Eadair Vw 13   18 A1
Binns Br 7   28 A2
Birchfield 14   53 D3
Birchs La 14   53 C3
Birchview Av 24   48 A2
Birchview Cl 24   48 A2
Birchview Ct 24
   off Treepark Rd   48 A2
Birchview Dr 24   48 A2
Birchview Hts 24
   off Birchview Dr   48 A2
Birchview Lawn 24
   off Birchview Av   48 A2
Birchview Ri 24
   off Birchview Dr   48 A2
Bird Av 14   53 C1
Bishop St 8   36 A3
Blackberry La 6   44 A1
Blackditch Rd 10   32 A2
Blackhall Par 7   58 A2
Blackhall Pl 7   35 C1
Blackhall St 7   35 C1
Blackheath Av 3   30 B2
Blackheath Ct 3   31 C2
Blackheath Dr 3   30 B2
Blackheath Gdns 3   30 B2
Blackheath Gro 3   30 B2
Blackheath Pk 3   30 B2
Blackhorse Av 7   26 A2
Blackhorse Br 12   33 D3
Blackhorse Gro 7   26 B3
Blackhorse Ind Est 7   26 B3
Blackhorse Sta 12   33 D3
Blackpitts 8   35 D3
Blackrock Business Pk
   Black.   55 D2
Blackrock Shop Cen
   Black.   55 D1
Blackrock Sta Black.   55 D1
Black St 7   34 B1
Blackwater Rd 11   27 C1
Blarney Pk 12   42 B2
Blessington Ct 7
   off Blessington St   28 A3
Blessington St 7   27 D3
Bloom Cotts 8   35 D3
Bloomfield Av
   (Donnybrook) 4   44 B1
Bloomfield Av 8   35 D3
Bloomfield Pk 8   43 D1
Bluebell Av 12   32 B3
Bluebell Ind Est 12   40 A1

Bluebell Rd 12   41 C1
Bluebell St 12   41 C1
Blythe Av 3
   off Church Rd   37 C1
Boden Wd 14   51 C3
Bolton St 1   58 B1
Bond Dr 3   38 A1
Bond Rd 3   29 D3
Bond St 8   35 C2
Bonham St 8   35 C2
Boolavogue Rd 3   37 C1
Booterstown Av Boot.   54 B1
Booterstown Pk Boot.   54 B2
Booterstown Sta Boot.   47 C3
Botanic Av 9   28 A1
Botanic Gdns 11   27 D1
Botanic Ms 9   27 D1
Botanic Pk 9   28 A1
Botanic Rd 9   27 D2
Botanic Vil 9
   off Botanic Rd   28 A1
Bothar An Easa
   (Watermill Rd) 5   15 D3
Bothar Baile Thormod
   (Ballyfermot Rd) 10   32 A2
Bothar Chille Na Manac
   (Walkinstown Rd) 12   41 C2
Bothar Coilbeard
   (Con Colbert Rd) 8   34 A2
Bothar Coilbeard
   (Con Colbert Rd) 10   33 D2
Bothar Dhroichead
   Chiarduibh
   (Cardiffsbridge Rd) 11   10 A1
Bothar Drom Finn
   (Drumfinn Rd) 10   32 A2
Bothar Loch Con
   (Lough Conn Rd) 10   32 A1
Bothar Phairc An Bhailtini
   (Villa Pk Rd) 7   26 A2
Bothar Raitleann
   (Rathland Rd) 12   42 B3
Boundary Rd 3   30 A3
Bow Br 8   34 B2
Bow La E 2   58 C4
Bow La W 8   34 B2
Bow St 7   58 A2
Boyne La 2   59 F4
Boyne Rd 11   10 B3
Boyne St 2   59 F3
Brabazon Row 8   35 D3
Brabazon Sq 8
   off Gray St   58 A4
Brabazon St 8
   off The Coombe   58 A4
Brackens La 2   59 E2
Braemor Av 14   52 A2
Braemor Dr 14   52 A2
Braemor Gro 14   52 A2
Braemor Pk 14   52 A1
Braemor Rd 14   52 A2
Brainborough Ter 8
   off South Circular Rd   35 C3
Braithwaite St 8   35 C2
Branch Rd N   38 B1
Branch Rd N
   Extension 3   38 B1
Branch Rd S 1   38 B1
Brandon Rd 12   41 D1
Breakwater Rd S 1   38 B1
Bregia Rd 7   27 C2
Bremen Av 4   38 A2
Bremen Gro 4   38 A2
Bremen Rd 4   38 A2
Brendan Behan Ct 1
   off Russell St   28 B3
Brendan Rd 4   45 C2
Brian Av 3   29 C1
Brian Boru Av 3   31 C3
Brian Boru St 3   31 C2
Brian Rd 3   29 C2
Brian Ter 3   29 C2
Briarfield Gro 5   16 B2
Briarfield Rd 5   16 A2
Briarfield Vil 5   16 B2
Brickfield Dr 12   34 B3
Brickfield La 8   35 C3
Bride Rd 8   58 B4
Bride St 8   58 B4
Bridgecourt Office
   Pk 12   40 B2
Bridgefoot St 8   58 A3
Bridge St 4   37 D2

Bridge St Lwr 8	58	A3
Bridge St Upr 8	58	A3
Bridgewater Quay 8	34	A1
Brighton Av 3	29	D2
Brighton Av 6	43	D3
Brighton Av Black.	56	B3
Brighton Gdns 6	43	D3
Brighton Grn 6	43	C3
Brighton Rd 6	43	D3
Brighton Sq 6	43	D3
Brighton Vale Black.	56	A2
Britain Pl 1	28	A3
Britain Quay 2	37	D2
Broadstone 7	27	D3
Broadstone Av 7		
off Phibsborough Rd	27	D3
Brookfield 6	15	C2
Brookfield 6	44	B3
Brookfield Black.	55	D2
Brookfield Av Black.	55	D2
Brookfield Est 12	42	B3
Brookfield Pl Black.	55	D2
Brookfield Rd 8	34	B2
Brookfield St 8	34	B2
Brookfield Ter Black.	55	D2
Brooklands 4	46	A2
Brooklawn 3	30	A2
Brooklawn Black.	55	C2
Brooklawn Av D.L.	56	A3
Brooklawn Wd D.L.	56	A3
Brookmount Av 24	49	C3
Brookmount Lawns 24		
off Tallaght Rd	49	C3
Brook Pk Ct Black.	56	B3
Brookvale Downs 14	51	C1
Brookvale Rd 4	45	C2
Brookvale Rd 14	51	C2
Brookville 11	10	B1
Brookville Cres 5	14	B1
Brookville Pk (Artane) 5	14	B2
Brookville Pk		
(Coolock) 5	15	C1
Brookwood Av 5	14	B3
Brookwood Cres 5	15	C3
Brookwood Dr 5	14	B3
Brookwood Glen 5	15	C3
Brookwood Gro 5	14	B3
Brookwood Hts 5	14	B3
Brookwood Lawn 5	15	C3
Brookwood Meadow 5	14	B3
Brookwood Ri 5	15	C3
Brookwood Rd 5	14	B3
Broombridge Rd 7	26	B1
Broombridge Sta 7	26	B1
Broomhill Business		
Pk 24	48	A2
Broomhill Rd 24	48	A2
Broom Hill Ter 24	48	A2
Brown St N 7	58	A1
Brown St S 8	35	C3
Brunswick Pl 2		
off Pearse St	37	C2
Brunswick St N 7	58	A1
Brusna Cotts Black.	55	D2
Buckingham St Lwr 1	28	B3
Buckingham St Upr 1	28	B3
Bulfin Gdns 8	34	A2
Bulfin Rd 8	34	A2
Bulfin St 8	34	A3
Bull All St 8	58	B4
Bunratty Av 17	14	B1
Bunratty Dr 17	14	A1
Bunratty Rd 17	14	A1
Bunting Rd 12	41	C2
Burgess La 7		
off Haymarket	58	A2
Burgh Quay 2	59	D2
Burke Pl 8	34	B2
Burleigh Ct 4	36	B3
Burlington Gdns 4	36	B3
Burlington Rd 4	44	B1
Burris Ct 8		
off School Ho La W	58	B3
Burrowfield Rd 13	18	A1
Burrow Rd 13	18	B1
Busáras Sta 1	59	F1
Bushfield Av 4	45	C2
Bushfield Pl 4	44	B1
Bushfield Ter 4	44	B2
Bushy Pk Gdns 6	51	C1
Bushy Pk Rd 6	51	C1
Buterly Business Pk 5	14	A2
Butt Br 1	59	E2
Butterfield Av 14	50	B2
Butterfield Cl 14	50	B3
Butterfield Ct 14	51	C2
Butterfield Cres 14	51	C2
Butterfield Dr 14	51	C3
Butterfield Gro 14	50	B2
Butterfield Meadow 14	50	B3
Butterfield Orchard 14	51	C3
Butterfield Pk 14	50	B3
Byrnes La 1	58	C2

C

Cabra Dr 7	27	C2
Cabra Gro 7	27	C2
Cabra Pk 7	27	D2
Cabra Rd 7	26	B2
Cadogan Rd 3	29	C2
Calderwood Av 9	13	C3
Calderwood Gro 9	13	C3
Calderwood Rd 9	29	C1
Caledon Rd 3	29	C3
Callary Rd Still.	54	A2
Calmount Rd 12	40	B3
Camac Pk 12	40	B1
Camac Ter 8		
off Bow Br	34	B2
Camberley Elms 14	52	A2
Camberley Oaks 14	52	A3
Cambridge Av 4	38	A2
Cambridge Rd 4	37	D2
Cambridge Rd		
(Rathmines) 6	44	A2
Cambridge Sq 4	37	D2
Cambridge Ter 6	44	B1
Cambridge Vil 6		
off Belgrave Rd	44	A2
Camden Lock 4		
off South Docks Rd	37	D2
Camden Mkt 2		
off Camden St Lwr	36	A3
Camden Pl 2	36	A3
Camden Row 8	36	A3
Camden St Lwr 2	36	A3
Camden St Upr 2	36	A3
Cameron Sq 8	34	B2
Cameron St 8	35	C3
Campbell's Ct 7		
off Little Britain St	58	B1
Campbells Row 1		
off Portland St N	28	B3
Canal Rd 6	44	A1
Canal Ter 12	33	C3
Canal Wk 10	32	A3
Cannon Rock Vw 13	21	C2
Canon Lillis Av 1	29	C3
Canon Mooney Gdns 4		
off Cambridge Rd	37	D2
Canon Troy Ct 20	32	B1
Capel St 1	58	C1
Cappagh Av 11	10	A1
Cappagh Dr 11	10	A1
Cappagh Rd 11	10	A1
Captains Av 12	42	A2
Captains Dr 12	42	A2
Captains Rd 12	42	A2
Caragh Rd 7	26	B3
Carberry Rd 9	13	C3
Cardiff Br 7		
off Phibsborough Rd	27	D3
Cardiff Castle Rd 11	10	A1
Cardiffsbridge Av 11	9	D2
Cardiffsbridge Gro 11		
off Cappagh Rd	10	A1
Cardiffsbridge Rd		
(Bothar Dhroichead		
Chiarduibh) 11	10	A1
Cardiffs La 2	37	C2
Cards La 2		
off Townsend St	59	E3
Carleton Rd 3	29	D2
Carlingford Par 2	37	C2
Carlingford Pl 2		
off Carlingford Par	37	C2
Carlingford Rd 9	28	A2
Carlisle Av 4	45	C1
Carlisle St 8	35	D3
Carlton Ct 3	30	A2
Carlton Ms 4		
off Shelbourne Av	37	D3
Carmans Hall 8	58	A4
Carndonagh Dr 13	16	B1
Carndonagh Lawn 13	16	B1
Carndonagh Pk 13	16	B1
Carndonagh Rd 13	16	B1
Carnew St 7	27	C3
Carnlough Rd 7	26	B2
Caroline Row 4		
off Bridge St	37	D2
Carraroe Av 13	16	A1
Carrickbrack Heath 13	19	C2
Carrickbrack Hill 13	19	C3
Carrickbrack Lawn 13	19	C3
Carrickbrack Pk 13	19	C3
Carrickbrack Rd 13	19	C3
Carrick Brennan Lawn		
Black.	56	B3
Carrickbrennan Rd		
Black.	56	B3
Carrickmount Av 14	52	A3
Carrickmount Dr 14	52	A3
Carrick Ter 8	34	B3
Carrigallen Dr 11		
off Carrigallen Rd	10	B3
Carrigallen Pk 11		
off Carrigallen Rd	10	B3
Carrigallen Rd 11	10	B3
Carriglea Ind Est 12	41	C1
Carrow Rd 12	33	D3
Carysfort Av Black.	55	D2
Carysfort Hall Black.	55	D3
Carysfort Pk Black.	55	D3
Casana Vw 13	21	C3
Casement Cl 11	10	A1
Casement Dr 11	10	A1
Casement Grn 11	10	A1
Casement Gro 11	10	A1
Casement Pk 11	10	A1
Casement Rd		
(Finglas S) 11	10	B2
Casement Rd		
(Finglas W) 11	10	A1
Cashel Av 12	42	B2
Cashel Business Cen 12	42	B3
Cashel Rd 12	42	A2
Casimir Av 6W	43	C2
Casimir Ct 6W	43	D2
Casimir Rd 6W	43	C2
Casino Pk 3	29	D1
Casino Rd 3	29	C1
Castilla Rd 3	31	C2
Castle Av 3	30	B2
Castlebyrne Pk Black.	55	D3
Castle Ct 3	30	A1
Castle Ct Boot.	54	B1
Castledawson Av Boot.	55	C1
Castle Elms 17	14	B1
Castleforbes Ind Est 3	37	D1
Castleforbes Rd 1	37	D1
Castle Gate 15	24	B1
Castle Gro 3	30	B1
Castlekevin Rd 5	14	A1
Castleknock Grn 15	24	A1
Castleknock Lo 15	24	A1
Castleknock Pk 15	24	A1
Castleknock Pines		
Lwr 15	8	A3
Castleknock Pines		
Upr 15	8	A3
Castleknock Rd 15	24	B1
Castleknock Village		
Cen 15	24	A1
Castlelands, The 14	51	D2
Castle Lawns Est 24	48	B3
Castle Mkt 2		
off Drury St	58	C4
Castle Pk 24	48	B3
Castle Pk Black.	56	B3
Castle Pk Est 24	48	B3
Castle Rd 3	30	B2
Castleside Dr 14	51	D2
Castle St 2	58	B3
Castletimon Av 5	13	D1
Castletimon Dr 5	13	D1
Castletimon Gdns 5	13	D1
Castletimon Grn 5	13	D1
Castletimon Pk 5	13	D1
Castletimon Rd 5	13	D1
Castletymon Ct 24	48	B3
Castleview 5	14	A2
Castlewood Av 6	44	A2
Castlewood Cl 6		
off Castlewood Av	44	A2
Castlewood La 6	44	A2
Castlewood Pk 6	44	A2
Castlewood Pl 6	44	A2
Castlewood Ter 6	44	A2
Cathal Brugha St 1	59	D1
Cathedral La 8	35	D3
Cathedral St 1	59	D1
Cathedral Vw Ct 8		
off Cathedral Vw Wk	35	D3
Cathedral Vw Wk 8	35	D3
Catherines La 7		
off Church St Upr	58	B1
Catherine St 8		
off Ash St	58	A4
Cavalry Row 7	35	C1
Cavendish Row 1		
off Parnell St	28	A3
Ceannchor Rd 13	22	C3
Ceannt Fort 8	34	B2
Cecil Av 3	29	D2
Cecilia St 2		
off Temple La S	58	C3
Cedar Ct 6W	43	C3
Cedar Hall 6		
off Prospect La	45	C3
Cedarmount Rd Still.	54	A3
Cedar Pk 13	16	A1
Cedars, The D.L.	56	A3
Cedar Sq Black.	55	C3
Cedar Wk 5	16	A2
Cedarwood Av 11	11	C1
Cedarwood Cl 11	11	C1
Cedarwood Gro 11	11	C1
Cedarwood Pk 11	11	C1
Cedarwood Ri 11	11	C1
Ceide Dun Eanna		
(Ennafort Dr) 5	15	C3
Ceide Gleannaluinn		
(Glenaulin Dr) 20	32	A1
Ceide Phairc An Bhailtini		
(Villa Pk Dr) 7	26	A2
Celestine Av 4	37	D2
Celtic Pk Av 9	13	D3
Celtic Pk Rd 9	13	D3
Chamber St 8	35	D3
Chancery La 8	58	C4
Chancery Pl 7	58	B2
Chancery St 7	58	B2
Chanel Av 5	14	B2
Chanel Gro 5	14	B1
Chanel Rd 5	14	A2
Chapel Av 4	37	D2
Chapelizod Bypass 20	32	A1
Chapelizod Ct 20	32	A1
Chapelizod Hill Rd 20	32	A1
Chapelizod Ind Est 10	32	B1
Chapelizod Rd 8	33	C1
Chapelizod Rd 20	33	C1
Chapel La 1	58	C1
Charlemont 13	13	D3
Charlemont Av D.L.	57	D3
Charlemont Ct 2	44	A1
Charlemont Gdns 2		
off Charlemont St	36	A3
Charlemont Mall 2	44	A1
Charlemont Par 3	29	C3
Charlemont Pl 2	44	A1
Charlemont Rd 3	29	D2
Charlemont Sq 2		
off Charlemont St	36	A3
Charlemont Sta 1	44	A1
Charlemont St 2	36	A3
Charles La 1	28	B3
Charles St Gt 1	28	B3
Charles St W 7	58	B2
Charleston Av 6	44	A2
Charleston Rd 6	44	A2
Charleville 14	52	B2
Charleville 16	50	A3
Charleville Av 3	29	C3
Charleville Mall 1	28	B3
Charleville Rd 6	43	D2
Charleville Rd 7	27	C2
Charleville Sq 14	50	B2
Charlotte Quay 4	37	C2
Charlotte Way 2	36	A3
Charlton Lawn 14	53	D2
Chatham Row 2		
off William St S	59	D4

84

Name	Ref
Chatham St 2	59 D4
Chaworth Ter 8	
off Hanbury La	58 A3
Cheaters La 2	
off Redmonds Hill	36 A3
Cheeverstown Cen 6W	50 A3
Chelmsford La 6	44 B1
Chelmsford Rd 6	44 B1
Chelsea Gdns 3	31 C2
Cheltenham Pl 6	
off Portobello Br	44 A1
Cherbury Ct Boot.	54 B2
Cherbury Gdns Boot.	54 B2
Cherbury Ms Boot.	54 B2
Cherry Ct 6W	43 C3
Cherryfield Av 6	44 B2
Cherryfield Av 12	41 D3
Cherryfield Dr 12	41 D3
Cherryfield Rd 12	41 C3
Cherrygarth Still.	54 B3
Cherry Gro 12	41 D3
Cherrymount Cres 3	29 D1
Cherrymount Gro 3	29 D1
Cherrymount Pk 7	27 D2
Chesterfield Av 8	25 D3
Chesterfield Av 15	24 B1
Chesterfield Cl 15	24 B1
Chesterfield Copse 15	24 B1
Chesterfield Gro 15	24 B1
Chesterfield Pk 15	24 B1
Chesterfield Vw 15	24 B1
Chester Rd 6	44 A1
Chestnut Ct 9	13 D2
Chestnut Rd 12	40 A2
Chestnut Rd Still.	54 A2
Christ Ch Cath 8	58 B3
Christchurch Pl 8	58 B3
Church Av (Irishtown) 4	37 D3
Church Av (Rathmines) 6	44 A3
Church Av 8	34 B3
Church Av (Glasnevin) 9	12 A3
Church Av N (Drumcondra) 9	28 B1
Church Ct 15	24 A1
Churchfields 14	52 B1
Church Gdns 6	44 A2
Churchgate Av 3	31 C3
Churchill Ter 4	45 D1
Church La 2	
off College Grn	59 D3
Church La (Rathfarnham) 14	51 C2
Church La S 8	
off Kevin St Lwr	36 A3
Church Pk Av 6W	43 C2
Church Pk Ct 6W	43 C2
Church Pk Dr 6W	43 C2
Church Pk Lawn 6W	43 C2
Church Pk Vw 6W	43 C2
Church Pk Way 6W	43 C2
Church Rd 3	37 C1
Church Rd 13	18 B2
Church Rd 7	58 B2
Church St (Finglas) 11	10 B2
Church St (Howth) 13	20 B2
Church St E 3	37 C1
Church St Upr 7	58 B1
Church Ter 7	
off Church St	58 B2
Churchtown Business Pk 14	52 A3
Churchtown Cl 14	52 B1
Churchtown Dr 14	52 B1
Churchtown Rd Lwr 14	52 B1
Churchtown Rd Upr 14	52 B3
Cian Pk 9	28 B1
Cill Eanna 5	15 D3
Citylink Business Pk 12	40 B1
City Quay 2	59 F2
Clanawley Rd 5	30 B1
Clanboy Rd 5	14 A3
Clanbrassil Cl 8	43 D1
Clanbrassil St Lwr 8	35 D3
Clanbrassil St Upr 8	43 D1
Clancarthy Rd 5	30 A1
Clancy Av 11	10 B1
Clancy Rd 11	11 C1
Clandonagh Rd 5	14 A3
Clanhugh Rd 5	30 A1
Clanmahon Rd 5	14 A3
Clanmaurice Rd 5	14 A3
Clanmoyle Rd 5	30 A1
Clanranald Rd 5	14 A3
Clanree Rd 5	14 A3
Clanwilliam Pl 2	37 C3
Clare La 2	59 E4
Claremont Av 9	11 C3
Claremont Ct 11	27 C1
Claremont Dr 11	11 D2
Claremont Pk (Pairc Clearmont) 4	38 A3
Claremont Rd 4	38 A3
Claremont Rd 13	19 C1
Clarence Mangan Rd 8	35 D3
Clarence St D.L.	57 C3
Clarendon Mkt 2	
off Chatham St	59 D4
Clarendon Row 2	
off Clarendon St	59 D4
Clarendon St 2	59 D4
Clare Rd 9	12 B3
Clare St 2	59 E4
Clareville Ct 11	27 D1
Clareville Gro 11	27 D1
Clareville Rd 6W	43 C2
Clarinda Pk N D.L.	57 D3
Clarke Ter 8	35 C3
Classons Br 14	52 B1
Claude Rd 9	28 A2
Clifden Rd 10	32 A2
Cliff Wk (Fingal Way) 13	21 D2
Clifton Av Black.	56 B3
Clifton La Black.	56 B3
Clifton Ms 6	44 A1
Clifton Ter Black.	56 B3
Cliftonville Rd 9	28 A1
Clinches Ct 3	29 C3
Clogher Rd 12	42 B1
Cloister Av Black.	55 D3
Cloister Gate Black.	55 D3
Cloister Grn Black.	55 D3
Cloister Gro Black.	55 C3
Cloister Pk Black.	55 C3
Cloisters, The 6W	43 C3
Cloisters, The 9	13 C3
Cloister Sq Black.	55 C3
Cloister Way Black.	55 D3
Clonard Rd 12	42 A1
Clonfadda Wd Boot.	54 B2
Clonfert Rd 12	42 B2
Clonlara Rd 4	38 A2
Clonliffe Av 3	28 B2
Clonliffe Gdns 3	28 B2
Clonliffe Rd 3	28 B2
Clonmacnoise Gro 12	42 B2
Clonmacnoise Rd 12	42 B2
Clonmel Rd 11	11 D1
Clonmel St 2	36 A3
Clonmore Rd 3	28 B3
Clonmore Rd Still.	54 A3
Clonmore Ter 3	28 B3
Clonrosse Ct 13	
off Elton Dr	15 D1
Clonrosse Dr 13	15 D1
Clonrosse Pk 13	
off Elton Dr	15 D1
Clonskeagh Br 14	45 C3
Clonskeagh Dr 14	45 C3
Clonskeagh Rd 6	45 C2
Clonskeagh Rd 14	45 C2
Clonskeagh Sq 14	45 C3
Clontarf Pk 3	31 C2
Clontarf Prom 3	30 A2
Clontarf Rd 3	29 D2
Clontarf Sta 3	29 D2
Clonturk Av 9	28 B1
Clonturk Gdns 9	28 B1
Clonturk Pk 9	28 B1
Cloonlara Cres 11	
off Cloonlara Rd	10 B3
Cloonlara Dr 11	
off Cloonlara Rd	10 B3
Cloonlara Rd 11	10 B3
Close, The 6W	50 A2
Close, The 9	13 D1
Close, The Still.	54 A2
Clover Hill Dr 10	32 A3
Clover Hill Rd 10	32 A3
Cloyne Rd 12	42 B2
Club Rd 22	40 A2
Clune Rd 11	10 B1
Clyde La 4	45 C1
Clyde Rd 4	45 C1
Coburg Pl 1	29 C3
Colepark Av 10	32 A3
Colepark Dr 10	32 B2
Colepark Grn 10	32 B2
Colepark Rd 10	32 A2
Coleraine St 7	58 B1
College Cres 6W	50 A1
College Dr 6W	50 A1
College Grn 2	59 D3
College La 2	59 F3
College Pk 6W	50 A1
College Rd 15	24 A1
College St 2	59 D3
College Vw 1 24	48 A3
Colliers Av 6	44 B2
Collins Av 9	13 D3
Collins Av E 5	14 A1
Collins Av Extension 9	12 A1
Collins Av W 9	12 B2
Collins Ct 5	13 D3
Collins Ct Black.	
off Sweetmans Av	55 D2
Collins Dr 11	11 C1
Collins Grn 11	11 C1
Collins Pk 9	13 D3
Collins Pl 11	11 C1
Collins Row 11	11 C2
Collins Wd 9	13 C2
Comeragh Rd 12	41 D1
Commons St 1	59 F2
Con Colbert Rd (Bothar Coilbeard) 8	34 A2
Con Colbert Rd (Bothar Coilbeard) 10	33 D2
Connaught St 7	27 D2
Connaught Ter 6	
off Rathgar Rd	43 D3
Connolly Av 8	34 A2
Connolly Gdns 8	34 A2
Connolly Luas Sta 1	59 F1
Connolly Sta 1	59 F1
Conor Clune Rd 7	25 D1
Conquer Hill Rd 3	31 C3
Conquer Hill Ter 3	31 C2
Constitution Hill 7	58 B1
Convent Av 3	29 C2
Convent La 14	51 C3
Convent Lawns 10	32 A2
Convent Rd Black.	55 D2
Convent Rd D.L.	57 D3
Convent Vw Cotts 7	26 A1
Conway Ct 2	
off Macken St	37 C2
Conyngham Rd 8	34 A1
Cook St 8	58 A3
Coolamber Ct 2 16	50 A3
Coolamber Pk 16	50 A3
Coolatree Cl 9	13 D2
Coolatree Pk 9	13 D2
Coolatree Rd 9	13 D2
Cooleen Av 9	13 C1
Coolevin La 8	
off Long La	35 D3
Cooley Rd 12	41 D1
Coolgariff Rd 9	13 C2
Coolgreena Cl 9	13 D2
Coolgreena Rd 9	13 D2
Coolock Av 5	14 B1
Coolock Cl 5	14 B1
Coolock Dr 17	14 B1
Coolock Grn 5	14 B1
Coolock Gro 5	14 B1
Coolock Ind Est 17	15 C1
Coolock Village 5	14 B2
Coolrua Dr 9	13 C1
Coombe, The 8	58 A4
Copeland Av 3	29 D1
Copeland Gro 3	29 D1
Cope St 2	59 D3
Copper All 8	58 B3
Coppinger Cl Black.	55 C3
Coppinger Glade Black.	55 C3
Coppinger Row 2	
off William St S	59 D4
Coppinger Wk Black.	55 C3
Coppinger Wd Black.	55 C3
Corballis Row 8	
off Kevin St Upr	58 B4
Cork Hill 7	58 C3
Cork St 8	35 C3
Cormac Ter 6W	51 C1
Corn Ex Pl 2	
off George's Quay	59 E2
Cornmarket 8	58 A3
Corporation St 1	59 E1
Corrib Rd 6W	42 B3
Corrig Ct 12	
off Lugaquilla Av	48 B1
Corrybeg 6W	50 A2
Cottage Pl 1	
off Portland Pl	28 A2
Coulson Av 6	43 D3
Court, The 3	
off Clontarf Rd	30 A2
Court, The 5	16 A3
Court, The 6W	50 A2
Court, The 9	13 C3
Court, The 13	18 A1
Courtyard, The 14	51 D2
Cowbooter La 13	21 C2
Cowley Pl 7	28 A2
Cow Parlour 8	35 C3
Cowper Downs 6	44 A3
Cowper Dr 6	44 B3
Cowper Gdns 6	44 B3
Cowper Rd 6	44 B3
Cowper Sta 6	44 B3
Cowper St 7	27 C3
Cowper Village 6	44 A3
Craigford Av 5	14 A3
Craigford Dr 5	14 A3
Craigmore Gdns Black.	56 A2
Crampton Bldgs 2	
off Temple Bar	58 C3
Crampton Ct 2	58 C3
Crampton Quay 2	59 D2
Crampton Rd 4	37 D3
Crane La 2	58 C3
Crane St 8	35 C2
Cranfield Pl 4	37 D3
Cranford Ct 4	46 A3
Cranmer La 4	37 C3
Crannagh 6	45 C3
Crannagh Castle 14	51 C2
Crannagh Ct 14	51 C2
Crannagh Gro 14	51 D2
Crannagh Pk 14	51 D2
Crannagh Rd 14	51 C2
Crannagh Way 14	51 D2
Crawford Av 9	28 A2
Creighton St 2	59 F3
Cremona Rd 10	32 A2
Cremore Av 11	11 D3
Cremore Cres 11	11 D3
Cremore Dr 11	11 D3
Cremore Hts 11	
off Ballygall Rd E	11 D2
Cremore Lawn 11	11 D3
Cremore Pk 11	11 D3
Cremore Rd 11	11 D3
Cremorne 16	50 A3
Crescent, The (Donnybrook) 4	45 C2
Crescent, The (Beaumont) 9	13 C2
Crescent, The (Whitehall) 9	13 C3
Crescent, The 13	18 A1
Crescent Dr 6W	50 A1
Crescent Gdns 3	29 C3
Crescent Pl 3	29 D2
Crescent Vil 9	28 A1
Crestfield Av 9	12 B2
Crestfield Cl 9	12 B2
Crestfield Dr 9	12 B2
Crestfield Pk 9	
off Crestfield Cl	12 B2
Crinan Strand 1	37 C1
Croaghpatrick Rd 7	26 A2
Crofton Av D.L.	57 C3
Crofton Rd D.L.	57 C2
Crofton Ter D.L.	57 C2
Croftwood Grn 10	32 A3
Croftwood Pk 10	32 A3
Croke Pk Ind Est 1	28 B3
Croker La 8	35 C2

Entry	Ref
Cromcastle Av 5	14 A1
Cromcastle Ct 5	14 A1
Cromcastle Dr 5	14 A1
Cromcastle Grn 5	14 A1
Cromcastle Pk 5	14 A1
Cromcastle Rd 5	14 A1
Cromwells Fort Rd 12.	41 C2
Cromwells Quarters 8	34 B2
Cross Av Boot.	55 C1
Cross Av D.L.	57 C3
Crossbeg Ind Est 24	40 A3
Cross Guns Br 11	27 D2
Cross Kevin St 8	36 A3
Crosslands Ind Est 22	40 A4
Crosstrees 13	21 C2
Crosthwaite Ter D.L.	57 C3
Crotty Av 12	41 D2
Crown All 2	
off Temple Bar	58 C3
Crow St 2	58 C3
Croydon Gdns 3	29 C1
Croydon Grn 3	29 C2
Croydon Pk Av 3	29 C1
Croydon Ter 3	29 C1
Crumlin Pk 12	42 A1
Crumlin Rd 12	42 A1
Crumlin Shop Cen 12	34 B3
Cuala Rd 7	27 C2
Cuckoo La 7	58 B2
Cuffe La 2	36 A3
Cuffe St 2	36 A3
Cullenswood Gdns 6	44 B2
Cullenswood Pk 6	44 B2
Cumberland Rd 2	36 B3
Cumberland St D.L.	57 C3
Cumberland St N 1	28 A3
Cumberland St S 2	59 F4
Curlew Rd 12	41 D1
Curved St 2	
off Eustace St	58 C3
Curzon St 8	36 A3
Custom Ho 1	59 E2
Custom Ho Quay 1	59 E2
Cymric Rd 4	38 A2
Cypress Downs 6W	50 A2
Cypress Dr 6W	50 A2
Cypress Garth 6W	50 A2
Cypress Gro N 6W	50 A2
Cypress Gro Rd 6W	50 A2
Cypress Gro S 6W	50 A2
Cypress Lawn 6W	50 A2
Cypress Pk 6W	50 A2
Cypress Rd Still.	54 A2

D

Entry	Ref
Dalcassian Downs 11	27 D2
Dale Ct Still.	54 A3
Dale Rd Still.	54 A3
Dame Ct 2	58 C3
Dame La 2	58 C3
Dame St 2	58 C3
Danes Ct 3	31 D2
Danesfort 3	30 B2
Daneswell Rd 9	28 A1
Dangan Av 12	42 A3
Dangan Dr 12	42 A3
Dangan Pk 12	42 A3
Danieli Dr 5	14 B3
Danieli Rd 5	14 B3
Daniel St 8	35 D3
Dargle Rd 9	28 A2
Darleys Ter 8	35 C3
Darley St 6	43 D1
Darling Est 7	25 D1
Dartmouth Ho Ind Est 10	32 B3
Dartmouth La 6	44 A1
Dartmouth Pl 6	44 A1
Dartmouth Rd 6	44 A1
Dartmouth Sq 6	44 A1
Dartmouth Ter 6	44 A1
Dartmouth Wk 6	
off Dartmouth Ter	44 A1
Dartry Cotts 6	52 A1
Dartry Pk 6	44 A3
Dartry Rd 6	44 A3
David Pk 9	28 A2
David Rd 9	28 A2
Davis Pl 8	
off Thomas Davis St S	58 B4
Davitt Rd 12	34 A3
Dawson Ct 2	
off Stephen St	58 C4
Dawson Ct Black.	55 C2
Dawson La 2	59 E4
Dawson St 2	59 D4
Deanstown Av 11	9 D2
Deanstown Dr 11	10 A2
Deanstown Grn 11	10 A2
Deanstown Pk 11	10 A2
Deanstown Rd 11	10 A2
Dean St 8	58 B4
Dean Swift Grn 11	11 D2
Dean Swift Rd 11	11 D2
Dean Swift Sq 8	
off Swifts All	58 A4
De Burgh Rd 7	34 B1
Decies Rd 10	32 A2
De Courcy Sq 9	27 D1
Deerpark Av 15	24 B1
Deerpark Cl 15	24 B1
Deerpark Dr 15	24 B1
Deerpark Lawn 15	24 B1
Deerpark Rd 15	24 B1
Deerpark Rd Still.	54 A2
Del Val Av 13	17 C2
Del Val Ct 13	17 C2
Delville Rd 11	11 D2
Delvin Rd 7	27 C2
Demesne 5	30 B1
Denmark St Gt 1	28 A3
Denzille La 2	59 F4
Denzille Pl 2	
off Denzille La	59 F4
Dermot O'Hurley Av 4	37 D2
Derravaragh Rd 6W	42 B3
Derry Dr 12	42 A2
Derrynane Gdns 4	37 D2
Derrynane Par 7	28 A2
Derry Pk 12	42 A2
Derry Rd 12	42 A2
Desmond Av D.L.	57 C3
Desmond St 8	35 D3
Devenish Rd 12	42 B2
Deverell Pl 1	59 E1
Deverys La 7	27 D2
De Vesci Ter D.L.	57 C3
Devoy Rd 8	34 A3
Digges La 2	
off Stephen St	58 C4
Digges St 2	36 A3
Digges St Lwr 2	
off Cuffe La	36 A3
Dingle Rd 7	26 B2
Dispensary La 14	51 C3
Distillery Rd 3	28 B2
Docklands Innovation Pk 3	29 D3
Dock Pl S 4	37 D2
Dock St S 4	
off Dock St S	37 C2
Dodderbank 14	44 B3
Dodder Dale 14	51 C2
Dodder Pk Dr 14	51 D1
Dodder Pk Gro 14	51 D1
Dodder Pk Rd 14	51 D1
Dodder Ter 4	37 D2
Doddervale 14	52 A1
D'Olier St 2	59 D2
Dollymount Av 3	31 D2
Dollymount Gro 3	31 C2
Dollymount Pk 3	31 D2
Dollymount Ri 3	31 D2
Dolphin Av 8	35 C3
Dolphin Mkt 8	
off Dolphin's Barn St	35 C3
Dolphin Rd 12	34 B3
Dolphin's Barn 8	35 C3
Dolphin's Barn St 8	35 C3
Dominick La 1	58 C1
Dominick Pl 1	58 C1
Dominick St D.L.	57 C3
Dominick St Lwr 1	58 C1
Dominick St Upr 7	27 D3
Domville Dr 6W	50 A2
Domville Rd 6W	50 A2
Donaghmede Av 13	16 B1
Donaghmede Dr 13	16 B1
Donaghmede Pk 13	16 B1
Donaghmede Rd 13	16 A1
Donaghmede Shop Cen 13	16 A1
Donard Rd 12	41 D1
Donelan Av 8	34 B2
Donnybrook Castle Ct 4	45 D2
Donnybrook Cl 4	45 D3
Donnybrook Grn 4	45 D3
Donnybrook Manor 4	45 C2
Donnybrook Rd 4	45 C2
Donnycastle 4	45 D2
Donnycarney Rd 9	13 D3
Donore Av 8	35 C3
Donore Rd 8	35 C3
Donore Ter 8	
off Brown St S	35 C3
Donovan La 8	
off Clanbrassil St Lwr	35 D3
Doon Av 7	27 C3
Doris St 4	37 C2
Dornden Pk Boot.	46 B3
Dorset La 1	28 A3
Dorset Pl 1	
off Dorset St Lwr	28 A3
Dorset St Lwr 1	28 A3
Dorset St Upr 1	28 A3
Dowkers La 8	35 D3
Dowland Rd 12	41 D2
Dowling's Ct 2	
off Lombard St E	59 F2
Dowling's Ct S 2	
off Lombard St E	59 F2
Downpatrick Rd 12	42 B1
Dowth Av 7	27 C2
Doyle's La 3	31 D2
Drapier Grn 11	11 D2
Drapier Rd 11	11 D2
Drayton Cl Black.	56 B3
Drimnagh Rd 12	41 D1
Drimnagh Sta 12	33 D3
Dromard Rd 12	41 D1
Dromawling Rd 9	13 D2
Dromdawn Av 9	13 C2
Dromeen Av 9	13 D2
Dromlee Cres 9	13 D2
Dromnanane Pk 9	13 D2
Dromnanane Rd 9	13 D2
Dromore Rd 12	42 A1
Drumalee Av 7	
off Drumalee Rd	27 C3
Drumalee Ct 7	
off Drumalee Rd	27 C3
Drumalee Dr 7	
off Drumalee Rd	27 C3
Drumalee Gro 7	
off Drumalee Rd	27 C3
Drumalee Pk 7	27 C3
Drumalee Rd 7	27 C3
Drumcliffe Dr 7	26 B2
Drumcliffe Rd 7	26 B2
Drumcondra Pk 3	28 A2
Drumcondra Rd Lwr 9	28 A2
Drumcondra Rd Upr 9	28 B1
Drumcondra Sta 3	28 B2
Drumfinn Pk 10	32 A2
Drumfinn Rd (Bothar Drom Finn) 10	32 A2
Drummartin Cl 14	53 D3
Drummartin Cres 1 14	53 D3
Drummartin Pk 14	53 D3
Drummartin Ter 14	53 D3
Drummond Pl 6	
off Mount Drummond Av	43 D1
Druncondra Br 9	28 B1
Drury St 2	58 C4
Dublin Ind Est 11	11 C3
Dublin Port Tunnel 3	29 D3
Dublin Rd 13	17 C2
Dufferin Av 8	35 D3
Duggan Pl 6	
off Rathmines Rd Upr	44 A2
Duke La 2	59 D4
Duke La Lwr 2	
off Duke St	59 D3
Duke Row 1	
off North Circular Rd	28 B3
Duke St 2	59 D4
Dunamase Boot.	55 C1
Dunard Av 7	26 B2
Dunard Ct 7	26 B2
Dunard Dr 7	26 B2
Dunard Pk 7	26 B3
Dunard Rd 7	26 B3
Dunard Wk 7	26 B3
Dunbo Ter 13	
off Church St	20 B2
Duncarrig 13	19 C2
Dundaniel Rd 5	13 D1
Dundrum Business Pk 14	53 C1
Dundrum Rd 14	52 B1
Dundrum Shop Cen 14	52 B3
Dundrum Sta 14	53 C3
Dungar Ter D.L.	
off Northumberland Av	57 D3
Dungriffan Rd 13	21 C3
Dun Laoghaire Sta D.L.	57 D2
Dunleary Hill D.L.	57 C3
Dunleary Rd D.L.	57 C2
Dunluce Rd 3	30 B1
Dunmanus Rd 7	26 B2
Dunne St 1	28 B3
Dunree Pk 5	15 C1
Dunsandle Ct 15	24 A1
Dunsandle Gro 15	24 A1
Dunseverick Rd 3	30 B1
Dunsink Av 11	10 A2
Dunsink Dr 11	10 A2
Dunsink Gdns 11	10 A2
Dunsink Grn 11	10 A2
Dunsink La 15	9 C2
Dunsink Pk 11	10 A2
Dunsink Rd 11	10 B2
Dunsoghly Av 11	9 D1
Dunsoghly Dr 11	9 D1
Dunsoghly Grn 11	9 D1
Dunville Av 6	44 A2
Dunville Ter 6	
off Mountpleasant Av Upr	44 A1
Durham Rd 4	46 A1
Durrow Rd 12	42 B2

E

Entry	Ref
Eagle Hill Black.	55 D2
Eagle Hill Av 6W	43 C3
Eagle Ter 2 16	53 C3
Earl Pl 1	59 D1
Earls Ct 7	26 B2
Earlscourt Ind Est 14	52 A3
Earlsfort Mans 2	
off Adelaide Rd	36 A3
Earlsfort Ter 2	36 A3
Earl St N 1	59 D1
Earl St S 8	58 A4
Eastern Breakwater 1	38 B2
East Link 4	37 D2
Eastmoreland La 4	37 C3
Eastmoreland Pl 4	37 C3
East Pt Business Pk 3	29 D3
East Rd 3	37 D1
East Rd Ind Est 3	37 D1
East Wall Rd 3	29 C2
Eastwood Cl 11	9 D2
Eastwood Cres 11	9 D2
Eastwood Pk 11	10 A2
Eaton Brae 14	52 A1
Eaton Pl Black.	56 A2
Eaton Rd 6W	43 C3
Eaton Sq 6W	43 C3
Eaton Sq Black.	56 A2
Ebenezer Ter 8	35 C3
Eblana Av D.L.	57 D3
Eblana Vil 1	
off Grand Canal St Lwr	37 C2
Eccles Ct 7	
off Eccles Pl	28 A3
Eccles Pl 7	28 A3
Eccles St 7	28 A3
Echlin St 8	35 C2
Edenbrook Ct 1 14	51 C3
Edenbrook Dr 14	50 B3
Edenbrook Pk 14	50 B3
Edenmore Av 5	15 D2
Edenmore Cres 5	15 D2
Edenmore Dr 5	15 D2
Edenmore Gdns 5	15 D2
Edenmore Grn 5	15 D2
Edenmore Gro 5	15 D2
Edenmore Pk 5	15 C2
Eden Pk Dr 14	53 D3
Eden Pk Rd 14	53 D3

86

Eden Quay *1* — 59 D2
Edenvale Rd *6* — 44 B2
Effra Rd *6* — 43 D2
Eglinton Ct *4* — 45 C2
Eglinton Pk *4* — 45 C2
Eglinton Rd *4* — 45 C2
Eglinton Sq *4* — 45 C2
Eglinton Ter *4* — 45 C2
Eglinton Ter *14* — 53 C3
Eldon Ter *8*
  off South Circular Rd — 35 C3
Elgin Rd *4* — 45 C2
Elizabeth St *3* — 28 B2
Elkwood *16* — 50 A3
Ellenfield Rd *9* — 13 C2
Ellesmere Av *7* — 27 C3
Ellis Quay *7* — 35 C1
Ellis St *7*
  off Benburb St — 35 C1
Elmcastle Cl *24* — 48 A2
Elmcastle Ct *24* — 48 A2
Elmcastle Dr *24* — 48 A2
Elmcastle Grn *24* — 48 A2
Elmcastle Pk *24* — 48 A2
Elmcastle Wk *24* — 48 A2
Elm Gro *Black.* — 55 D3
Elm Gro Cotts *7*
  off Blackhorse Av — 26 A2
Elm Mt Av *9* — 13 D3
Elm Mt Cl *9* — 13 D3
Elm Mt Ct *9* — 14 A3
Elm Mt Cres *9* — 13 D2
Elm Mt Dr *9* — 13 D3
Elm Mt Gro *9* — 13 D2
Elm Mt Hts *9* — 13 D2
Elm Mt Lawn *9* — 13 D2
Elm Mt Pk *9* — 13 D2
Elm Mt Ri *9* — 13 D2
Elm Mt Rd *9* — 13 D3
Elm Mt Vw *9* — 13 D2
Elm Pk *4* — 46 A2
Elmpark Av *6* — 44 B1
Elmpark Ter *6W* — 43 C3
Elm Rd *9* — 13 D3
Elm Rd *12* — 40 A2
Elms, The *4* — 46 A3
Elms, The *Black.* — 55 C2
Elmwood Av Lwr *6* — 44 B1
Elmwood Av Upr *6*
  off Elmwood Av Lwr — 44 B2
Elton Ct *13*
  off Elton Dr — 15 D1
Elton Dr *13* — 15 D1
Elton Pk *13* — 15 D1
Elton Wk *13*
  off Elton Dr — 15 D1
Ely Pl *2* — 36 B3
Ely Pl Upr *2*
  off Ely Pl — 36 B3
Embassy Lawn *14* — 45 C3
Emerald Cotts *4* — 37 C3
Emerald Pl *1*
  off Sheriff St Lwr — 37 C1
Emerald Sq *8* — 35 C3
Emerald St *1* — 37 C1
Emily Pl *1*
  off Sheriff St Lwr — 59 F1
Emmet Ct *8* — 33 D3
Emmet Rd *8* — 33 D2
Emmet Sq *Boot.* — 55 C1
Emmet St *1* — 28 B3
Emmet St
  (Haroldscross) *6* — 43 D1
Emor St *8* — 35 D3
Emorville Av *8* — 35 D3
Emorville Sq *8*
  off South Circular Rd — 35 C3
Empress Pl *1* — 28 B3
Enaville Rd *3* — 29 C2
Engine All *8* — 58 A4
Ennafort Av
  (Ascal Dun Eanna) *5* — 15 C3
Ennafort Ct *5* — 15 C3
Ennafort Dr
  (Ceide Dun Eanna) *5* — 15 C3
Ennafort Gro *5* — 15 C3
Ennafort Pk *5* — 15 C3

Ennafort Rd *5* — 15 C3
Ennel Av *5* — 15 C2
Ennel Dr *5* — 15 C2
Ennel Pk *5* — 15 C2
Ennis Gro *4* — 37 D3
Enniskerry Rd *7* — 27 D2
Erne Pl *2* — 37 C2
Erne Pl Little *2* — 59 F3
Erne St Lwr *2* — 37 C2
Erne St Upr *2* — 37 C2
Erne Ter Front *2*
  off Erne St Upr — 37 C2
Erne Ter Rere *2*
  off Erne St Upr — 37 C2
Errigal Gdns *12* — 41 D1
Errigal Rd *12* — 41 D1
Erris Rd *7* — 27 C2
Esmond Av *3* — 29 C2
Esposito Rd *12* — 41 D2
Essex Quay *8* — 58 B3
Essex St E *2* — 58 C3
Essex St W *8* — 58 C3
Estate Av *4* — 46 B3
Estate Cotts *4* — 37 C3
Eugene St *8* — 35 C3
Eustace St *2* — 58 C3
Everton Av *7* — 27 C3
Evora Cres *13* — 20 B2
Evora Pk *13* — 20 B2
Evora Ter *13*
  off St. Lawrence Rd — 20 B2
Ewington La *8* — 35 C2
Exchange Ct *2*
  off Dame St — 58 C3
Exchange St Lwr *8* — 58 B3
Exchange St Upr *8*
  off Lord Edward St — 58 C3
Exchequer St *2* — 58 C3

F
Fade St *2* — 58 C4
Fairbrook Lawn *14* — 51 C3
Fairfield Av *3* — 29 C3
Fairfield Pk *6* — 43 D3
Fairfield Rd
  (Glasnevin) *9* — 28 A1
Fairlawn Pk *11*
  off Fairlawn Rd — 10 B2
Fairlawn Rd *11* — 10 B2
Fairview *3* — 29 C2
Fairview Av
  (Irishtown) *4* — 37 D2
Fairview Av Lwr *3* — 29 C2
Fairview Av Upr *3* — 29 C2
Fairview Grn *3* — 29 C2
Fairview Pas *3*
  off Fairview Strand — 29 C2
Fairview Strand *3* — 29 C2
Fairview Ter *3* — 29 C2
Fairways *14* — 50 B2
Fairways Av *11* — 11 C2
Fairways Grn *11* — 11 C2
Fairways Gro *11* — 11 C2
Fairways Pk *11* — 11 C2
Faith Av *3* — 29 C3
Falcarragh Rd *9* — 12 B2
Farmhill Dr *14* — 53 C2
Farmhill Pk *14* — 53 D3
Farmhill Rd *14* — 53 C2
Farney Pk *4* — 38 A3
Farnham Cres *11* — 10 B2
Farnham Dr *11* — 10 B2
Farrenboley Cotts *14* — 52 B1
Farrenboley Pk *14* — 52 B1
Father Kitt Ct *12* — 42 B2
Father Matthew Br *8* — 58 A3
Fatima Mans *8* — 34 B3
Fatima Sta *8* — 35 C2
Faughart Rd *12* — 42 B2
Faussagh Av *7* — 26 B1
Faussagh Rd *7* — 27 C2
Fenian St *2* — 59 F4
Ferguson Rd *9* — 28 A1
Fergus Rd *6W* — 51 C1
Ferndale Av *11* — 11 C2
Ferndale Rd *11* — 11 C2
Fernhill Av *12* — 49 D1
Fernhill Pk *12* — 49 D1
Fernhill Rd *12* — 49 D1
Ferns Rd *12* — 42 B2
Fernvale Dr *12* — 41 D1
Ferrard Rd *6* — 43 D3
Ferrymans Crossing *1* — 37 C1

Fertullagh Rd *7* — 27 C2
Field Av *12* — 41 D2
Fields Ter *6*
  off Ranelagh Rd — 44 B1
Finches Ind Pk *12* — 41 C1
Findlater Pl *1*
  off Parnell St — 28 A3
Findlaters St *7* — 34 B1
Fingal Pl *7* — 27 C3
Fingal St *8* — 35 C3
Finglas Business Pk *11* — 11 C3
Finglas Pk *11* — 11 C1
Finglas Pl *11* — 10 B2
Finglas Rd *11* — 11 C3
Finglas Rd Old *11* — 11 C3
Finglas Shop Cen *11* — 10 B1
Finglaswood Rd *11* — 10 A1
Finlay Sq *4* — 54 A2
Finn St *7* — 27 C3
Finsbury Pk *14* — 52 B3
Firhouse Rd *16* — 49 D3
Firhouse Rd *24* — 49 D3
First Av *1* — 37 C1
First Av (Inchicore) *10* — 33 C2
Fishamble St *8* — 58 B3
Fitzgerald St *6* — 43 D1
Fitzgibbon La *1* — 28 B3
Fitzgibbon St *1* — 28 B3
Fitzmaurice Rd *11* — 11 D2
Fitzroy Av *3* — 28 A2
Fitzwilliam Ct *2*
  off Pembroke St Upr — 36 B3
Fitzwilliam La *2* — 36 B3
Fitzwilliam Pl *2* — 36 B3
Fitzwilliam Quay *4* — 37 D2
Fitzwilliam Sq E *2* — 36 B3
Fitzwilliam Sq N *2* — 36 B3
Fitzwilliam Sq S *2* — 36 B3
Fitzwilliam Sq W *2* — 36 B3
Fitzwilliam St
  (Ringsend) *4* — 37 D2
Fitzwilliam St Lwr *2* — 36 B3
Fitzwilliam St Upr *2* — 36 B3
Fleet St *2* — 59 D2
Fleming Pl *4* — 37 C3
Fleming Rd *9* — 28 A1
Flemings La *4*
  off Haddington Rd — 37 C3
Flemingstown Pk *14* — 52 B2
Fleurville *Black.* — 55 D3
Florence St *8*
  off Lennox St — 36 A3
Foley St *1* — 59 E1
Fontenoy St *7* — 27 D3
Fonthill Abbey *2 14* — 51 C3
Fonthill Ct *3 14* — 51 C3
Fonthill Pk *14* — 51 C3
Fonthill Rd *14* — 51 C3
Forbes La *8* — 35 C2
Forbes St *2* — 37 C2
Forest Av *24* — 48 A1
Forest Ct *24* — 48 A1
Forest Dr *24* — 48 A1
Forest Grn *24* — 48 A1
Forest Lawn *24* — 48 A1
Forest Pk *24* — 48 A1
Fortfield Av *6W* — 50 B1
Fortfield Ct *6W* — 50 B1
Fortfield Dr *6W* — 50 B2
Fortfield Gdns *6* — 44 A3
Fortfield Gro *6W* — 50 B1
Fortfield Pk *6W* — 50 B2
Fortfield Rd *6W* — 50 B1
Fortfield Ter *6* — 44 A3
Forth Rd *3* — 29 D3
Fortview Av *3* — 31 C3
Fosterbrook *Boot.* — 54 B1
Foster Cotts *7*
  off Phibsborough Rd — 27 D3
Foster Pl S *2* — 59 D3
Fosters, The *Still.* — 54 A2
Fosters Av *Still.* — 54 A2
Foster Ter *3* — 28 B3
Fountain Pl *7* — 35 C1
Fountain Rd *8* — 34 B1
Four Cts Sta *7* — 58 B2
Fourth Av *1* — 37 C1
Fownes St *2* — 59 D3
Foxfield Av *5* — 16 A2
Foxfield Cres *5* — 16 B2
Foxfield Dr *5* — 16 B2
Foxfield Grn *5* — 16 B2
Foxfield Gro *5* — 16 A2

Foxfield Hts *5* — 16 A2
Foxfield Lawn *5* — 16 B2
Foxfield Pk *5* — 16 B2
Foxfield Rd *5* — 16 B2
Foxfield St. John *5* — 16 B2
Foxhill Av *13* — 15 D1
Foxhill Ct *13* — 15 D1
Foxhill Cres *13* — 15 D1
Foxhill Dr *13* — 15 D1
Foxhill Lawn *13* — 15 D1
Foxhill Pk *13* — 15 D1
Foxhill Way *13* — 15 D1
Foxs La *5* — 16 B3
Foyle Rd *3* — 29 C2
Francis St *8* — 58 A3
Frankfort *14* — 52 B2
Frankfort Av *6* — 43 D2
Frankfort Ct *6* — 43 D3
Frankfort Pk *14* — 52 B2
Frascati Pk *Black.* — 55 D2
Frascati Rd *Black.* — 55 D2
Frascati Shop Cen
  Black. — 55 D2
Frederick Ct *1*
  off Hardwicke St — 28 A3
Frederick La *2* — 59 E4
Frederick La N *1* — 28 A3
Frederick St N *1* — 28 A3
Frederick St S *2* — 59 E4
Frenchmans La *1*
  off Gardiner St Lwr — 59 E1
Friarsland Av *14* — 53 C2
Friarsland Rd *14* — 53 C2
Friary Av *7* — 58 A2
Friel Av *10* — 32 A3
Fumbally La *8* — 35 D3
Furry Pk Ct *5* — 30 B1
Furry Pk Rd *5* — 30 B1
Furze Rd *8* — 24 B2

G
Gaelic St *3* — 29 C3
Gairdini Sheinleasa *9* — 12 A1
Galmoy Rd *7* — 27 C2
Galtymore Cl *12* — 33 D3
Galtymore Dr *12* — 34 A3
Galtymore Pk *12* — 41 D1
Galtymore Rd *12* — 34 A3
Gandon Cl *6W* — 43 D1
Garden Croath *Black.* — 55 D3
Garden La *8* — 58 A4
Gardiner La *1* — 28 B3
Gardiner Row *1* — 28 A3
Gardiner's Pl *1* — 28 A3
Gardiner St Lwr *1* — 28 B3
Gardiner St Mid *1* — 28 A3
Gardiner St Upr *1* — 28 A3
Gardini Lein
  (Lein Gdns) *5* — 15 D3
Gardini Phairc An
  Bhailtini
  (Villa Pk Gdns) *7* — 26 A2
Garrynure *6* — 44 B3
Garryowen Rd *10* — 32 B2
Gartan Av *9* — 28 A2
Garville Av *6* — 43 D3
Garville Av Upr *6* — 43 D3
Garville Rd *6* — 43 D3
Geoffrey Keating Rd *8*
  off O'Curry Rd — 35 D3
George's Av *Black.* — 55 D2
George's Hill *7* — 58 B2
George's La *7* — 58 A1
George's Pl *1* — 28 A3
George's Pl *Black.* — 55 D2
George's Pl *D.L.* — 57 C3
George's Quay *2* — 59 E2
George's St Lwr *D.L.* — 57 C3
George's St Upr *D.L.* — 57 D3
Georgian Village *15* — 24 A1
Geraldine St *7* — 27 D3
Geraldine Ter *6* — 44 B3
Gerald St *4* — 37 C2
Gilbert Rd *8* — 35 D3
Gilford Av *4* — 46 A1
Gilford Ct *4* — 46 A1
Gilford Dr *4* — 46 A1
Gilford Pk *4* — 46 A1
Gilford Rd *4* — 46 A1
Glandore Rd *9* — 13 C3
Glasanaon Ct *11*
  off Glasanaon Pk — 11 C2
Glasanaon Pk *11* — 11 C2

Glasanaon Rd *11*	11	C1
Glasaree Rd *11*	11	C1
Glasilawn Av *11*	11	D2
Glasilawn Rd *11*	11	C3
Glasmeen Rd *11*	11	C3
Glasnamana Pl *11*	11	C2
Glasnamana Rd *11*	11	C3
Glasnevin Av *11*	11	C1
Glasnevin *27*	27	D1
Glasnevin Business Pk *11*	10	A3
Glasnevin Ct *11*	11	C3
Glasnevin Downs *11*	11	C3
Glasnevin Dr *11*	11	D2
Glasnevin Hill *9*	12	A3
Glasnevin Pk *11*	11	D1
Glasnevin Wds *11*	11	D1
Glasson Ct *14*	52	B1
Glaunsharoon *4*	45	C2
Gleann Na Smol *D.L.*	56	A3
Glebe Vw *11*	10	B1
Gledswood Av *14*	53	C1
Gledswood Cl *14*	53	C1
Gledswood Dr *14*	53	C1
Gledswood Pk *14*	53	C1
Glenaan Rd *9*	12	B2
Glenabbey Rd *Still.*	54	A3
Glenanne *12*	42	B3
Glenard Av *7*	27	C3
Glenarm Av *9*	28	B2
Glenarm Sq *9*	28	A2
Glenarriff Rd *7*	25	D1
Glenart Av *Black.*	55	C3
Glenaulin *20*	24	A3
Glenaulin Dr (Ceide Glennaluinn) *20*	32	A1
Glenaulin Pk (Pairc Gleannaluinn) *20*	24	A3
Glenavy Pk *6W*	42	B3
Glenayle Rd *5*	15	D1
Glenayr Rd *6*	51	D1
Glenbeigh Pk *7*	26	B3
Glenbeigh Rd *7*	26	B3
Glenbower Pk *14*	52	B3
Glenbrook Pk *14*	51	C3
Glenbrook Rd *7*	9	D3
Glencarrig *13*	19	C1
Glencar Rd *7*	26	B3
Glencloy Rd *9*	12	B2
Glencorp Rd *9*	13	C2
Glendale Pk *12*	50	A1
Glendalough Rd *9*	28	A1
Glendhu Pk *7*	9	D3
Glendhu Rd *7*	9	D3
Glendoo Cl *12*		
off *Lugaquilla Av*	48	B1
Glendown Av *6W*	49	D1
Glendown Cl *6W*		
off *Glendown Gro*	49	D1
Glendown Ct *6W*	49	D1
Glendown Cres *6W*	49	D1
Glendown Grn *6W*		
off *Glendown Gro*	49	D1
Glendown Gro *6W*	49	D1
Glendown Lawn *6W*	50	A1
Glendown Pk *6W*	49	D1
Glendown Rd *6W*	49	D2
Glendun Rd *9*	12	B2
Glenealy Rd *12*	43	C1
Glenfarne Rd *5*	15	C1
Glengariff Par *7*	28	A2
Glenhill Av *11*	11	C2
Glenhill Ct *11*	11	C2
Glenhill Dr *11*	10	B2
Glenhill Gro *11*	11	C2
Glenhill Pk *11*	11	C2
Glenhill Vil *11*		
off *Glenhill Pk*	10	B2
Glenmalure Pk *8*	34	B3
Glenmalure Sq *6*	44	B3
Glenmore Rd *7*	26	B3
Glenomena Gro *Boot.*	54	A1
Glenomena Pk *Boot.*	46	A3
Glenshesk Rd *9*	13	C2
Glenties Dr *11*	10	A2
Glenties Pk *11*	10	A2
Glentow Rd *9*	12	B2
Glenvar Pk *Boot.*	55	C2
Glenview Ind Est *12*	34	B3
Glenview Lawn *24*	49	C3
Glenview Pk *24*	48	B3
Glenville Ind Est *Still.*	54	A2
Glenwood Rd *5*	15	C1

Gloucester La *1*		
off *Sean McDermott St Lwr*	28	B3
Gloucester Pl *1*	28	B3
Gloucester Pl Lwr *1*	28	B3
Gloucester Pl N *1*	28	B3
Gloucester Pl Upr *1*		
off *Gloucester Pl*	28	B3
Gloucester St S *2*	59	E2
Glovers All *2*	58	C4
Goatstown Av *14*	53	C2
Goatstown Rd *14*	53	D2
Golden Br *8*	33	D2
Goldenbridge Av *8*	34	A3
Goldenbridge Gdns *8*	34	A3
Goldenbridge Sta *12*	34	A3
Goldenbridge Ter *8*		
off *Connolly Av*	34	A3
Golden La *8*	58	B4
Goldsmith St *7*	27	D3
Gordon Pl *2*		
off *Richmond St S*	36	A3
Gordon St *4*	37	C2
Gorsefield Ct *5*	15	C2
Gortbeg Av *11*		
off *Gortbeg Rd*	10	B3
Gortbeg Dr *11*		
off *Gortbeg Rd*	10	B3
Gortbeg Pk *11*		
off *Gortbeg Rd*	10	B3
Gortbeg Rd *11*	10	B3
Gortmore Av *11*	10	B3
Gortmore Dr *11*	10	B3
Gortmore Pk *11*		
off *Gortmore Rd*	10	B3
Gortmore Rd *11*	10	B3
Government Bldgs *2*	59	E4
Gracefield Av *5*	15	C3
Gracefield Ct *5*	14	B3
Gracefield Rd *5*	14	B2
Grace O'Malley Dr *13*	20	B2
Grace O'Malley Rd *13*	20	B2
Grace Pk Av *3*	28	B1
Grace Pk Ct *3*	13	C2
Grace Pk Gdns *9*	28	B1
Grace Pk Hts *9*	13	C3
Grace Pk Meadows *9*	13	D3
Grace Pk Rd *9*	28	B1
Grace Pk Ter *9*	29	C1
Grafton St *2*	59	D4
Graham Ct *1*	28	A3
Granby La *1*	28	A3
Granby Pl *1*	58	C1
Granby Row *1*	28	A3
Grand Canal Bk *8*	35	C2
Grand Canal Bk (Ranelagh) *8*	44	A1
Grand Canal Business Cen *3*	33	C3
Grand Canal Harbour *8*		
off *James's St*	34	B2
Grand Canal Pl N *8*	35	C2
Grand Canal Quay *2*	37	C2
Grand Canal St Lwr *2*	37	C2
Grand Canal St Upr *4*	37	C3
Grand Canal Vw *8*	34	A3
Grand Par *6*	44	A1
Grange Cl *13*	17	C1
Grange Downs *14*	51	D3
Grange Dr *13*	17	C1
Grangegorman Lwr *7*	58	A1
Grangegorman Upr *7*	27	C3
Grange Par *13*	17	C1
Grange Pk *14*	51	C3
Grange Pk Av *5*	16	A2
Grange Pk Cl *5*	16	A2
Grange Pk Cres *5*	16	A2
Grange Pk Dr *5*	16	A2
Grange Pk Grn *5*	16	A2
Grange Pk Gro *5*	16	A2
Grange Pk Ri *5*	16	A2
Grange Pk Rd *5*	16	A2
Grange Pk Wk *5*	16	A2
Grange Rd *13*	16	A1
Grange Rd *14*	51	C2
Grange Rd *16*	51	C3
Grange Way *13*	17	C1
Granite Pl *4*	45	D1
Granite Ter *8*		
off *Inchicore Ter S*	33	D2
Grantham Pl *8*	36	A3
Grantham St *8*	36	A3

Grants Row *2*	37	C2
Grattan Br *1*	58	C2
Grattan Ct E *2*		
off *Grattan St*	37	C2
Grattan Cres *8*	33	D2
Grattan Par *9*	28	A2
Grattan Pl *2*		
off *Grattan St*	37	C2
Grattan St *2*	37	C2
Gray Sq *8*		
off *Gray St*	58	A4
Gray St *8*	58	A4
Great Clarence Pl *2*	37	C2
Great Western Av *7*		
off *North Circular Rd*	27	D3
Great Western Sq *7*	27	D3
Great Western Vil *7*	27	D3
Greek St *7*	58	B2
Green, The *9*	13	D1
Greenacre Ct *16*	49	D3
Greencastle Av *17*	14	B1
Greencastle Par *17*	15	C1
Greendale Av *5*	16	B2
Greendale Rd *5*	16	B2
Greendale Shop Cen *5*	16	B2
Greenfield Cres *4*	45	D3
Greenfield Manor *4*	45	D3
Greenfield Pk *4*	45	D3
Greenfield Rd *13*	18	B1
Greenfield Rd *Still.*	54	B2
Greenhills Business Cen *24*	48	B2
Greenhills Business Pk *24*	48	B3
Greenhills Ind Est *12*	41	C3
Greenhills Rd *12*	40	B3
Greenhills Rd *24*	48	B2
Greenlands, The *14*	51	D3
Greenlea Av *6W*	50	B1
Greenlea Dr *6W*	50	B1
Greenlea Gro *6W*	50	B1
Greenlea Pk *6W*	50	B1
Greenlea Rd *6W*	50	B1
Greenmount Av *12*	43	D1
Greenmount Ct *12*		
off *Greenmount Av*	43	D1
Greenmount La *12*	43	D1
Greenmount Lawns *5*	51	C1
Greenmount Rd *6*	43	D3
Greenmount Sq *12*		
off *Greenmount La*	43	D1
Greenore Ter *2*		
off *Grattan St*	37	C2
Green Pk *14*	52	A1
Green Rd *Black.*	55	C2
Green St *7*	58	B1
Green St E *2*	37	D2
Green St Little *7*	58	B2
Greentrees Dr *12*	49	D1
Greentrees Pk *12*	41	D3
Greentrees Rd *12*	41	D3
Greenville Av *8*	35	D3
Greenville Rd *D.L.*	56	A3
Greenville Ter *8*	35	D3
Greenwich Ct *6*	44	A2
Grenville La *1*	28	A3
Grenville St *1*	28	A3
Greygates *Still.*	54	B2
Greys La *13*	21	C3
Griffith Av *9*	12	B3
Griffith Av *11*	11	D3
Griffith Br *8*	34	A3
Griffith Cl *11*	11	C3
Griffith Ct *3*	29	C1
Griffith Downs *9*	12	B3
Griffith Dr *11*	11	C2
Griffith Lawns *9*	12	A3
Griffith Par *11*	11	C2
Griffith Rd *11*	11	C2
Griffith Sq *8*		
off *Wesley Pl*	35	D3
Griffith Sq S *8*		
off *South Circular Rd*	35	C3
Griffith Wk *7*	29	C1
Grosvenor Ct *3*	30	B1
Grosvenor Ct *6W*	50	A1
Grosvenor Lo *6*	43	D2
Grosvenor Pk *6*	43	D2
Grosvenor Pl *6*	43	D2
Grosvenor Rd *6*	43	D2
Grosvenor Sq *6*	43	D1
Grosvenor Ter *D.L.*	57	C3
Grosvenor Vil *6*	43	D2

Grotto Av *Boot.*	55	C1
Grotto Pl *Boot.*	54	B1
Grove, The *5*	16	A3
Grove, The *9*	13	C3
Grove Av *6*		
off *Grove Rd*	43	D1
Grove Av (Finglas) *11*	11	C1
Grove Av *Black.*	55	C2
Grove Ho Gdns *Black.*	55	C3
Grove Lawn *Black.*	55	C3
Grove Pk *6*	43	D1
Grove Pk Av *11*	11	C1
Grove Pk Cres *11*	11	D1
Grove Pk Dr *11*	11	C1
Grove Pk Rd *11*	11	C1
Grove Rd (Rathmines) *6*	43	D1
Grove Rd (Finglas) *11*	11	C1
Grove Wd *11*	11	C1
Guild St *1*	37	C1
Guinness Enterprise Cen *8*	35	C2
Gulistan Cotts *6*	35	C2
Gulistan Pl *6*	44	A1
Gulistan Ter *6*	44	A1
Gurteen Av *10*	32	A2
Gurteen Pk *10*	32	A2
Gurteen Rd *10*	32	A1

H

Haddington Pl *4*	37	C3
Haddington Rd *4*	37	C3
Haddinton Ter *D.L.*	57	D3
Haddon Pk *3*		
off *Seaview Av N*	30	A2
Haddon Rd *3*	30	A2
Hadleigh Ct *15*	8	A3
Hadleigh Grn *15*	8	A3
Hadleigh Pk *15*	8	A3
Hagans Ct *2*	36	B3
Haigh Ter *D.L.*	57	D3
Halliday Rd *7*	35	C1
Halliday Sq *7*	35	C1
Halston St *7*	58	B1
Hamilton St *8*	35	C3
Hammond La *7*	58	A2
Hammond St *8*	35	D3
Hampstead Av *9*	12	A2
Hampstead Ct *9*	12	A2
Hampstead Pk *9*	12	A3
Hampton Ct *3*	31	C1
Hampton Cres *Boot.*	54	B1
Hampton Grn *7*	26	B2
Hampton Pk *Boot.*	54	B2
Hanbury La *8*	58	A3
Hannaville Pk *6W*	43	C3
Hanover La *8*	58	B4
Hanover Quay *2*	37	C2
Hanover Sq W *8*		
off *Hanover La*	58	B4
Hanover St E *2*	59	F3
Hanover St W *8*		
off *Ash St*	58	A4
Ha'penny Br *1*	59	D2
Harbour Ct *1*		
off *Marlborough St*	59	D2
Harbourmaster Pl *1*	59	F1
Harbour Rd *13*	20	B1
Harbour Rd *D.L.*	57	D3
Harbour Ter *D.L.*	57	C2
Harbour Vw *13*		
off *St. Lawrence Rd*	21	C2
Harcourt Grn *2*	36	A3
Harcourt La *2*		
off *Harcourt Rd*	36	A3
Harcourt Rd *2*	36	A3
Harcourt St *2*	36	A3
Harcourt Sta *2*	36	A3
Harcourt St *2*	36	A3
Harcourt Ter *2*	36	B3
Harcourt Ter La *2*	36	B3
Hardbeck Av *12*	41	C2
Hardiman Rd *9*	28	A1
Hardwicke Pl *1*	28	A3
Hardwicke St *1*	28	A3
Harlech Cres *14*	53	D2
Harlech Downs *14*	53	D2
Harlech Gro *14*	53	D2

88

Entry	Ref
Harlech Vil 14	53 D2
Harman St 8	35 C3
Harmonstown Rd 5	15 C3
Harmonstown Sta 5	15 C3
Harmony Av 4	45 C2
Harmony Row 2	37 C2
Harold Rd 7	35 C1
Harolds Cross Rd 6W	43 D1
Haroldville Av 8	35 C3
Harrington St 8	36 A3
Harrison Row 6	43 D3
Harry St 2	59 D4
Harty Av 12	41 D2
Harty Ct 12	41 D2
Harty Pl 8	35 D3
Harvard 14	53 D2
Hastings St 4	37 D2
Hatch La 2	36 A3
Hatch Pl 2 off Hatch La	36 A3
Hatch St Lwr 2	36 A3
Hatch St Upr 2	36 A3
Havelock Pl 4 off Bath Av	37 D3
Havelock Sq E 4	37 D3
Havelock Sq N 4	37 D3
Havelock Sq S 4	37 D3
Havelock Sq W 4	37 D3
Havelock Ter 4 off Bath Av	37 D3
Haven, The 9	12 A3
Haverty Rd 3	29 D2
Hawkins St 2	59 E2
Hawthorn Av 3	29 D2
Hawthorn Lawn 15	8 A3
Hawthorn Lo 15	8 A3
Hawthorn Manor 1 Black.	55 D3
Hawthorn Ter 3	29 C3
Hayden Sq 4	54 A2
Haymarket 7	58 A2
Hazelbrook Ct 6W	43 C3
Hazelbrook Dr 8	42 B3
Hazelbrook Pk 24	48 B2
Hazelbrook Rd 6W	42 B3
Hazelcroft Gdns 11 off Hazelcroft Rd	10 B2
Hazelcroft Pk 11 off Hazelcroft Rd	10 B2
Hazelcroft Rd 11	10 B2
Hazeldene 4	45 D2
Hazel Pk 12	42 B3
Hazel Rd 9	13 D3
Hazelwood Ct 5	14 A1
Hazelwood Dr 5	14 A2
Hazelwood Gro 5	14 A2
Hazelwood Pk 5	14 A2
Headford Gro 14	52 A3
Healthfield Rd 6	43 D3
Healy St 1 off Rutland Pl N	28 B3
Heath, The 6W	50 A2
Heath Cres 7	25 D1
Heathfield Black.	56 B3
Heath Gro 7	26 A1
Heidelberg 14	53 D2
Hellers Copse Black.	55 C3
Hendrick La 7 off Benburb St	35 C1
Hendrick Pl 7	35 C1
Hendrick St 7	35 C1
Henley Ct 14	52 B2
Henley Pk 14	52 B2
Henley Vil 14	52 B2
Henrietta La 1	27 D3
Henrietta Pl 1	58 B1
Henrietta St 1	58 B1
Henry Pl 1	59 D1
Henry Rd 10	32 A3
Henry St 1	58 C1
Herbert Av 4	46 B3
Herbert Cotts 4	45 D1
Herbert La 2	37 C3
Herberton Dr 12	34 B3
Herberton Pk 8	34 B3
Herberton Rd 8	34 B3
Herberton Rd 12	34 B3
Herbert Pk 4	45 C1
Herbert Pl 2	37 C3
Herbert Rd 4	37 D3
Herbert St 2	36 B3
Heuston Luas Sta 8	35 C1
Heuston Sta 8	34 B1
Hewardine Ter 1 off Killarney St	28 B3
Heytesbury La 4	45 C1
Heytesbury Pl 8 off Long La	35 D3
Heytesbury St 8	36 A3
Hibernian Av 3	29 C3
Hibernian Ind Est 24	48 A3
Highfield Ct 6	43 D3
Highfield Gro 6	44 A3
Highfield Pk 14	52 B2
Highfield Rd 6	43 D3
High Pk 9	13 C3
High St 8	58 B3
Hill, The Black.	57 C3
Hill, The Still.	55 C3
Hillcrest 6W	50 A3
Hillcrest Pk 11	11 D1
Hillsbrook Av 12	41 D3
Hillsbrook Cres 12	41 D3
Hillsbrook Dr 12	42 A3
Hillsbrook Gro 12	41 D3
Hillside Dr 14	51 D2
Hillside Vw 5	17 C2
Hill St 1	28 A3
Hilltop Shop Cen 5	15 D2
Hoeys Ct 2 off Castle St	58 B3
Hogan Av 2	37 C2
Hogan Pl 2	37 C2
Holles Row 2	59 F4
Holles St 2	59 F4
Hollybank Av 6	44 B2
Hollybank Rd 9	28 A1
Hollybrook Ct 3 off Hollybrook Rd	30 A2
Hollybrook Ct Dr 3	30 A2
Hollybrook Gro 3	29 D2
Hollybrook Pk 3	30 A2
Hollybrook Rd 3	30 A2
Holly Rd 9	29 D1
Hollywood Dr 14	53 D1
Hollywood Pk 14	53 D3
Holycross Av 3	28 B2
Holyrood Pk 4 off Sandymount Av	46 A1
Holywell Av 13	16 A1
Holywell Cres 13	16 A1
Holywell Rd 13	16 A1
Home Fm Pk 9	28 B1
Home Fm Rd 9	12 A3
Home Vil 4	45 C1
Homeville 6	44 A2
Hope Av 3	29 C3
Hope St 4	37 C2
Hopkins Sq 4	54 A2
Horseman's Row 1 off Parnell St	28 A3
Horton Ct 6W	51 C1
Hotel Yd 1	58 C2
Howard St 4	37 C2
Howth Junct 5	16 B1
Howth Rd 3	29 D2
Howth Rd 5	15 C3
Howth Rd (Howth) 13	19 D1
Howth Sta 13	20 B1
Howth Vw Pk 13	16 A1
H.S. Reilly Br 11	10 A3
Huband Br 4	37 C3
Huband Rd 12	41 C1
Hughes Rd E 12	41 D2
Hughes Rd N 12	41 D2
Hughes Rd S 12	41 D2
Hume Cen 10	32 A3
Hume St 2	36 B3
Huxley Cres 8	35 C3
Hyacinth St 3	29 C3
Hyde Pk 6W	50 B2
Hyde Pk Av Black.	55 C2
Hyde Pk Gdns Black.	55 C2
Hyde Sq 4	54 A1

I

Entry	Ref
I.D.A. Ind Cen 7	27 C3
Idrone Ter Black.	55 D2
ILAC Cen 1	58 C1
Imaal Rd 7	27 C2
Inagh Rd 10	32 A2
Inchicore Par 8	33 D2
Inchicore Rd 8	34 A2
Inchicore Sq 8	33 D2
Inchicore Ter N 8	33 D2
Inchicore Ter S 8	33 D2
Infirmary Rd 7	34 B1
Ingram Rd 8	35 D3
Innisfallen Par 7	28 A2
Innismaan Rd 9	12 B2
Innismore 12	41 D2
Inns Quay 7	58 B2
Invermore Gro 13 off Carraroe Av	16 A1
Inverness Rd 3	29 C2
Inver Rd 7	26 B2
Iona Cres 9	28 A1
Iona Dr 9	28 A2
Iona Pk 9	28 A2
Iona Rd 9	27 D2
Iona Vil 9	28 A1
Iris Gro Still.	54 A2
Irishtown Rd 4	37 D2
Irvine Cres 3 off Church Rd	37 C1
Irvine Ter 3	37 C1
Irwin Ct 8	34 B2
Irwin St 8	34 B2
Island St 8	35 C1
Island Vw 5	17 C2
Island Vil 2 off Hogan Av	37 C2
Isolda Rd 4	38 A2
Ivar St 7	35 C1
Iveagh Bldgs 8 off Kevin St Upr	35 D3
Iveagh Gdns 12	42 A1
Iveleary Rd 9	12 B2
Iveragh Ct 4	37 D3
Iveragh Rd 9	12 B2

J

Entry	Ref
James Joyce Ct 3	17 C2
James Larkin Rd 3	47 C1
James Larkin Rd 5	16 A3
James McCormack Gdns 13	18 A1
James Pl E 2	36 B3
James's Gate 8 off James's St	34 B2
James's Sta 8	34 B2
James's St 8	34 B2
James's St E 2	36 B3
James St N 3	29 C3
Jamestown Av 8	33 C3
Jamestown Business Pk 11	10 B1
Jamestown Ind Est 8	33 C3
Jamestown Rd (Inchicore) 8	33 C3
Jamestown Rd (Finglas) 11	10 B1
Jamestown Sq 10	33 C3
Janelle Shop Cen 11	10 B2
Jane Vil D.L. off Tivoli Rd	57 C3
Jerome Connor Pl 7 off Sullivan St	34 B1
Jervis La Lwr 1	58 C2
Jervis La Upr 1	58 C1
Jervis Sta 1	58 C2
Jervis St 1	58 C1
Jetty Rd 1	38 B1
John Dillon St 8	58 B4
John F. Kennedy Av 12	40 A1
John F. Kennedy Dr 12	40 B1
John F. Kennedy Ind Est 12	40 A1
John F. Kennedy Pk 12	40 A1
John F. Kennedy Rd 12	40 A1
John McCormack Av 12	41 D2
Johns La W 8	58 A3
Johnsons Ct 2 off Grafton St	59 D4
Johnsons Pl 2 off King St S	59 D4
Johnstown Pk 11	11 D2
John St S 8	35 C2
John St W 8	58 A3
Jones's Rd 3	28 B2
Josephine Av 7 off Leo St	28 A3
Joshua La 2 off Dawson St	59 D4
Joyce Rd 9	28 A1
Joy St 4 off Barrow St	37 C2

K

Entry	Ref
KCR Ind Est 12	42 B3
Keadeen Av 12	48 B1
Kearns Pl 8	34 B2
Keeper Rd 12	34 B3
Kells Rd 12	42 B2
Kelly's Av D.L.	57 C3
Kellys Row 1	28 A3
Kempton Av 7	25 D1
Kempton Ct 7	25 D1
Kempton Grn 7	25 C1
Kempton Gro 7	25 C1
Kempton Heath 7	25 D1
Kempton Lawn 7	25 D1
Kempton Pk 7	25 D1
Kempton Ri 7	25 D1
Kempton Vw 7	25 D1
Kempton Way 7	25 D1
Kenilworth La 6	43 D2
Kenilworth Rd 6	43 C2
Kenilworth Rd 6	43 D2
Kenilworth Sq E 6	43 D2
Kenilworth Sq N 6	43 D2
Kenilworth Sq S 6	43 D2
Kenilworth Sq W 6	43 D2
Kenmare Par 1 off Dorset St Lwr	28 A2
Kennington Cl 6W	49 C2
Kennington Cres 6W	49 C2
Kennington Lawn 6W	49 C2
Kennington Rd 6W	49 C2
Keogh Sq 8	33 D2
Kerlogue Rd 4	38 A2
Kevanagh Av 10	32 A3
Kevin St Lwr 8	36 A3
Kevin St Upr 2	58 B4
Kickam Rd 8	34 A2
Kilakea Cl 12 off Tibradden Dr	48 B1
Kilakea Dr 12 off Tibradden Dr	48 B1
Kilbarrack Av 5	17 C2
Kilbarrack Gdns 5	17 C2
Kilbarrack Gro 5	16 B2
Kilbarrack Ind Est 5	16 B1
Kilbarrack Par 5	16 B1
Kilbarrack Rd 5	16 A1
Kilbarrack Shop Cen 5	16 A2
Kilbarrack Sta 5	16 B1
Kilbarrack Way 5	16 B1
Kilbarron Av 5	13 D1
Kilbarron Dr 5	13 D1
Kilbarron Pk 5	13 D1
Kilbarron Rd 5	13 D1
Kilbride Rd 5	30 B1
Kildare Pk 12	42 A1
Kildare Rd 12	42 B1
Kildare St 2	59 E4
Kildonan Av 11	10 A1
Kildonan Dr 11	10 A1
Kildonan Rd 11	10 A1
Kilfenora Rd 12	42 B2
Kilkieran Ct 7	26 B1
Kilkieran Rd 7	26 B1
Killala Rd 7	26 B2
Killan Rd 3	37 C1
Killarney Av 1	28 B3
Killarney Par 7	28 A2
Killarney St 1	28 B3
Killeen Rd 6	44 A2
Killeen Rd 10	40 A1
Killeen Rd 12	40 A1
Killester Av 5	30 B1
Killester Ct 5	14 B3
Killester Pk 5	14 B3
Killester Sta 5	30 B1
Kilmacud Pk Still.	54 A3
Kilmacud Rd Upr 14	53 D3
Kilmainham Br 8	34 A2
Kilmainham La 8	34 A2
Kilmashogue Cl 12 off Kilmashogue Dr	48 B1
Kilmashogue Dr 12	48 B1
Kilmashogue Gro 12	48 B1
Kilmore Av 5	14 A1
Kilmore Cl 5	14 A1
Kilmore Cres 5	14 A1

Kilmore Dr 5　14 A1
Kilmore Rd 5　14 A2
Kilmorony Cl 13　16 A1
Kilnamanagh Rd 12　41 C2
Kilnamarragh Shop
　Cen 24　48 A2
Kilohan Gro 12　49 C1
Kilrock Rd 13　21 C1
Kilshane Rd 11　9 D2
Kilvere 14　50 B2
Kilworth Rd 12　33 D3
Kimmage Ct 6W　42 B3
Kimmage Gro 6W　43 C3
Kimmage Rd Lwr 6W　43 C2
Kimmage Rd W 12　42 A3
Kinahan St 7　34 B1
Kincora Av 3　30 A2
Kincora Ct 3　31 C2
Kincora Dr 3　30 B2
Kincora Gro 3　30 B2
Kincora Pk 3　30 B2
Kincora Rd 3　30 B2
Kingram La 2　36 B3
Kings Av 3　29 C3
Kings Hall 20　32 B1
Kings Inns St 1　58 C1
Kingsland Par 8　44 A1
Kingsland Pk Av 8　44 A1
King St N 7　58 B1
King St S 2　59 D4
Kingswood Sta 24　48 A1
Kinvara Av 7　25 D1
Kinvara Dr 7　25 D1
Kinvara Gro 7　25 D1
Kinvara Pk 7　25 D1
Kinvara Rd 7　25 D1
Kippure Av 12　48 B1
Kippure Pk 11　10 A3
Kirkwood 4　46 A1
Kirwan St 7　35 C1
Kirwan St Cotts 7
　off Kirwan St　27 C3
Kitestown Rd 13　21 C3
Knapton Ct D.L.
　off Vesey Pl　57 C3
Knapton Lawn D.L.　57 C3
Knapton Rd D.L.　57 C3
Knights Br 3　30 B2
Knockcullen 16　50 A3
Knockcullen Dr 16　50 A3
Knockcullen Lawn 16　50 A3
Knockcullen Pk 16　50 A3
Knocklyon Av 16　49 D3
Knocklyon Dr 16　50 A3
Knocklyon Ms 16　49 D3
Knockmaroon Hill 20　24 A3
Knockmaroon Rd 15　24 A3
Knocknarea Av 12　42 A1
Knocknarea Rd 12　41 D1
Knocknashee 14　53 D3
Knock Riada 20　32 B1
Kor Dev Pk 12　40 B3
Kyber Rd 8　25 D3
Kyle-Clare Rd 4　38 A2
Kylemore Av 10　32 A3
Kylemore Dr 10　32 B3
Kylemore Pk Ind Est 10　32 B3
Kylemore Pk N 10　32 A3
Kylemore Pk S 10　32 B3
Kylemore Pk W 10　32 B3
Kylemore Rd 10　32 B2
Kylemore Rd 10　32 B2
Kylemore Rd 20　32 A1
Kylemore Sta 12　40 B1

L

Laburnum Rd 14　45 C3
Lad La 2　36 B3
Lagan Rd 11　10 B3
Lakelands, The 14　51 C2
Lakelands Pk 6W　51 C1
Lally Rd 10　33 C2
Lambay Rd 9　12 A3
Lambourne Village 3　30 B2
Lambs Ct 8
　off James's St　34 B2
Landen Rd 10　32 B3
Landscape Av 14　52 A2
Landscape Cres 14　52 A2
Landscape Gdns 14　52 A2
Landscape Pk 14　52 A2
Landscape Rd 14　52 A2
Landys Ind Est 16　50 A3

Langrishe Pl 1
　off Summerhill　28 B3
Lansdowne Gdns 4
　off Shelbourne Rd　37 D3
Lansdowne Hall 4
　off Tritonville Rd　37 D3
Lansdowne La 4　37 D3
Lansdowne Pk 4　37 C3
Lansdowne Pk 16　50 A3
Lansdowne Rd 4　37 C3
Lansdowne Rd
　Stadium 4　37 D3
Lansdowne Rd Sta 4　37 D3
Lansdowne Ter 4
　off Serpentine Av　45 D1
Lansdowne Valley
　Cres 12
　off Kilworth Rd　41 D1
Lansdowne Valley
　Rd 12　41 C1
Lansdowne Village 4　37 D3
Lansdown Valley Pk 12　33 D3
Laracor Gdns 13　16 A1
Laragh Cl 13　16 A1
Laragh Gro 13
　off Laragh Cl　16 A1
Larchfield 14　52 B2
Larchfield Pk 14　53 C2
Larchfield Rd 14　53 C2
Larch Gro 6　44 B2
Larkfield Av 6W　43 C2
Larkfield Gdns 6W　43 C2
Larkfield Gro 6W　43 C2
Larkfield Pk 6W　43 C2
Larkhill Rd 9　12 A2
La Touche Dr 12　33 C3
La Touche Rd 12　41 C1
Lauders La 13　18 B1
Laundry La 6W　43 D2
Laurel Av 14　52 B3
Laurel Dr 14　52 B3
Laurel Rd 14　52 B3
Laurels, The 6W　43 C3
Laurels, The 14　52 B3
Laurelton 6　51 D1
Laurence Brook 20　32 B1
Lavarna Gro 6W　50 B1
Lavarna Rd 6W　42 B3
Lavista Av (Killester) 5　30 B1
La Vista Av 13　19 C3
Lawn, The 11　10 B1
Lea Cres 4　46 A1
Leahys Ter 4　38 A3
Lea Rd 4　46 A1
Le Bas Ter 6
　off Leinster Rd W　43 D2
Le Broquay Av 10　32 A3
Lee Rd 11　27 C1
Leeson Cl 2　36 B3
Leeson La 2　36 B3
Leeson Pk 6　44 B1
Leeson Pk Av 6　44 B1
Leeson Pl 2　36 B3
Leeson St Br 2　36 B3
Leeson St Lwr 2　36 B3
Leeson St Upr 4　44 B1
Leeson Village 6　44 B1
Le Fanu Dr 10　32 A3
Le Fanu Rd 10　32 A2
Leicester Av 6　43 D2
Leighlin Rd 12　42 B2
Lein Gdns
　(Gardini Lein) 5　15 D3
Lein Pk 5　15 C2
Lein Rd 5　15 C2
Leinster Av 3　29 C3
Leinster La 2
　off Leinster St S　59 E4
Leinster Lawn 14　53 C1
Leinster Mkt 2
　off D'Olier St　59 D2
Leinster Pl 6　43 D2
Leinster Rd 6　43 D2
Leinster Rd W 6　43 D2
Leinster Sq 6　44 A2
Leinster St E 3　29 C3
Leinster St N 7　27 D2
Leinster St S 2　59 E4
Leitrim Pl 4
　off Grand Canal
　St Upr　37 C3
Leix Rd 7　27 C2
Leland Pl 1　37 C1

Lemon St 2　59 D4
Lennox Pl 8　44 A1
Lennox St 8　36 A3
Lentisk Lawn 13　16 A1
Leo Av 7
　off Leo St　28 A3
Leo St 7　28 A3
Leslies Bldgs 7　27 D3
Leukos Rd 4　38 A2
Le Vere Ter 6　43 D1
Liberty La 8　36 A3
Library Rd D.L.　57 C3
Liffey Dockyard 1　37 D1
Liffey St 10　33 C2
Liffey St Lwr 1　58 C2
Liffey St Upr 1　58 C2
Liffey St W 7
　off Benburb St　35 C1
Limekiln Av 12　49 C1
Limekiln Cl 12　49 D1
Limekiln Dr 12　49 D1
Limekiln Gro 12　41 D3
Limekiln La 12　49 D1
Limekiln Pk 12　49 D1
Limekiln Rd 12　49 C1
Lime St 2　37 C2
Limewood Av 5　15 D1
Limewood Pk 5　15 D1
Limewood Rd 5　15 D1
Lincoln La 7　58 A2
Lincoln Pl 2　59 E4
Linden Black.　55 C3
Linden Gro Black.　55 C3
Linden Vale Black.　55 D3
Lindsay Rd 9　27 D2
Linenhall Par 7　58 B1
Linenhall Ter 7　58 B1
Lisburn St 7　58 B1
Liscannor Rd 7　26 B1
Lisle Rd 12　41 D2
Lismore Rd 12　42 B2
Lissadel Av 12　34 A3
Lissadel Ct 12　42 A1
Lissadel Dr 12　42 A1
Lissadel 12　42 A1
Lissenfield 6　44 A1
Litten La 1　59 D2
Little Britain St 7　58 B1
Little Strand St 7　58 B2
Loftus La 1　58 C1
Lombard Ct 2　59 F2
Lombard St E 2　59 F3
Lombard St W 8　35 D3
Lomond Av 3　29 C2
London Br 4　37 D3
Londonbridge Dr 4
　off Londonbridge Rd　37 D3
Londonbridge Rd 4　37 D3
Longdale Ter 9　12 A1
Longford La 8
　off Longford St Gt　58 C4
Longford Pl Black.　57 C3
Longford St Gt 8　58 C4
Longford St Little 2　58 C4
Longford Ter Black.　56 B3
Long La 7　28 A3
Long La (Tenter Flds) 8　35 D3
Long La Gro 8　35 D3
Long Mile Rd 12　40 B2
Longs Pl 8　35 C2
Longwood Av 8　35 D3
Longwood Pk 14　51 D3
Lorcan Av 9　13 C1
Lorcan Cres 9　13 C1
Lorcan Dr 9　13 C1
Lorcan Grn 9　13 D1
Lorcan Gro 9　13 C1
Lorcan O'Toole Pk 12　42 A3
Lorcan Pk 9　13 C1
Lorcan Rd 9　13 C1
Lorcan Vil 9　13 D1
Lord Edward St 2　58 B3
Lord's Wk 8　26 A3
Loreto Av 14　51 D3
Loreto Ct 14　51 D3
Loreto Cres 14　51 D3
Loreto Pk 14　51 D3
Loreto Rd 8　35 C3
Loreto Row 14　51 D3
Loreto Ter 14　51 D3
Lorne Ter 8
　off Brookfield Rd　34 B2
Lotts 1　59 D2

Lough Conn Av 10　32 A1
Lough Conn Dr 10　32 A1
Lough Conn Rd
　(Bothar Loch Con) 10　32 A1
Lough Conn Ter 10　32 A1
Lough Derg Rd 5　15 D2
Lourdes Rd 8　35 C3
Louvain 14　53 D2
Louvain Glade 14　53 D2
Love La E 2　37 C3
Lower Dodder Rd 14　51 D1
Lower Glen Rd 15　24 A3
Lower Kilmacud Rd 14　53 D3
Lower Kilmacud Rd
　Still.　54 A3
Luby Rd 8　34 A2
Lucan Rd 20　24 A3
Lugaquilla Av 12　48 B1
Luke St 2　59 E2
Lullymore Ter 8　35 C3
Lurgan St 7　58 B1
Lynchs La 10　32 B2
Lynchs Pl 7　27 D3
Lyndon Gate 7　26 A2

M

M50 Business Pk 24　48 A1
Mabbot La 1　59 E1
Mabel St 3　28 B2
Macartney Br 2　36 B3
McAuley Av 5　15 C2
McAuley Dr 5　15 C2
McAuley Pk 5　15 C2
McAuley Rd 5　15 C2
McCabe Vil Boot.　54 B1
McCarthy's Bldgs 7
　off Cabra Rd　27 D2
McDowell Av 8　34 B2
McKee Dr 7　26 B3
McKee Pk 7　26 B3
McKee Rd 11　10 B1
Macken St 2　37 C2
Macken Vil 2　37 C2
Mackies Pl 2　36 B3
McMahon St 8　35 D3
McMorrough Rd 6W　43 C3
Madeleine Ter 8　33 D2
Madison Rd 8　34 B3
Magennis Pl 2　59 F3
Magennis Sq 2
　off Pearse St　59 F3
Magenta Hall 9　13 C1
Mageough Home 6　44 A3
Mahers Pl 2
　off Macken St　37 C2
Maiden Row 20　32 B1
Main Rd 24　48 A3
Main Rd Tallaght 24　48 B3
Main St (Raheny) 5　15 D3
Main St (Finglas) 11　10 B1
Main St (Howth) 13　21 C2
Main St (Dundrum) 14　52 B3
Main St
　(Rathfarnham) 14　51 C2
Main St 20　32 B1
Main St 24　48 A3
Main St Black.　55 D2
Malachi Rd 7　35 C1
Malahide Rd 3　29 D2
Malahide Rd 5　14 A3
Malahide Rd 17　15 C1
Mallin Av 8　35 C3
Malone Gdns 4　37 D2
Malpas Pl 8
　off Malpas St　35 D3
Malpas St 8　35 D3
Malpas Ter 8
　off Malpas St　35 D3
Mander's Ter 6
　off Ranelagh Rd　44 B1
Mangerton Rd 12　41 C1
Mannix Rd 9　28 A1
Manor Av 6W　50 B1
Manor Pl 7　35 C1
Manor St 7　27 C3
Mansion Ho 2　59 D4
Maolbuille Rd 11　12 A2

Maple Dr 6W	43	C3
Maple Rd 14	45	C3
Maples, The 14	53	C1
Maples, The D.L.	56	A3
Maquay Br 4	37	C3
Maretimo Gdns E Black.	56	A2
Maretimo Gdns W Black.		
off Newtown Av	56	A2
Maretimo Pl Black.		
off Newtown Av	56	A2
Maretimo Rd Black.		
off Newtown Av	56	A2
Maretimo Vil Black.		
off Newtown Av	55	D2
Margaret Pl 4	37	D2
Marguerite Rd 9	28	A1
Marian Cres 14	50	B3
Marian Dr 14	50	B2
Marian Gro 14	50	B3
Marian Pk 13	17	C1
Marian Pk		
(Rathfarnham) 14	50	B3
Marian Rd 14	50	B3
Marine Dr 4	38	A3
Marine Rd D.L.	57	D3
Mariners Cove 13	21	C3
Mariner's Port 1	37	C1
Marine Ter D.L.	57	D3
Marino Av 3	29	D1
Marino Grn 3	29	D1
Marino Mart 3	29	D2
Marino Pk 3	29	C2
Marino Pk Av 3	29	C2
Marion Vil 8	35	C2
Market St S 8	35	C2
Marks All W 8	58	B4
Marks La 2	59	F3
Mark St 2	59	F3
Marlborough Ms 2	26	B3
Marlborough Pl 1	59	D1
Marlborough Rd		
(Donnybrook) 4	44	B2
Marlborough Rd 7	26	B3
Marlborough St 1	59	D1
Marne Vil 7	27	D3
Marrowbone La 8	35	C2
Marrowbone La Cl 8	35	C2
Marshalsea La 8	35	C2
Martello Av D.L.	57	D3
Martello Ms 4	46	B2
Martello Ter Boot.	55	C1
Martello Vw 4	38	A3
Martello Wd 4	46	B1
Martin Savage Pk 15	9	C3
Martin Savage Rd 7	25	D2
Martins Row 20	24	B3
Martin St 8	44	A1
Maryfield Av 5	14	A2
Maryfield Coll 9	13	C3
Maryfield Cres 5	14	A2
Maryfield Dr 5	14	A2
Mary's Abbey 7	58	B2
Mary's La 7	58	B2
Mary St 1	58	C2
Mary St Little 7	58	B2
Maryville Rd 5	15	C3
Mask Av		
(Ascal Measc) 5	14	B2
Mask Cres 5	14	B2
Mask Dr 5	14	B2
Mask Grn 5	14	B2
Mask Rd 5	14	B2
Mastersons La 2		
off Charlemont St	36	A3
Mather Rd N Still.	54	A2
Mather Rd S Still.	54	A2
Maunsell Pl 7		
off Mountjoy St	28	A3
Maxwell Rd 6	44	A2
Maxwell St 8	35	C3
Mayfield 6	51	D1
Mayfield Rd		
(Terenure) 6W	43	C3
Mayfield Rd		
(Kilmainham) 8	34	B3
May La 7	58	A2
Mayola Ct 14	52	B2
Mayor St Lwr 1	37	C1
Mayor St Upr 1	37	D1
May St 3	28	B2
Maywood Av 5	16	A3
Maywood Cl 5	16	A3
Maywood Cres 5	16	A3
Maywood Dr 5	16	A3
Maywood Gro 5	16	A3
Maywood La 5	16	A3
Maywood Pk 5	16	A3
Maywood Rd 5	16	A3
Meades Ter 2	37	C2
Meadowbank 6	51	D1
Meadowbrook Av 13	17	D1
Meadowbrook Lawn 13	17	D1
Meadowbrook Pk 13	17	D1
Meadow Pk Av 14	52	A3
Meadows, The 5	15	C3
Meath Pl 8	58	A4
Meath Sq 8		
off Gray St	58	A4
Meath St 8	58	A4
Meehan Sq 4	54	A1
Meetinghouse La 7		
off Mary's Abbey	58	C2
Mellifont Av D.L.	57	D3
Mellowes Av 11	10	A1
Mellowes Ct 11	10	B1
Mellowes Cres 11	10	A1
Mellowes Pk 11	10	A1
Mellowes Rd 11	10	A1
Mellows Br 8	35	C1
Melrose Av 3	29	C2
Melvin Rd 6W	43	C3
Memorial Rd 1	59	E2
Mercer St Lwr 2	58	C4
Mercer St Upr 2	36	A3
Merchamp 3	31	C2
Merchants Quay 8	35	C1
Merchants Rd 3	37	D1
Merlyn Dr 4	46	A2
Merlyn Pk 4	46	A2
Merlyn Rd 4	46	A2
Merrion Cres Boot.	46	B3
Merrion Gro Boot.	54	B1
Merrion Pk Boot.	54	B1
Merrion Pl 2	59	E4
Merrion Rd 4	45	D1
Merrion Row 2	36	A3
Merrion Shop Cen 4	46	A2
Merrion Sq E 2	59	F4
Merrion Sq N 2	59	F4
Merrion Sq S 2	59	F4
Merrion Sq W 2	59	F4
Merrion Strand 4	46	B2
Merrion Ter 2		
off Clare St	59	F4
Merrion St Upr 2	36	B3
Merrion Vw Av 4	46	A2
Merrion Village 4	46	A2
Merrywell Ind Est 22	40	A3
Merton Av 8	35	C3
Merton Cres 6	44	B3
Merton Dr 6	44	B3
Merton Rd 6	44	B3
Merton Wk 6	44	B3
Merville Av 3	29	C2
Mespil Rd 4	36	B3
Mews, The 3	30	B2
Mews, The		
(Dollymount) 3	31	D2
Middle Third 5	30	B1
Military Rd		
(Rathmines) 6	44	A1
Military Rd		
(Kilmainham) 8	34	B2
Military Rd		
(Phoenix Pk) 8	33	C1
Millbourne Av 9	28	A1
Millbrook Av 5	15	D1
Millbrook Ct 8	34	B2
Millbrook Dr 13	15	D1
Millbrook Gro 13	15	D1
Millbrook Rd 13	15	D1
Millbrook Village 6		
off Prospect La	45	C3
Millennium Br 1	58	C2
Millgate Dr 12	49	D1
Mill La 8		
off Newmarket	35	D3
Mill La 15	9	C3
Millmount Av 9	28	A1
Millmount Gro 14	52	B1
Millmount Pl 9	28	B1
Millmount Ter		
(Drumcondra) 9		
off Millmount Av	28	B1
Millmount Ter		
(Dundrum) 14		
off Millmount Gro	52	B1
Millmount Vil 9	28	A1
Mill St 8	35	D3
Milltown Av 6	44	B3
Milltown Br Rd 14	44	B3
Milltown Dr 14	52	A2
Milltown Gro 14	52	A2
Milltown Hill 6		
off Milltown Rd	44	B3
Milltown Path 6	44	B3
Milltown Rd 6	44	B3
Milltown Sta 6	44	B3
Millwood Pk 5	15	D1
Millwood Vil 5	15	D1
Misery Hill 2	37	C2
Moatfield Av 5	15	C1
Moatfield Pk 5	15	C1
Moatfield Rd 5	15	C1
Moeran Rd 12	41	D2
Monck Pl 7	27	D3
Monkstown Cres Black.	56	B3
Monkstown Gate Black.	57	C3
Monkstown Rd Black.	56	A2
Monkstown Valley		
Black.	56	B3
Montague Ct 2		
off Protestant Row	36	A3
Montague La 2	36	A3
Montague St 2	36	A3
Montpelier Dr 7	34	B1
Montpelier Gdns 7	34	B1
Montpelier Hill 7	34	B1
Montpelier Par Black.	56	A3
Montpelier Pk 7	35	C1
Montpelier Pl Black.	35	C1
Montrose Av 5	13	D2
Montrose Cl 5	13	D2
Montrose Cres 5	14	A1
Montrose Dr 5	13	D1
Montrose Gro 5	13	D2
Montrose Pk 5	13	D2
Moore La 1	59	D1
Moore St 1	59	D1
Morehampton La 4	45	C1
Morehampton Rd 4	45	C1
Morehampton Sq 4	45	C1
Morehampton Ter 4	45	C1
Morgan Pl 7		
off Inns Quay	58	B2
Morning Star Av 7	58	B2
Morning Star Rd 8	35	C3
Mornington Gro 5	14	B2
Mornington Rd 6	44	B2
Morrogh Ter 3	29	C1
Moss St 2	59	E2
Mountain Vw Av 6		
off Harolds Cross Rd	43	D2
Mountain Vw Cotts 6	44	B2
Mountain Vw Dr 14	52	A3
Mountain Vw Pk 14	52	A3
Mountain Vw Rd 6	44	A1
Mount Albion Rd 14	52	A3
Mount Albion Ter 1 14	52	A3
Mount Annville Pk 14	54	A3
Mount Annville Rd 14	53	D3
Mount Annville Wd 14	54	A3
Mount Annville		
Lawn 14	53	D3
Mount Argus Cl 6W	43	C2
Mount Argus Ct 6W	43	C2
Mount Argus Cres 6W	43	C2
Mount Argus Gro 6W	43	C2
Mount Argus Pk 6W	43	C2
Mount Argus Rd 6W	43	C2
Mount Argus Ter 6W	43	C2
Mount Argus Vw 6W	43	C2
Mount Argus Way 6W	43	C2
Mount Brown 8	34	B2
Mount Carmel Av 14	53	C2
Mount Carmel Rd 14	53	C2
Mount Dillon Ct 5	53	C2
Mountdown Dr 12	49	D1
Mountdown Pk 12	49	D1
Mountdown Rd 12	49	D1
Mount Drummond		
Av 6	43	D1
Mount Drummond		
Sq 6	43	D1
Mount Eden Rd 4	45	C2
Mount Harold Ter 6	43	D2
Mountjoy Cotts 7	28	A2
Mountjoy Par 1		
off North Circular Rd	28	B3
Mountjoy Pl 1	28	B3
Mountjoy Prison		
Cotts 7		
off Cowley Pl	28	A2
Mountjoy Sq E 1	28	B3
Mountjoy Sq N 1	28	A3
Mountjoy Sq S 1	28	A3
Mountjoy Sq W 1	28	A3
Mountjoy St 7	27	D3
Mountjoy St Mid 7	27	D3
Mount Merrion Av		
Black.	54	B2
Mount Olive Gro 5	16	A1
Mount Olive Pk 5	16	A1
Mount Olive Rd 5	16	A1
Mountpleasant Av		
Lwr 6	44	A1
Mountpleasant Av		
Upr 6	44	A1
Mountpleasant		
Bldgs 6	44	A1
Mountpleasant Par 6		
off Mountpleasant		
Pl	44	A1
Mountpleasant Pl 6	44	A1
Mountpleasant Sq 6	44	A1
Mount Prospect Av 3	31	C2
Mount Prospect Dr 3	31	C1
Mount Prospect Gro 3	31	D1
Mount Prospect		
Lawns 3	31	C2
Mount Prospect Pk 3	31	C2
Mount Sandford 6	45	C2
Mount Shannon Rd 8	34	B3
Mount St Cres 2	37	C3
Mount St Lwr 2	37	C2
Mount St Upr 2	36	B3
Mount Tallant Av 6W	43	C3
Mount Tallant Ter 6		
off Harolds Cross Rd	43	D1
Mount Temple Rd 7	35	C1
Mount Town Rd		
Upr D.L.	57	C3
Mourne Rd 12	34	B3
Moyclare Av 13	17	D1
Moyclare Cl 13	17	D1
Moyclare Dr 13	17	D1
Moyclare Gdns 13	18	A1
Moyclare Pk 13	17	D1
Moyclare Rd 13	17	D1
Moy Elta Rd 3	29	C3
Moyle Rd 11	26	B1
Moyne Rd 6	44	B2
Moynihan Ct 24	48	B3
Muckross Av 12	41	D3
Muckross Cres 12	41	D3
Muckross Dr 12	42	A3
Muckross Grn 12	42	A3
Muckross Gro 12	41	D3
Muckross Par 7		
off Killarney Par	28	A2
Muckross Rd 12	41	D3
Muirfield Dr 12	41	C1
Mulcahy Keane Est 12	41	D3
Mulgrave St D.L.	57	D3
Mulroy Rd 7	27	C1
Mulvey Pk 14	53	C2
Munster St 7	27	D2
Murrays Cotts 10		
off Sarsfield Rd	33	D2
Murtagh Rd 7	35	C1
Museum Sta 1	35	C1
Muskerry Rd 10	32	B2
Myra Cotts 8	34	A2

N

Naas Rd 12 — 40 A2
Naas Rd Business Pk 12 — 41 C1
Naas Rd Ind Pk 12 — 41 C1
Nanikin Av 5 — 15 D3
Nash St 8 — 33 C3
Nashville Pk 13 — 21 C2
Nashville Rd 13 — 21 C2
Nassau Pl 2 — 59 E4
Nassau St 2 — 59 D3
Navan Rd 7 — 25 D1
Navan Rd 15 — 8 A3
Neagh Rd 6W — 43 C3
Nelson St 7 — 28 A3
Nephin Rd 7 — 26 A2
Nerneys Ct 1 — 28 A3
Neville Rd 6 — 44 A3
New Bride St 8 — 36 A3
Newbridge Av 4 — 37 D3
Newbridge Dr 4 — 37 D3
Newbrook Av 13 — 16 B1
Newbrook Rd 13 — 16 B1
New Ch St 7 — 58 A2
Newcomen Av 3 — 29 C3
Newcomen Br 3 — 29 C3
Newcomen Ct 3
  off North Strand Rd — 29 C3
New Gra Rd 7 — 27 C2
Newgrove Av 4 — 38 A3
New Ireland Rd 8 — 34 B3
New Lisburn St 7
  off Coleraine St — 58 B1
Newmarket 8 — 35 D3
Newmarket St 8 — 35 D3
Newport St 8 — 35 C2
New Rd (Inchicore) 8 — 33 C3
New Rd 13 — 21 C3
New Row S 8 — 35 D3
New Row Sq 8 — 58 B4
New St Gdns 8 — 35 D3
New St S 8 — 35 D3
Newtown Av Black. — 56 A2
Newtown Cotts 17 — 15 C1
Newtown Dr 13 — 15 C1
Newtown Pk 24 — 48 B3
Newtownpark Av Black. — 55 D3
Newtown Vil Black. — 56 A2
New Wapping St 1 — 37 C1
Niall St 7 — 27 C3
Nicholas Av 7
  off Church St — 58 B1
Nicholas Pl 8
  off Patrick St — 58 B4
Nicholas St 8 — 58 B4
Nore Rd 11 — 26 B1
Norfolk Mkt 1
  off Parnell St — 28 A3
Norfolk Rd 7 — 27 D2
Norseman Pl 7 — 35 C1
North Av Still. — 54 A2
Northbrook Av 6 — 44 B1
Northbrook Av Lwr 1
  off North Strand Rd — 29 C3
Northbrook Av Upr 3 — 29 C3
Northbrook La 6 — 44 B1
Northbrook Rd 6 — 44 A1
Northbrook Ter 3 — 29 C3
Northbrook Vil 6
  off Northbrook Rd — 44 A1
Northbrook Wk 6 — 44 B1
North Circular Rd 1 — 28 A3
North Circular Rd 7 — 28 A2
Northcote Av D.L. — 57 C3
Northcote Pl D.L. — 57 C3
North Dublin Docklands 1 — 38 A1
North Gt Clarence St 1 — 28 B3
North Gt Georges St 1 — 28 A3
Northland Dr 11 — 11 C3
Northland Gro 11 — 11 C3
North Quay Extension 1 — 37 D1
North Rd 8 — 25 C1
North Rd Number 1 1 — 38 A1
North Strand Rd 1 — 29 C3
North Strand Rd 3 — 29 C3
Northumberland Av D.L. — 57 D3
Northumberland Pk D.L. — 57 D3
Northumberland Pl D.L.
  off Northumberland Av — 57 D3
Northumberland Rd 4 — 37 C3
North Wall Quay 1 — 37 C1
Nortons Av 7 — 27 D3
Norwood Pk 6 — 44 B2
Nottingham St 3 — 29 C3
Nugent Rd 14 — 52 A3
Nutgrove Av (Ascal An Charrain Chno) 14 — 51 D3
Nutgrove Cres 14 — 52 A3
Nutgrove Enterprise Pk 14 — 52 A3
Nutgrove Office Pk 14 — 52 A3
Nutgrove Pk 14 — 53 C1
Nutgrove Shop Cen 14 — 52 A3
Nutgrove Way 14 — 52 A3
Nutley Av 4 — 45 D2
Nutley La 4 — 46 A3
Nutley Pk 4 — 46 A3
Nutley Rd 4 — 45 D2
Nutley Sq 4 — 45 D3

O

Oak Apple Grn 6 — 43 D3
Oakdown Rd 14 — 52 A3
Oakfield Pl 8 — 35 D3
Oaklands Cres 6 — 44 A3
Oaklands Dr 4 — 45 D1
Oaklands Dr 6 — 44 A3
Oaklands Pk 4 — 45 D1
Oaklands Ter 4
  off Serpentine Av — 45 D1
Oaklands Ter 6 — 43 D3
Oak Lawn Castle. — 8 A3
Oakley Gro Black. — 55 D3
Oakley Pk 3 — 31 C2
Oakley Pk Black. — 55 D3
Oakley Rd 6 — 44 B1
Oak Lo 15 — 24 A1
Oak Pk Av 9 — 13 C1
Oak Pk Cl 9 — 13 C1
Oak Rd 9 — 29 D1
Oaks, The 3 — 31 D2
Oaks, The 14 — 52 B3
Oakwood Av 11 — 11 C1
Obelisk Gro Black. — 55 D3
Obelisk Wk Black. — 55 D3
O'Brien Rd 12 — 41 D2
O'Brien's Pl N 9 — 28 A1
O'Brien's Ter 9
  off Prospect Rd — 27 D2
Observatory La 6
  off Rathmines Rd Lwr — 44 A1
O'Carolan Rd 8 — 35 D3
O'Connell Av 7 — 27 D3
O'Connell Br 1 — 59 D2
O'Connell Gdns 4 — 37 D3
O'Connell St Lwr 1 — 59 D1
O'Connell St Upr 1 — 59 D1
O'Curry Av 8 — 35 D3
O'Curry Rd 8 — 35 D3
O'Daly Rd 9 — 12 A3
Odd Lamp Rd 8 — 25 D2
O'Devaney Gdns 7 — 34 B1
O'Donoghue St 8 — 33 C3
O'Donovan Rd 8 — 35 D3
O'Donovan Rossa Br 8
  off Winetavern St — 58 B3
O'Dwyer Rd 12 — 41 D2
Offaly Rd 7 — 27 C2
Offington Av 13 — 19 C1
Offington Ct 13 — 19 C1
Offington Dr 13 — 19 C2
Offington Lawn 13 — 19 C2
Offington Pk 13 — 19 C1
O'Hogan Rd 10 — 33 C2
Olaf Rd 7 — 35 C1
Old Br Rd 16 — 50 A2
Old Cabra Rd 7 — 26 B2
Old Camden St 2
  off Harcourt Rd — 36 A3
Old Castle Av 13 — 19 C3
Old Co Glen 12 — 42 B1
Old Co Rd 12 — 42 A1
Old Dublin Rd Still. — 54 B3
Old Dunleary D.L. — 57 C3
Old Fm, The 14 — 53 D3
Old Kilmainham 8 — 34 A2
Old Kilmainham Village 8 — 34 B2
Old Malahide Rd 5 — 14 B1
Old Mill Ct 8 — 35 D3
Old Mountpleasant 6
  off Mountpleasant Pl — 44 A1
Old Navan Rd 12 — 40 B1
Old Orchard 14 — 50 A3
Old Rectory Pk 14 — 53 C3
Old Sawmills Ind Est 12 — 41 C3
Oldtown Av 9 — 12 A1
Oldtown Pk 9 — 12 A1
Oldtown Rd 9 — 12 A1
O'Leary Rd 8 — 34 A3
Olivemount Gro 14 — 53 C1
Olivemount Rd 14 — 53 C1
Oliver Bond St 8 — 58 A3
Oliver Plunkett Av (Irishtown) 4 — 37 D2
Olney Cres 6W — 51 C1
Omni Pk 9 — 12 B1
Omni Pk Shop Cen 9 — 12 B1
O'Moore Rd 10 — 33 C2
O'Neachtain Rd 9 — 28 A1
O'Neill's Bldgs 8 — 36 A3
Ontario Ter 6 — 44 A1
Ophaly Ct 14 — 53 C2
O'Quinn Av 8 — 34 B2
O'Rahilly Par 1
  off Moore St — 59 D1
Orchard, The 3 — 29 C2
Orchard, The 5 — 14 B3
Orchard, The 6W — 42 B3
Orchard Cotts 2 Black. — 55 D3
Orchard La 6 — 44 A1
Orchard Rd 3 — 29 C2
Orchard Rd 5 — 16 B3
Orchard Rd 6 — 44 A3
Orchardston 14 — 50 B3
Orchardstown Av 14 — 50 B3
Orchardstown Dr 14 — 50 A3
Orchardstown Rd 14 — 50 B3
Orchardstown Vil 14 — 50 B3
Ordnance Survey Rd 8 — 24 B2
O'Reilly's Av 8 — 34 B2
Oriel Pl 1 — 29 C3
Oriel St Lwr 1 — 37 C1
Oriel St Upr 1 — 37 C1
Ormeau St 4
  off Gordon St — 37 C2
Ormond Mkt Sq 7
  off Ormond Quay Upr — 58 B2
Ormond Quay Lwr 1 — 58 C2
Ormond Quay Upr 7 — 58 B2
Ormond Rd N 9 — 28 B1
Ormond Rd S (Rathmines) 6 — 44 A2
Ormond Sq 7 — 58 B2
Ormond St 8 — 35 C3
Orpen Cl Black. — 55 D3
Orpen Dale Black. — 55 C3
Orwell Gdns 14 — 52 A1
Orwell Pk 6 — 52 A1
Orwell Pk Av 6W — 49 D2
Orwell Pk Cl 6W — 49 D2
Orwell Pk Cres 6W — 49 D2
Orwell Pk Dale 6W — 49 D2
Orwell Pk Dr 6W — 49 D2
Orwell Pk Glade 6W — 49 D2
Orwell Pk Glen 6W — 49 D2
Orwell Pk Grn 6W — 49 D2
Orwell Pk Gro 6W — 49 D2
Orwell Pk Hts 6W — 49 D2
Orwell Pk Lawns 6W — 49 D2
Orwell Pk Ri 6W — 49 D2
Orwell Pk Vw 6W — 49 D2
Orwell Pk Way 6W — 49 D2
Orwell Rd 6 — 43 D3
Orwell Rd 6W — 49 D2
Orwell Rd 14 — 52 A1
Orwell Shop Cen 6W — 49 D2
Orwell Wds 6 — 52 A1
Oscar Sq 8 — 35 D3
Osprey Av 6W — 49 C1
Osprey Dr 6W — 49 D2
Osprey Lawn 6W — 49 D1
Osprey Pk 6W — 49 D2
Osprey Rd 6W — 49 D2
Ossory Rd 3 — 29 C3
Ossory Sq 8 — 35 D3
Ostman Pl 7 — 27 C3
O'Sullivan Av 3 — 28 B2
Oswald Rd 4 — 38 A3
Oulton Rd 3 — 30 B2
Our Ladys Cl 8 — 35 C2
Our Lady's Rd 8 — 35 C3
Ovoca Rd 8 — 35 D3
Owendore Av 14 — 51 C2
Owendore Cres 14 — 51 C2
Owens Av 8 — 34 B2
Owenstown Pk 4 — 54 A3
Oxford Rd 6 — 44 A1
Oxford Ter 3
  off Church Rd — 37 C1
Oxford Ter 1
  off Oxford Rd — 44 A1
Oxmantown La 7
  off Blackhall Pl — 35 C1
Oxmantown Rd 7 — 27 C3
Oxmantown Rd Lwr 7
  off Arbour Hill — 35 C1

P

Pacelli Av 13 — 17 C2
Packenham D.L. — 57 C3
Paddock, The 7 — 25 C1
Pairc Baile Munna 11 — 11 D1
Pairc Clearmont (Claremont Pk) 4 — 38 A3
Pairc Gleannaluinn (Glenaulin Pk) 20 — 24 A3
Pakenham Rd Black. — 56 B3
Pakerton D.L.
  off Sloperton — 57 C3
Palace St 2
  off Dame St — 58 C3
Palmerston Gdns 6 — 44 A3
Palmerston Gro 6 — 45 C3
Palmerston La 6 — 44 A3
Palmerston Pk 6 — 44 A3
Palmerston Pl 7 — 27 D3
Palmerston Rd 6 — 44 A2
Palmerston Vil 6 — 44 A3
Palms, The 14 — 53 D2
Paradise Pl 7 — 28 A3
Park, The 9 — 13 D2
Park Av 4 — 46 A1
Park Av 16 — 51 C3
Park Cres 8 — 26 A2
Park Cres 12 — 42 A3
Park Dr 6 — 44 B2
Parkgate Pl Business Cen 8 — 34 B1
Parkgate St 8 — 34 B1
Parkhill Way 24 — 48 A2
Parklands, The 14 — 51 C2
Park La 4 — 46 A1
Park La 20 — 32 B1
Park La E 2 — 59 E3
Park Lawn 3 — 31 D1
Parkmore Dr 6W — 50 B1
Parkmore Ind Est 22 — 40 B2
Park Pl 8
  off South Circular Rd — 34 A1
Park Rd 7 — 25 D1
Park Rd D.L. — 57 D3
Park Shop Cen 7 — 27 C3
Park St 10 — 33 C2
Park Ter 8 — 58 A4
Parkvale 13 — 17 D1
Parkview 7 — 26 B3
Park Vw 15 — 24 A1
Parkview Av (Haroldscross) 6 — 43 D2
Park Vw Av (Rathmines) 6 — 44 A2
Park Vil 15 — 8 A3
Park Vil Black. — 55 C3
Parkway Business Cen 24 — 40 A3
Park W Ind Pk 10 — 32 A3
Parliament Row 2
  off Fleet St — 59 D2
Parliament St 2 — 58 C3
Parnell Av 12
  off Parnell Rd — 43 D1
Parnell Ct 12 — 43 D1
Parnell Pl 1 — 28 A3
Parnell Rd 12 — 35 C3
Parnell Sq E 1 — 28 A3

Parnell Sq N 1	28	A3
Parnell Sq W 1	28	A3
Parnell St 1	58	C1
Partridge Ter 8	33	C3
Patrician Vil Black.	55	C3
Patrick Doyle Rd 14	52	B1
Patricks Row Black.		
off Carysfort Av	55	D2
Patrick St 8	58	B4
Patrick St D.L.	57	D3
Patrickswell Pl 11	10	B2
Patriotic Ter 8		
off Brookfield Rd	34	B2
Paul St 7	58	A2
Pea Fld Boot.	55	C2
Pearse Gro 2		
off Great Clarence Pl	37	C2
Pearse Ho 2	59	F3
Pearse Sq 2	37	C2
Pearse Sta 2	59	F3
Pearse St 2	59	E3
Pecks La 15	8	A3
Pembroke Cotts (Donnybrook) 4	45	C2
Pembroke Cotts (Ringsend) 4	37	D2
Pembroke Cotts (Dundrum) 14	53	C3
Pembroke Cotts Boot.	54	B1
Pembroke Gdns 4	37	C3
Pembroke La 2	36	B3
Pembroke La 4	37	C3
Pembroke Pk 4	45	C1
Pembroke Rd 4		
off Pembroke St Upr	36	B3
Pembroke Rd 4	37	C3
Pembroke Row 2	36	B3
Pembroke St 4	37	D2
Pembroke St Lwr 2	36	B3
Pembroke St Upr 2	36	B3
Penrose St 4	37	C2
Percy French Rd 12	41	D2
Percy La 4	37	C3
Percy Pl 4	37	C3
Peter Row 8	58	C4
Petersons Ct 2	59	F2
Peters Pl 2	36	A3
Peter St 8	58	C4
Petrie Rd 8	35	D3
Phibsborough 7	27	D2
Phibsborough Av 3	27	D3
Phibsborough Pl 7	27	D3
Phibsborough Rd 7	27	D3
Philipsburgh Av 3	29	C2
Philipsburgh Ter 3	29	C1
Philomena Ter 4	37	D2
Phoenix Av 15	8	A3
Phoenix Ct 7		
off Cavalry Row	35	C1
Phoenix Ct 15	8	A3
Phoenix Dr 15	8	A3
Phoenix Gdns 15	8	A3
Phoenix Manor 7	26	B3
Phoenix Pl 15		
off Phoenix Av	8	A3
Phoenix St 7	58	A2
Phoenix St 10	33	C2
Phoenix Ter Boot.	55	C1
Pigeon Ho Rd 4	37	D2
Pig La 1	28	B3
Piles Bldgs 8		
off Golden La	58	B4
Piles Ter 2		
off Sandwith St Upr	59	F3
Pimlico 8	58	A4
Pimlico Sq 8		
off The Coombe	58	A4
Pim St 8	35	C2
Pinebrook Av 5	14	A3
Pinebrook Cres 5		
off Pinebrook Av	14	A2
Pinebrook Gro 5		
off Pinebrook Rd	14	A3
Pinebrook Ri 5	14	A3
Pinebrook Rd 5	14	A3
Pine Gro 16	50	A3

Pine Haven Boot.	55	C1
Pine Hurst 7	26	B2
Pine Rd 4	38	A2
Pines, The 5	14	B3
Pinewood Av 11	11	D1
Pinewood Cres 11	11	D1
Pinewood Dr 11	11	D1
Pinewood Grn 11	11	D1
Pinewood Gro 11	11	D1
Pinewood Pk 14	50	B3
Pinewood Vil 11	11	D1
Pleasants La 8	36	A3
Pleasants Pl 8	36	A3
Pleasants St 8	36	A3
Plunkett Rd 11	10	A1
Poddle Pk 12	42	B3
Polo Rd 8	26	A3
Poolbeg St 2	59	E2
Poole St 8	35	C2
Poplar Row 3	29	C2
Poplars, The D.L.	56	A3
Portland Cl 1	28	B3
Portland Pl 1	28	A2
Portland Row 1	28	B3
Portland St N 1	28	B3
Portmahon Dr 8	34	B3
Portobello Br 6	44	A1
Portobello Harbour 8	44	A1
Portobello Pl 8	44	A1
Portobello Rd 8	43	D1
Portobello Sq 8		
off Clanbrassil St Upr	43	D1
Portside Business Cen 3	29	D3
Port Side Ct 3	29	C3
Potato Mkt 7		
off Green St Little	58	B2
Powers Ct 2		
off Warrington Pl	37	C3
Powers Sq 8		
off John Dillon St	58	B4
Prebend St 7	58	B1
Preston St 1	28	B3
Price's La 2	59	D2
Prices La 6	44	A1
Priestfield Cotts 8	35	C3
Priestfield Dr 8		
off South Circular Rd	35	C3
Priestfield Ter 8		
off South Circular Rd	35	C3
Primrose Av 7	27	D3
Primrose Hill D.L.	57	C3
Primrose St 7	27	D3
Prince Arthur Ter 6	44	A2
Prince of Wales Ter 4	45	D1
Princes St N 1	59	D2
Princes St S 2	59	F2
Princeton 14	53	D2
Priory, The 7	26	A1
Priory Av Black.	55	C2
Priory Dr Black.	54	B3
Priory E 7	26	A1
Priory Gro Black.	54	B3
Priory Hall Black.	54	B3
Priory N 7	26	A1
Priory Rd 6W	43	C2
Priory W 7	26	A1
Probys La 1	58	C2
Proby Sq Black.	55	D3
Promenade Rd 3	30	A3
Prospect Av 7	27	D1
Prospect Cem 11	27	D1
Prospect La 6	45	C3
Prospect Rd 9	27	D2
Prospect Sq 9	27	D1
Prospect Ter (Sandymount) 4		
off Beach Rd	38	A3
Prospect Way 7	27	D1
Protestant Row 2	36	A3
Prouds La 2	59	D4
Prussia St 7	27	C3
Purser Gdns 6	44	A2

Q

Quarry Dr 12	41	D3
Quarry Rd (Cabra) 7	27	C2
Queens Rd D.L.	57	D3
Queens Sq D.L.	57	D3
Queen St 7	58	A2

Quinns La 2	36	B3

R

Rafters Av 12	42	A1
Rafters La 12	42	A1
Rafters Rd 12	42	A1
Raglan La 4	45	C1
Raglan Rd 4	45	C1
Raheen Dr 10	32	A3
Raheen Pk 10	32	A3
Raheny Pk 5	16	A3
Raheny Rd 5	15	D2
Raheny Sta 5	15	D3
Railway Av 8		
off Tyrconnell Rd	33	D3
Railway Av (Inchicore) 8	33	C3
Railway Av 13	18	A1
Railway Cotts 4		
off Serpentine Av	45	D1
Railway St 1	28	B3
Railway Ter 2		
off Grattan St	37	C2
Rainsford Av 8	35	C2
Rainsford St 8	35	C2
Raleigh Sq 12	42	A1
Ramillies Rd 10	32	B2
Ramleh Cl 6	45	C3
Ramleh Pk 6	45	C3
Ramleh Vil 6	44	B3
Ranelagh Av 6	44	B1
Ranelagh Rd 6	44	A1
Ranelagh Sta 6	44	A1
Raphoe Rd 12	42	A1
Rathdown Av 6W	51	C1
Rathdown Ct 6W	43	C3
Rathdown Cres 6W	51	C1
Rathdown Dr 6W	51	C1
Rathdown Pk 6W	51	C1
Rathdown Rd 7	27	D3
Rathdown Sq 7	27	C3
Rathdown Vil 6W	51	C1
Rathdrum Rd 12	43	C1
Rathfarnham Gate 14	51	C2
Rathfarnham Mill 14	51	C2
Rathfarnham Pk 14	51	C1
Rathfarnham Rd 6W	51	C1
Rathfarnham Rd 14	51	C1
Rathfarnham Shop Cen 14	50	B2
Rathfarnham Wd 14	51	D2
Rathgar Av 6	43	D2
Rathgar Pk 6	43	D3
Rathgar Rd 6	43	D3
Rathland Rd (Bothar Raitleann) 12	42	B3
Rathlin Rd 9	12	A3
Rathmines Av 6	44	A2
Rathmines Rd Lwr 6	44	A1
Rathmines Rd Upr 6	44	A1
Rathmore Pk 5	16	A3
Rath Row 2	59	E2
Rathvale Av 13	15	C1
Rathvale Dr 13	15	C1
Rathvale Gro 13		
off Rathvale Av	15	C1
Rathvale Pk 13	15	C1
Rathvilly Dr 11	10	A2
Rathvilly Pk 11	10	A2
Rathvilly Rd 11	10	A2
Ratoath Av (Ascal Ratabhachta) 11	9	D2
Ratoath Dr 11	9	D1
Ratoath Est 11	26	A1
Ratoath Rd 7	26	B2
Ratoath Rd 11	9	D2
Ratra Rd 7	25	D1
Ravensdale Cl 12	42	B3
Ravensdale Pk 12	42	B3
Ravensdale Rd 3	29	D3
Raymond St 8	35	D3
Red Brick Ter 3 Black.	55	D3
Redcourt Oaks 3	31	D2
Red Cow Business Pk 22	40	A2
Red Cow La 7	58	A1
Redesdale Cres Still.	54	A3
Redesdale Rd Still.	54	A3
Redmonds Hill 2	36	A3
Redwood Av 24	48	A2
Redwood Cl 24		
off Redwood Av	48	A2
Redwood Ct 14	52	A2

Redwood Gro Boot.	55	C2
Redwood Hts 24		
off Redwood Pk	48	A2
Redwood Pk 24	48	A2
Redwood Ri 24		
off Redwood Pk	48	A2
Redwood Vw 24		
off Redwood Av	48	A2
Reginald Sq 8		
off Gray St	58	A4
Reginald St 8	58	A4
Rehoboth Av 8	35	C3
Rehoboth Pl 8	35	C3
Reillys Av 8		
off Dolphin's Barn St	35	C3
Reuben Av 8	34	B3
Reuben St 8	35	C3
Rialto Br 8	34	B3
Rialto Bldgs 8		
off Rialto Cotts	34	B3
Rialto Cotts 8	34	B3
Rialto Dr 8	34	B3
Rialto Sta 8	34	B3
Rialto St 8	34	B3
Ribh Av 5	15	C3
Ribh Rd 5	15	C3
Richelieu Pk 4	46	A2
Richmond Av Black.	56	B3
Richmond Av N 3	29	C2
Richmond Av S 6	44	B3
Richmond Cotts 1	28	B3
Richmond Cotts (Inchicore) 8	34	A2
Richmond Cotts N 1		
off Richmond Cotts	28	B3
Richmond Ct 6	52	B1
Richmond Cres 1	28	B3
Richmond Est 3	29	C2
Richmond Grn Black.	56	B3
Richmond Gro Black.	56	B3
Richmond Hill 6	44	A1
Richmond Hill Black.	56	B3
Richmond La 1		
off Russell St	28	B3
Richmond Ms 6	44	A1
Richmond Par 1	28	B3
Richmond Pk Black.	56	B3
Richmond Pl 6	44	A1
Richmond Pl S 2		
off Richmond St S	44	A1
Richmond Rd 3	28	B1
Richmond Row 8	44	A1
Richmond Row S 2		
off Richmond St S	36	A3
Richmond St N 1	28	B3
Richmond St S 2	36	A3
Richview Office Pk 14	45	C3
Richview Pk 6	44	B3
Ringsend Br 4	37	D2
Ringsend Pk 4	37	D2
Ringsend Rd 4	37	C2
Ring St 8	33	C3
Ring Ter 8	33	C3
Rise, The (Drumcondra) 9	12	A3
Rise, The Still.	54	B2
River Gdns 9	12	A3
River Rd 11	9	D3
River Rd 15	9	D3
Riversdale Av 6	51	D1
Riversdale Gro 6W	42	B3
Riversdale Ind Est 12	40	B1
Riverside Cotts 6W	50	B2
Riverside Dr 14	51	D2
Riverside Wk 4	45	C3
Riverston Abbey 7	26	A1
Riverview Ct 20	32	B1
Road Number 1 1	38	A1
Road Number 2 1	38	A1
Road Number 3 1	38	A1
Robert Emmet Br 12	43	D1
Robert Pl 3		
off Clonliffe Rd	28	B2
Robert St 3		
off Clonliffe Rd	28	B2
Robert St 8	35	C2
Robinhood Business Pk 22	40	A2
Robinhood Ind Est 22	40	B2
Robinhood Rd 22	40	B2
Robinsons Ct 8	58	A4
Rockfield Av 12	49	D1
Rockfield Dr 12	42	A3

Name	Pg	Grid
Rockford Pk D.L.	56	A3
Rock Hill Black.	55	D2
Rock Rd Boot.	46	B3
Rockville Cres D.L.	56	A3
Rockville Dr D.L.	56	A3
Rockville Pk D.L.	56	A3
Rockville Rd D.L.	56	A3
Roebuck Av Still.	54	B2
Roebuck Castle 14	53	D1
Roebuck Downs 14	53	C2
Roebuck Dr 12	41	D3
Roebuck Hall 14	53	D2
Roebuck Rd 14	53	C1
Roger's La 2	36	B3
Roncalli Rd 13	17	C2
Roosevelt Cotts 3	26	A2
Rope Wk Pl 4	37	D2
Rory O'More Br 8	35	C1
Rosary Gdns E D.L.	57	C3
Rosary Gdns W D.L.	57	C3
Rosary Rd 8	35	C3
Rosary Ter 4	37	D2
Rosbeg Ct 13	17	C2
Rose Glen Av 5	16	B2
Rose Glen Rd 5	16	A2
Rosemount 12	52	B2
Rosemount Av 5	14	B3
Rosemount Ct 14	53	C2
Rosemount Ct Boot.	54	B1
Rosemount Cres 14	53	C1
Rosemount Pk 14	53	C2
Rosemount Rd 7	27	D3
Rosemount Ter Boot.	54	B1
Rosevale Ct 5 off Brookwood Glen	15	C3
Rosevale Mans 5	15	C3
Rosmeen Gdns D.L.	57	D3
Rossmore Av 6W	49	D2
Rossmore Av 10	32	A2
Rossmore Cl 6W	49	D3
Rossmore Cres 6W	49	D2
Rossmore Dr 6W	49	D2
Rossmore Dr 10	32	A1
Rossmore Gro 6W	49	D2
Rossmore Lawns 6W	49	D2
Rossmore Pk 6W	49	D2
Rossmore Rd 6W	49	D2
Rossmore Rd 10	32	A1
Ross Rd 8	58	B4
Ross St 7	26	B3
Rostrevor Rd 6	51	D1
Rostrevor Ter 6	51	D1
Rothe Abbey 8	34	A3
Rowanbyrn D.L.	56	A3
Rowan Hall 6 off Prospect La	45	C3
Rowan Pk Av Black.	56	A3
Royal Canal Bk 7	27	D3
Royal Canal Ter 7	27	D3
Royal Liver Retail Pk 12	40	B1
Royal Ter 3 off Inverness Rd	29	C2
Royse Rd 7	27	D2
Royston 12	42	A3
Rugby Rd 6	44	A1
Rugby Vil 6 off Rugby Rd	44	A1
Rushbrook Av 6W	49	D2
Rushbrook Ct 6W	49	D2
Rushbrook Dr 6W	49	D2
Rushbrook Gro 6W	49	D2
Rushbrook Pk 6W	49	D2
Rushbrook Vw 6W	49	C2
Rushbrook Way 6W	49	D2
Russell Av 3	28	A2
Russell Av E 3	29	C3
Russell St 1	28	B3
Rutland Av 12	43	C1
Rutland Gro 12	43	C1
Rutland Pl 3 off Clontarf Rd	30	B3
Rutland Pl N 1	28	B3
Rutland Pl W 1	28	A3
Rutland St Lwr 1	28	B3
Rutledges Ter 8	35	C3
Ryders Row 1 off Parnell St	58	C1

S

Name	Pg	Grid
Sackville Av 3	28	B3
Sackville Gdns 3	28	B3
Sackville La 1 off O'Connell St Lwr	59	D1
Sackville Pl 1	59	D2
St. Agnes Pk 12	42	A2
St. Agnes Rd 12	42	A2
St. Aidan's Dr 14	53	D2
St. Aidan's Pk 3	29	D2
St. Aidan's Pk Av 3	29	D2
St. Aidan's Pk Rd 3	29	D2
St. Alban's Pk 4	46	B2
St. Alban's Rd 8	35	D3
St. Alphonsus Av 9	28	A2
St. Alphonsus Rd 9	28	A2
St. Andoens Ter 8 off Cook St	58	A3
St. Andrew's La 2 off Trinity	59	D3
St. Andrew's St 2	59	D3
St. Annes 12	42	A3
St. Anne's Av 5	15	D3
St. Anne's Dr 5	15	D3
St. Anne's Rd 8	35	C3
St. Anne's Rd N 9	28	A2
St. Anne's Sq Black.	55	D2
St. Anne's Ter 5	15	D3
St. Anthony's Cres 12	41	C3
St. Anthony's Pl 1 off Temple St N	28	A3
St. Anthony's Rd 8	34	B3
St. Aongus Cres 24	48	B2
St. Aongus Grn 24	48	B2
St. Aongus Gro 24	48	B2
St. Aongus Lawn 24	48	B2
St. Aongus Rd 24	48	B2
St. Assam's Av 5	16	A3
St. Assam's Dr 5	16	A3
St. Assam's Pk 5	16	A3
St. Assam's Rd E 5	16	A3
St. Assam's Rd W 5	16	A3
St. Attracta Rd 7	27	C2
St. Audoens Ter 8 off School Ho La W	58	B3
St. Augustine St 8	58	B3
St. Barnabas Gdns 3	29	C3
St. Brendan's Av 5	14	B2
St. Brendan's Cotts 4	37	D2
St. Brendan's Cres 12	49	C1
St. Brendan's Dr 5	14	B2
St. Brendan's Pk 5	15	C2
St. Brendan's Ter 5	14	B1
St. Brendan's Ter D.L. off Library Rd	57	C3
St. Bricin's Pk 7	35	C1
St. Bridget's Av 3	29	C3
St. Bridget's Dr 12	41	C3
St. Brigid's Ct 5 off St. Brigid's Dr	14	B3
St. Brigid's Cres 5	14	B2
St. Brigid's Dr 5	14	B3
St. Brigids Flats 14	45	C3
St. Brigids Gdns 1	37	C1
St. Brigids Grn 5	14	B3
St. Brigids Gro 5	14	B3
St. Brigids Lawn 5	14	B3
St. Brigid's Rd 5	14	B3
St. Brigid's Rd Lwr 9	28	A2
St. Brigid's Rd Upr 9	28	A2
St. Brigids Shop Mall 5	14	B2
St. Broc's Cotts 4	45	C2
St. Canice's Pk 11	11	D2
St. Canice's Rd 11	11	D2
St. Catherine's Av 8	35	C3
St. Catherine's La W 8	58	A3
St. Clare's Av 6 off Harolds Cross Rd	43	D1
St. Clare's Ter 6 off Mount Drummond Av	43	D1
St. Clement's Rd 9	28	A2
St. Columbanus Av 14	52	B1
St. Columbanus Pl 14	52	B1
St. Columbanus Rd 14	52	B1
St. Columba's Rd 12	41	C3
St. Columba's Rd Lwr 9	28	A2
St. Columba's Rd Upr 9	28	A2
St. Conleth's Rd 12	41	C3
St. Davids 5	14	A3
St. Davids Pk 5	14	A3
St. David's Ter 7 off Blackhorse Av	26	B3
St. Davids Ter (Glasnevin) 9	12	A3
St. Davids Wd 5	12	A3
St. Declan Rd 3	29	C1
St. Declan Ter 3	29	D1
St. Donagh's Cres 13	16	A1
St. Donagh's Pk 13	16	B1
St. Donagh's Rd 13	16	A1
St. Eithne Rd 7	27	C2
St. Elizabeth's Ct 7 off North Circular Rd	27	C3
St. Enda's Dr 14	51	C3
St. Enda's Pk 14	51	C3
St. Enda's Rd 6	43	C3
St. Finbar's Cl 12	49	C1
St. Finbar's Rd 7	26	B1
St. Fintan Rd 7	27	C2
St. Fintan's Cres 13	19	C3
St. Fintan's Gro 13	19	C3
St. Fintan's Pk 13	19	C3
St. Fintan's Rd 13	19	C3
St. Fintan Ter 7	27	C1
St. Gabriels Ct 3	31	D2
St. Gabriel's Rd 3	31	D2
St. Gall Gdns N 14	52	B1
St. Gall Gdns S 14	52	B1
St. George's Av 3	28	B2
St. Gerard's Rd 12	41	C3
St. Helena's Dr 11	10	B2
St. Helena's Rd 11	10	B2
St. Helen's Rd Boot.	54	B1
St. Helens Wd Boot.	54	B2
St. Ignatius Av 7	28	A2
St. Ignatius Rd 7	28	A2
St. Ita's Rd 9	28	A1
St. James Pl 8	33	D2
St. James's Av 3	28	B2
St. James's Av 8	35	C2
St. James's Pl 8 off Tyrconnell Rd	33	D3
St. James's Rd 12	41	C3
St. James's Ter 8	35	C3
St. James's Wk 8	34	B3
St. Jarlath Rd 7	27	C2
St. Johns 4	46	A2
St. John's Av 8 off John St S	58	A4
St. John's Ct 3	30	A1
St. John's Ct 5	14	A1
St. John's Pk D.L.	57	C3
St. John's Rd 4	46	A1
St. John's Rd W 8	34	A2
St. John St 8 off Blackpitts	35	D3
St. Johns Wd 3	30	B2
St. Joseph's Av 3	28	B2
St. Joseph's Av 9	28	A2
St. Josephs Av 7	27	C3
St. Josephs Gro 14	53	C3
St. Joseph's Par 7	28	A3
St. Joseph's Pl 7 off Dorset St Upr	28	A3
St. Joseph's Rd 7	27	C3
St. Joseph's Rd 12	41	C3
St. Joseph's Sq 3 off Vernon Av	31	C2
St. Joseph's St 7 off Synnott Pl	28	A3
St. Joseph's Ter 1 off North Circular Rd	28	B3
St. Joseph's Ter 3	29	C2
St. Kevins Ct 6	44	A3
St. Kevins Gdns 6	44	A3
St. Kevin's Par 8	35	D3
St. Kevins Pk (Rathgar) 6	44	A3
St. Kevin's Rd 8	43	D1
St. Killian's Av 12	40	B3
St. Laurence Gro 20	32	B1
St. Laurence Rd 20	32	B1
St. Laurence's Mans 1	37	C1
St. Laurences Pk Still.	54	B3
St. Laurence St N 1 off Sheriff St Lwr	59	F1
St. Lawrence Gro 3	30	A2
St. Lawrence Pl 1 off Sheriff St Lwr	59	F1
St. Lawrence Rd (Clontarf) 3	30	A2
St. Lawrence Rd (Howth) 13	20	B2
St. Lawrences Ct 3	30	A2
St. Lawrence St 1 off Sheriff St Lwr	59	F1
St. Lawrence Ter 13	21	C2
St. Luke's Cres 14	52	B1
St. Magdalene Ter 4	37	D2
St. Malachy's Dr 12	41	C3
St. Malachy's Rd 9	28	A1
St. Margaret's Av 5	16	B2
St. Margaret's Av N 1 off North Circular Rd	28	B3
St. Margaret's Ter 8	35	C3
St. Martin's Dr 12	42	B3
St. Martin's Pk 12	42	B2
St. Mary's Av (Rathfarnham) 14	51	C2
St. Mary's Av N 7	28	A3
St. Mary's Av W 10	33	D2
St. Mary's Cres 12	41	D1
St. Mary's Dr 12	41	D1
St. Mary's La 4	37	C3
St. Mary's Pk 12	41	D2
St. Mary's Pk 15	9	D2
St. Mary's Pl 13 off Main St	21	C2
St. Mary's Pl N 7	28	A3
St. Mary's Rd 3	29	C3
St. Mary's Rd 12	41	D2
St. Mary's Rd 13 off Main St	21	C2
St. Mary's Rd N 3	29	C3
St. Mary's Rd S 4	37	C3
St. Mary's St D.L.	57	C3
St. Mary's Ter 7	28	A3
St. Mel's Av 12	49	C1
St. Michael's Est 8	34	A3
St. Michael's Hill 8	58	B3
St. Michael's La 8 off High St	58	B3
St. Michael's Rd 9	28	A1
St. Michael's Ter 8	35	D3
St. Michan's St 7	58	B2
St. Mobhi Boithirin 9	12	A3
St. Mobhi Ct 9	12	A3
St. Mobhi Dr 9	28	A1
St. Mobhi Gro 9	28	A1
St. Mobhi Rd 9	28	A1
St. Mobhis Br 9	28	A1
St. Nessan's Ter 13 off Tuckett's La	20	B2
St. Nicholas Pl 8	58	B4
St. Pappin Grn 11	11	D2
St. Pappin Rd 11	11	D2
St. Patrick Av 3 off North Strand Rd	29	C3
St. Patrick's Cl 8	58	B4
St. Patrick's Cotts 14	51	C3
St. Patrick's Par 9	28	A2
St. Patrick's Rd 9	28	A2
St. Patrick's Rd 12	41	C3
St. Patrick's Ter 1 off Russell St	28	B3
St. Patrick's Ter 3 off North Strand Rd	29	C3
St. Patrick's Ter 8	33	D2
St. Patrick's Vil 4	37	D2
St. Peters Av 7	27	D2
St. Peters Cl 7	27	D3
St. Peter's Cres 12	41	D3
St. Peter's Dr 12	41	D3
St. Peter's Rd 7	27	D2
St. Peter's Rd 12	41	C3
St. Peter's Ter 13	20	B2
St. Philomena's Rd 11	27	D2
St. Stephen's Grn 2	36	B3
St. Stephen's Grn N 2	59	D4
St. Stephen's Grn Pk 2	36	A3
St. Stephen's Grn Shop Cen 2	59	D4
St. Stephen's Grn S 2	36	A3
St. Stephen's Grn Sta 2	59	D4
St. Stephen's Grn W 2	36	A3
St. Teresa's La 12	42	A3
St. Teresa's Pl 9 off Prospect Av	27	D1
St. Teresa's Rd 9	27	D1
St. Teresa's Rd (Crumlin) 12	42	A3
St. Theresa Gdns 8	35	C3
St. Thomas' Mead Still.	54	B2
St. Thomas' Rd (Tenter Flds) 8	35	D3
St. Thomas' Rd Still.	54	A2

St. Thomas's Av 7
 off Constitution Hill 58 B3
St. Vincent's Pk Black. 56 A2
St. Vincent St N 7 27 D3
St. Vincent St S
 (Tenter Flds) 8 35 D3
St. Vincent St W 8 33 D2
Salamanca 14 53 D2
Sallymount Av 6 44 B1
Sallymount Gdns 6 44 B1
Sally's Br 8 43 C1
Salthill & Monkstown
 Sta Black. 56 B2
Salzburg 14 53 D2
Sampsons La 1 58 C1
Sandford Av
 (Donnybrook) 4 45 C2
Sandford Av 8 35 C3
Sandford Cl 6 44 B2
Sandford Gdns 4 45 C2
Sandford Gdns 8
 off Donore Av 35 C3
Sandford Rd 6 44 B2
Sandford Ter 6 44 B2
Sandon Cove 3 30 B2
Sandwith Pl 2 59 F3
Sandwith St Lwr 2 59 F3
Sandwith St Upr 2 59 F3
Sandymount Av 4 45 D1
Sandymount Castle
 Dr 4 46 A1
Sandymount Castle
 Rd 4 46 A1
Sandymount Grn 4 38 A3
Sandymount Rd 4 38 A3
Sandymount Sta 4 46 A1
Sans Souci Pk Boot. 54 A1
Santa Sabina Manor 13 19 C2
Santry Hall Ind Est 9 12 B1
Sarah Pl 8 34 A1
Sarsfield Quay 7 35 C1
Sarsfield Rd 8 33 D2
Sarsfield Rd 10 33 C2
Sarsfield St 7 27 D3
Sarto Lawn 13 17 C1
Sarto Pk 13 17 C1
Sarto Ri 13 17 C2
Sarto Rd 13 17 C2
Saul Rd 12 42 B1
School Av 5 14 B3
Schoolhouse La 2 59 D4
School Ho La W 8 58 B3
School St 8 35 C2
Seabury 4 46 B1
Seacliff Av 13 17 D1
Seacliff Dr 13 17 C1
Seacliff Rd 13 17 C1
Seacourt 3 31 C2
Seafield Av 3 31 C2
Seafield Av Black. 56 B3
Seafield Cl Boot. 54 A1
Seafield Ct 13 18 A1
Seafield Cres Boot. 54 B1
Seafield Down 3 31 D2
Seafield Dr Boot. 54 A1
Seafield Gro 3 31 D2
Seafield Rd Boot. 54 B1
Seafield Rd E 3 31 C2
Seafield Rd W 3 30 B2
Seafort Av 4 38 A3
Seafort Cotts 4
 off Seafort Av 38 A3
Seafort Gdns 4 38 A3
Seafort Vil 4
 off Seafort Av 38 A3
Seagrange Rd 13 17 C1
Seamus Ennis Rd 11 10 B1
Sean Heuston Br 8 34 B1
Sean McDermott St
 Lwr 1 28 B3
Sean McDermott St
 Upr 1 59 D1
Sean More Rd 4 38 A3
Sean O'Casey La 1 28 B3
Seapark 3 31 C2
Seapark Dr 3 31 C2

Seapark Rd 3 31 C2
Seapoint Av Black. 56 A2
Seapoint Sta Black. 56 A2
Seaview Av 3 29 C3
Seaview Av N 3 30 A2
Sea Vw Ter 4 45 D2
Seaview Ter 13 21 C2
Second Av 1 37 C1
Selskar Ter 6 44 A1
Serpentine Av 4 45 D1
Serpentine Pk 4 37 D3
Serpentine Rd 4 37 D3
Serpentine Ter 4 45 D1
Seven Oaks 9 12 B3
Seville Pl 1 29 C3
Seville Ter 1 28 B3
Shamrock Cotts 1
 off Shamrock Pl 29 C3
Shamrock Pl 1 29 C3
Shamrock St 7
 off Primrose St 27 D3
Shamrock Ter 1 29 C3
Shamrock Vil 6W 43 D2
Shanard Av 9 12 A1
Shanard Rd 9 12 A1
Shanboley Rd 9 13 C1
Shandon Cres 7 27 D2
Shandon Dr 7 27 D2
Shandon Gdns 7 27 C1
Shandon Pk 7 27 D2
Shandon Pk Black. 56 A2
Shandon Rd 7 27 D2
Shangan Av 9 12 B1
Shangan Gdns 9 12 B1
Shangangh Rd 9 28 A2
Shangan Grn 9 12 B1
Shangan Pk 9 12 B1
Shangan Rd 9 12 A1
Shanglas Rd 9 13 C1
Shanid Rd 6W 43 D2
Shanliss Av 9 12 B1
Shanliss Dr 9 12 B1
Shanliss Gro 9 12 B1
Shanliss Pk 9 12 A1
Shanliss Rd 9 12 B1
Shanliss Wk 9 12 B1
Shanliss Way 9 12 B1
Shannon Ter 8 34 B2
Shanrath Rd 9 13 C1
Shantalla Av 9 13 C2
Shantalla Dr 9 13 C2
Shantalla Pk 9 13 C2
Shantalla Rd 9 13 C2
Shanvarna Rd 9 13 C1
Shaws La 4 37 D3
Shaw St 2 59 E3
Shelbourne Av 4 37 D3
Shelbourne La 4 37 C3
Shelbourne Rd 4 37 D3
Shellysbanks Rd 4 38 B3
Shelmalier Rd 3 29 C3
Shelmartin Av 3 29 C2
Shelmartin Ter 3 29 C1
Shelton Dr 12 42 A3
Shelton Gdns 12 42 A3
Shelton Gro 12 42 A3
Shelton Pk 12 42 A3
Sheriff St Lwr 1 59 F1
Sheriff St Upr 1 37 D1
Sherkin Gdns 9 12 B3
Sherrard Av 1 28 A2
Sherrard St Lwr 1 28 A3
Sherrard St Upr 1 28 A3
Shielmartin Dr 13 19 C3
Shielmartin Pk 13 22 A2
Shielmartin Rd 13 22 A2
Ship St Gt 8 58 C3
Ship St Little 8 58 B3
Shrewsbury 4 46 A1
Shrewsbury Pk 4 46 A1
Shrewsbury Rd 4 45 D2
Sibthorpe La 6 44 B2
Sigurd Rd 7 27 C3
Silloge Av 11 11 D1
Silloge Gdns 11 12 A1
Silloge Rd 11 12 A1

Silver Birches 14 53 C3
Silverwood Dr 6W
 off Templeville Dr 50 A2
Silverwood Dr 14 50 B3
Silverwood Rd 14 50 B3
Simmon's Ct 4
 off Simmonscourt
 Castle 45 D1
Simmonscourt Av 4 45 D2
Simmonscourt Castle 4 45 D1
Simmonscourt Rd 4 45 D1
Simmonscourt Ter 4 45 D1
Simonscourt Sq 4 45 D1
Simonscourt Vw 4 45 D1
Sion Hill Boot. 55 C1
Sion Hill Av 6W 43 C3
Sion Hill Ct 9 13 C3
Sion Hill Rd 9 13 C3
Sir John Rogersons
 Quay 2 37 C1
Sitric Rd 7 35 C1
Skellys La 5 13 D2
Skippers All 8 58 B3
Skreen Rd 7 26 A2
Slademore Cl 13 15 D1
Slademore Dr 13 15 D1
Slade Row 7 35 C1
Slane Rd 12 42 B1
Slaney Cl 11 27 C1
Slaney Rd 11 27 C1
Slemish Rd 7 26 A2
Slievebloom Pk 12 41 D1
Slievebloom Rd 12 41 D1
Slievemore Rd 12 42 A1
Slievenamon Rd 12 34 A3
Slieve Rua Dr Still. 54 A3
Sloperton D.L. 57 C3
Slopes, The D.L. 57 C3
Smithfield 7 58 A2
Smithfield Sta 7 58 A2
Smiths Vil D.L. 57 C3
Somerset St 4
 off Doris St 37 D2
Somerville Av 12 41 D2
Somerville Grn 12 41 D2
Somerville Pk 12 41 D2
Sommerville 14 52 B2
Sorbonne 14 53 D2
South Av Still. 54 A3
South Bk Rd 4 38 B2
South Circular Rd 8 34 A1
Southdene Black. 56 B3
South Docks Rd 4 37 D2
Southern Cross Av 8 34 A2
South Gt Georges St 2 58 C4
South Hill 6 44 A3
South Hill Av Boot. 54 B2
South Hill Pk Boot. 54 B2
South Lotts Rd 4 37 D3
South Rd Number 4 1
 off Alexandra Rd 38 B1
Southwood Pk Boot. 55 C2
Spade Enterprise
 Cen 7 35 C1
Spafield Ter 4 45 D1
Spa Rd
 (Kilmainham) 8 33 D2
Spa Rd (Phoenix Pk) 8 26 A3
Spawell Br 16 50 A3
Spencer Dock 1 37 C1
Spencer St N 3
 off South Circular Rd 35 C3
Spencer St N 3 29 C3
Sperrin Rd 12 33 D3
Spire Vw 6 43 D2
Spire Vw La 6 43 D2
Spitalfields 8 58 A4
Springdale Rd 5 15 C1
Springfield 7 26 A2
Springfield Av 6W 50 B2
Springfield Cres 6W 50 B2
Springfield Dr 6W 50 B2
Springfield Pk 6W 50 B2
Springfield Rd 6W 50 B2
Spring Gdn La 2 59 E3
Spring Gdn St 3 29 C3
Square, The 4 37 D2
Square, The 6W 43 C2
Stable La 2
 off Harcourt St 36 A3
Stable La 2
 off Londonbridge Rd 37 D3

Stables, The Boot. 54 B1
Stamer St 8 36 A3
Stanford Grn 12 41 D2
Stanhope Cen 7 27 D3
Stanhope Grn 7 35 C1
Stannaway Av 12 42 A2
Stannaway Dr 12 42 B2
Stannaway Rd 12 42 A2
Station Rd 5 15 D3
Station Rd 13 18 A1
Steeples, The 10 33 C2
Steevens La 8 35 C2
Stella Av 9 12 A3
Stephens La 2 37 C3
Stephens Pl 2
 off Stephens La 37 C3
Stephens Rd 8 34 A3
Stephen St 2 58 C4
Stephen St Upr 8 58 C4
Stiles Ct, The 3
 off The Stiles Rd 30 A2
Stiles Rd, The 3 30 A2
Stillorgan Pk Black. 55 C3
Stillorgan Pk Av Black. 55 C3
Stillorgan Rd 4 45 D2
Stillorgan Rd Still. 54 B2
Stillorgan Shop Cen
 Still. 54 B3
Stirling Pk 14 52 A1
Stirrup La 7
 off Beresford St 58 B1
Stockton Ct 15 8 A3
Stockton Dr 15 24 A1
Stockton Grn 15 24 A1
Stockton Gro 15 24 A1
Stockton Lawn 15 8 A3
Stockton Pk 15 24 A1
Stonepark Abbey 14 51 D3
Stonepark Ct 14 51 D3
Stonepark Dr 14 51 D3
Stonepark Grn 14 51 D3
Stonepark Orchard 14 51 D3
Stoneview Pl D.L. 57 D3
Stoneybatter 7 35 C1
Stoney Rd 3
 off East Wall Rd 29 C3
Stoney Rd
 (Dundrum) 14 53 C3
Store St 1 59 E1
Stormanstown Rd 11 11 D2
Stradbrook Gdns Black. 56 A3
Stradbrook Lawn D.L. 56 A3
Stradbrook Rd D.L. 56 A3
Strand Rd
 (Sandymount) 4 38 A3
Strand Rd 13 19 C2
Strand St 4 37 D2
Strand St Gt 1 58 C2
Strandville Av E 3 30 A2
Strandville Av N 3 29 C3
Strandville Ho 3 30 A2
Strangford Gdns 3 29 C3
Strangford Rd E 3 29 C3
Streamville Rd 13 16 A1
Suffolk St 2 59 D3
Suir Rd 8 34 A2
Suir Rd Sta 12 34 A3
Sullivan St 7 34 B1
Summerhill 1 28 B3
Summerhill Par 1 28 B3
Summerhill Par D.L. 57 D3
Summerhill Pl 1 28 B3
Summerhill Rd D.L. 57 D3
Summer Pl 1 28 B3
Summer St N 1 28 B3
Summer St S 8 35 C2
Summerville 3 30 B2
Summerville Pk 6 44 A2
Sunbury Gdns 6 44 A3
Sundrive Pk 12 43 C2
Sundrive Rd 12 42 B1
Sundrive Shop Cen 12 43 C2
Sunnybank Ter 14 52 B3
Sunshine Ind Est 12 42 A1
Superquinn Shop
 Cen 12 41 C2
Susan Ter 8 35 D3
Susanville Rd 3 28 B2
Sussex Rd 4 44 B1
Sussex St D.L. 57 D3
Sussex Ter Lwr 4
 off Mespil Rd 36 B3

Sussex Ter Upr 4	
off Leeson St Upr	36 B3
Sutton Ct 13	17 D1
Sutton Cross Shop Cen 13	18 B1
Sutton Downs 13	17 D2
Sutton Gro 13	17 D1
Sutton Lawns 13	17 D1
Sutton Pk 13	17 D1
Sutton Sta 13	18 A1
Swan Pl 4	
off Morehampton Rd	45 C1
Swan Shop Cen 6	44 A2
Swans Nest Av 5	16 B1
Swans Nest Ct 5	16 B1
Swans Nest Rd 5	16 A1
Swanville Pl 6	44 A2
Swanward Business Cen 24	40 A3
Swanward Ct 12	43 C1
Swan Yd 2	
off Harry St	59 D4
Sweeneys Ter 8	
off Mill St	35 D3
Sweetmans Av Black.	55 D2
Sweetmount Av 14	52 B3
Sweetmount Dr 14	52 B3
Sweetmount Pk 14	52 B3
Swifts All 8	58 A4
Swifts Row 7	
off Ormond Quay Upr	58 B2
Swilly Rd 7	26 B2
Swords Rd 9	12 B3
Swords St 7	27 C3
Sybil Hill Av 5	15 C3
Sybil Hill Rd 5	15 C3
Sycamore Cres Still.	54 B2
Sycamore Dr 24	48 A1
Sycamore Pk 24	48 A1
Sycamore Rd 12	40 A2
Sycamore Rd Still.	54 B2
Sycamore St 2	58 C3
Sydenham Ms D.L.	57 D3
Sydenham Rd (Sandymount) 4	45 D1
Sydenham Rd (Dundrum) 14	53 C3
Sydenham Vil 14	53 C3
Sydney Av Black.	55 D2
Sydney Par Av 4	46 A2
Sydney Par Sta 4	46 A2
Sydney Ter Black.	55 D2
Sykes La 8	43 D3
Synge La 8	36 A3
Synge Pl 8	36 A3
Synge St 8	36 A3
Synnott Pl 7	28 A3
Synnott Row 7	28 A2

T

Tailor's Mkt 8	58 B3
Talbot La 1	
off Talbot St	59 D1
Talbot Lo Black.	55 C3
Talbot Mem Br 1	59 E2
Talbot Pl 1	59 E1
Talbot St 1	59 D1
Tallaght Enterprise Cen 24	48 A3
Tallaght Rd 24	49 C3
Tallagt Rd 6W	49 D3
Tamarisk Av 24	48 A1
Tamarisk Cl 24	
off Tamarisk Way	48 A1
Tamarisk Ct 24	48 A2
Tamarisk Dale 24	
off Tamarisk Dr	48 A1
Tamarisk Dr 24	48 A1
Tamarisk Gro 24	
off Tamarisk Pk	48 A2
Tamarisk Hts 24	48 A2
Tamarisk Lawn 24	48 A2
Tamarisk Pk 24	48 A2
Tamarisk Vw 24	
off Tamarisk Pk	48 A2
Tamarisk Wk 24	
off Tamarisk Dr	48 A1
Tamarisk Way 24	48 A1
Taney Av 14	53 C3
Taney Ct 14	53 C3
Taney Cres 14	53 C3
Taney Dr 14	53 C3
Taney Gro 14	53 D3
Taney Lawn 14	53 C3
Taney Manor 14	53 C3
Taney Pk 14	53 C3
Taney Ri 14	53 C3
Taney Rd 14	53 C3
Tara Hill Cres 14	51 C3
Tara Hill Gro 14	51 C3
Tara Hill Rd 14	51 C3
Tara Lawn 13	16 A1
Tara St 2	59 E2
Tara St Sta 2	59 E2
Taylors La 8	35 C2
Temple Bar 2	58 C3
Temple Cotts 7	27 D3
Temple Ct 7	35 C1
Temple Cres Black.	56 A2
Temple Gdns 6	44 A3
Temple La N 1 Black.	56 A2
Temple La N 1	28 A3
Temple La S 2	35 C2
Temple Manor Av 12	49 C1
Temple Manor Cl 12	49 C1
Temple Manor Ct 12	49 C1
Temple Manor Dr 12	49 C1
Temple Manor Gro 12	49 C1
Temple Manor Way 12	49 C1
Templemore Av 6	43 D3
Templeogue Lo 6W	49 D2
Templeogue Rd 6W	50 B2
Templeogue Wd 6W	50 A2
Temple Pk 6	44 B3
Temple Pk Av Black.	56 A2
Temple Pl 6	44 B1
Temple Rd 6	44 A3
Temple Rd Black.	55 D2
Temple Sq 6	44 A3
Temple St N 1	28 A3
Temple St W 7	35 C1
Temple Vil 6	
off Palmerston Rd	44 A2
Templeville Av 6W	50 A2
Templeville Dr 6W	50 A2
Templeville Pk 6W	50 B2
Templeville Rd 6W	49 D1
Terenure Pk 6W	43 C3
Terenure Pl 6W	51 C1
Terenure Rd E 6	43 C3
Terenure Rd N 6W	43 C3
Terenure Rd W 6W	42 B3
Terminal Rd N 1	39 C1
Thatch Rd, The 9	13 C2
Third Av 1	37 C1
Third Av 8	
off Dolphin's Barn	35 C3
Thomas Ct 8	35 C2
Thomas Davis St S 8	58 B4
Thomas Davis St W 8	33 D3
Thomas La 1	
off O'Connell St Upr	59 D1
Thomas Moore Rd 12	41 C2
Thomas St E 4	37 D2
Thomas St W 8	35 C2
Thomond Rd 10	32 B2
Thormanby Lawns 13	21 C2
Thormanby Lo 13	21 D3
Thormanby Rd 13	21 C2
Thormanby Wds 13	21 C3
Thorncastle St 4	37 D2
Thorncliffe 14	52 B1
Thorncliffe Pk 14	52 A1
Thorndale Av 9	
off Elm Mt Rd	14 A3
Thorndale Ct 9	13 C2
Thorndale Cres 9	
off Elm Mt Rd	14 A3
Thorndale Dr 5	12 A3
Thorndale Gro 5	12 A3
Thorndale Lawns 9	
off Elm Mt Rd	14 A3
Thorndale Pk 9	
off Elm Mt Rd	14 A3
Thornhill Rd Still.	54 A3
Thornville Av 5	16 B2
Thornville Dr 5	16 B2
Thornville Pk 5	16 B2
Thornville Rd 5	16 B2
Thor Pl 7	35 C1
Three Rock Cl 12	48 B1
Thundercut All 7	
off Smithfield	58 A1
Tibradden Cl 12	
off Tibradden Dr	48 B1
Tibradden Dr 12	48 B1
Tibradden Gro 12	
off Tibradden Dr	48 B1
Timber Quay 1	38 A1
Tinkler's Path 8	24 B2
Tivoli Av 6W	43 D2
Tivoli Rd D.L.	57 C3
Tivoli Ter E D.L.	57 C3
Tivoli Ter N D.L.	57 C3
Tivoli Ter S D.L.	57 C3
Tolka Cotts 11	11 C3
Tolka Est Rd 11	11 C3
Tolka Quay 1	37 D1
Tolka Quay Rd 1	38 B1
Tolka Rd 3	28 B2
Tolka Vale 11	11 C3
Tolka Valley Business Pk 11	10 B3
Tolka Valley Ind Est 11	10 B3
Tolka Valley Rd 11	10 A3
Tolka Vw Ter 11	11 C3
Tom Clarke Ho 3	29 C2
Tom Kelly Rd 2	44 A1
Tonduff Cl 12	
off Lugaquilla Av	48 B1
Tonguefield Rd 12	42 B2
Tonlegee Av 5	15 D1
Tonlegee Dr 5	15 C1
Tonlegee Rd 5	15 C1
Torlogh Gdns 3	29 C2
Torlogh Par 3	29 C1
Tourmakeady Rd 9	12 B2
Tower Av 14	43 D3
Tower Rd 15	24 A2
Tower Vw Cotts 11	27 D1
Townsend St 2	59 E2
Trafalgar La Black.	56 A2
Trafalgar Ter Black.	56 A2
Tram Ter 3	31 C3
Tramway Cotts 7	27 D2
Tramway Ct 13	
off Station Rd	18 A1
Tramway Ter 4	46 A1
Tramway Vil 6W	43 C3
Tranquility Gro 5	14 A1
Treepark Av 24	48 A2
Treepark Cl 24	48 A2
Treepark Dr 24	48 A2
Treepark Rd 24	48 A2
Trees Av Still.	54 B3
Trees Rd Lwr Still.	54 B3
Trees Rd Upr Still.	54 A3
Trevor Ter 2	
off Grattan St	37 C2
Trimbleston 14	53 D2
Trimleston Av Boot.	46 B3
Trimleston Dr Boot.	46 B3
Trimleston Gdns Boot.	46 B3
Trimleston Pk Boot.	46 B3
Trimleston Rd Boot.	54 B1
Trim Rd 5	13 D1
Trinity Coll Enterprise Cen 2	37 C2
Trinity St 2	59 D3
Trinity Ter 3	29 C2
Tritonville Av 4	38 A3
Tritonville Ct 4	37 D3
Tritonville Cres 4	38 A3
Tritonville Rd 4	37 D3
Tryconnell Pk 12	33 D2
Tuckett's La 13	20 B2
Tudor Rd 6	44 B3
Turnberry 13	17 D1
Turrets, The 4	37 D3
Turrets Flats 6	
off Rathmines Rd Upr	44 A2
Tuscany Downs 5	15 D2
Tuscany Pk 13	17 D1
Tymon La 24	49 C2
Tymon N Av 24	48 B2
Tymon N Gdns 24	48 B3
Tymon N Grn 24	48 B2
Tymon N Gro 24	48 B2
Tymon N Lawn 24	48 B2
Tymon N Pk 24	48 B2
Tymon N Rd 24	48 B2
Tymonville Av 24	48 A2
Tymonville Ct 24	48 A2
Tymonville Cres 24	48 A2
Tymonville Dr 24	48 A2
Tymonville Gro 24	48 B2
Tymonville Rd 24	48 B2
Tyrconnell Rd 8	33 D3
Tyrconnell St 8	33 D3
Tyrconnell Vil 8	
off Grattan Cres	33 D2
Tyrone Pl 8	33 D3

U

Ulster St 7	27 D2
Ulster Ter 1 Still.	55 C3
Upper Cliff Rd 13	21 C2
Uppercross Rd 8	34 B3
Upper Glen Rd 15	24 B3
Ushers Island 8	35 C1
Ushers Quay 8	58 A3
Usher St 8	58 A3

V

Valentia Par 7	28 A2
Valentia Rd 9	12 A3
Valeview Cres 11	10 A2
Valeview Dr 11	10 A2
Valeview Gdns 11	10 A2
Valley Pk Av 11	9 D2
Valley Pk Dr 11	9 D3
Valley Pk Rd 11	9 D3
Vauxhall Av 8	35 C3
Vavasour Sq 4	37 C3
Venetian Hall 5	14 B3
Ventry Dr 7	26 B1
Ventry Pk 7	26 B1
Ventry Rd 7	26 B1
Verbena Av 13	17 C2
Verbena Gro 13	17 C1
Verbena Lawns 13	17 C1
Verbena Pk 13	17 C1
Vergemount 6	
off Clonskeagh Rd	45 C3
Vergemount Hall 6	45 C3
Vergemount Pk 6	45 C2
Vernon Av (Clontarf) 3	31 C2
Vernon Av 6	
off Frankfort Av	43 D2
Vernon Ct 3	31 C3
Vernon Dr 3	31 C1
Vernon Gdn 3	31 C2
Vernon Gro 3	31 C2
Vernon Gro (Rathgar) 6	44 A3
Vernon Heath 3	31 C1
Vernon Par 3	
off Clontarf Rd	30 A2
Vernon Pk 3	31 C2
Vernon Ri 3	31 C1
Vernon St 8	35 D3
Vernon Ter 6	
off Frankfort Av	44 A3
Veronica Ter 4	37 D2
Verschoyle Ct 2	
off Verschoyle Pl	37 C3
Verschoyle Pl 2	37 C3
Vesey Ms D.L.	57 C3
Vesey Pl D.L.	57 C3
Vicar St 8	58 A4
Victoria Av 4	45 C2
Victoria Br 2	37 C2
Victoria Quay 8	35 C1
Victoria Rd (Clontarf) 3	30 A2
Victoria Rd (Terenure) 6	51 D1
Victoria St 8	35 D3
Victoria Ter 3	
off Clontarf Rd	31 C3
Victoria Ter 14	52 B3
Victoria Vil 3	29 D2
Victoria Vil (Rathgar) 6	43 D3
Viking Pl 7	
off Arbour Hill	35 C1
Viking Rd 7	35 C1
Village, The 5	16 A3
Village, The 9	12 B3
Village Ct 14	51 C2
Village Grn 24	48 A3
Villa Pk Av (Ascal Pairc An Bhailtini) 7	26 A2
Villa Pk Dr (Ceide Pairc An Bhailtini) 7	26 A2
Villa Pk Gdns (Gardini Pairc An Bhailtini) 7	26 A2

Villa Pk Rd (Bothar Pairc
An Bhailtini) 7 26 A2
Villiers Rd 6 44 A3
Vincent Ter 9 28 A1
Violet Hill Dr 11 11 C3
Violet Hill Pk 11 11 C3
Violet Hill Rd 11 11 C3
Virginia Dr 11
off Virginia Pk 10 A2
Virginia Pk 11 10 A2

W

Wad Br 9 12 A2
Wadelai Grn 11 12 A2
Wadelai Rd 11 11 D2
Wade's Av 5 15 D3
Wainsfort Av 6W 50 A1
Wainsfort Cres 6W 50 A1
Wainsfort Dr 6W 42 A3
Wainsfort Gdns 6W
off Wainsfort Cres 50 A1
Wainsfort Gro 6W 50 B1
Wainsfort Pk 6W 50 A1
Wainsfort Rd 6W 50 A1
Waldemar Ter 14 52 B3
Waldrons Br 6 52 A1
Walk, The 6W 50 A2
Walkinstown Av 12 41 C2
Walkinstown Cres 12 41 C2
Walkinstown Cross 12 41 C2
Walkinstown Dr 12 41 C2
Walkinstown Grn 12 41 C2
Walkinstown Mall 12 41 C2
Walkinstown Par 12 41 C2
Walkinstown Pk 12 41 C2
Walkinstown Rd
(Bothar Chille
Na Manac) 12 41 C2
Wallace Rd 12 41 D2
Walnut Av 9 12 B3
Walnut Ct 9 12 B3
Walnut Lawn 9 12 B3
Walnut Pk 9 12 B3
Walnut Ri 9 12 B3
Walsh Rd 9 12 A3
Waltham Ter Black. 55 C2
Walworth Rd 8
off Victoria Rd 43 D1
Wards Hill 8 35 D3
Warners La 6 36 B3
Warren Grn 13 18 A1
Warrenmount 8 35 D3
Warrenmount Pl 8 35 D3
Warrenpoint 3 30 A2
Warren St 8 44 A1
Warrington La 2
off Warrington Pl 37 C3
Warrington Pl 2 37 C3
Warwick Ter 6
off Sallymount Av 44 B1
Wasdale Gro 6 51 D1
Wasdale Pk 6 51 C1
Washington La 14 50 B3
Washington Pk 14 50 B2
Washington St 8 35 D3
Watercourse 6W 49 D2
Waterfall Av 3 28 B2
Waterfall Rd 5 15 D3
Waterloo Av 3 29 C3
Waterloo La 4 44 B1
Waterloo Rd 4 45 C1
Watermill Av 5 15 D3
Watermill Dr 5 15 D3
Watermill Lawn 5 16 A3
Watermill Pk 5 15 D3
Watermill Rd (Bothar
An Easa) 5 15 D3
Watling St 8 35 C2
Waverley Av 3 29 C2
Waverley Business
Pk 12 40 B1
Waverley Ter 6
off Kenilworth Rd 43 D2
Weaver La 7
off Phibsborough Rd 27 D3
Weavers Sq 8 35 D3
Weaver's St 8 58 A4

Wellesley Pl 1
off North Circular Rd 28 B3
Wellington La 4 45 C1
Wellington La 6W 49 D2
Wellington Pk 6W 49 D1
Wellington Pl
(Donnybrook) 4 45 C1
Wellington Pl N 7 27 D3
Wellington Quay 2 58 C3
Wellington Rd 4 45 C1
Wellington Rd 6W 49 D2
Wellington Rd 8 34 A1
Wellington St D.L. 57 C3
Wellington St Lwr 7 28 A3
Wellington St Upr 7 27 D3
Wellmount Av 11 10 A2
Wellmount Ct 11 10 A2
Wellmount Cres 11 10 A2
Wellmount Dr 11 10 A2
Wellmount Grn 11 10 A2
Wellmount Par 11 10 A2
Wellmount Pk 11 10 A2
Wellmount Rd 11 10 A2
Wellpark Av 9 12 B3
Wentworth Ter 2
off Hogan Pl 37 C2
Werburgh St 8 58 B3
Wesley Pl 8 35 D3
Wesley Rd 6 43 D3
Westbourne Rd 6W 51 C1
Westbrook 12 42 A3
Westbrook Rd 14 52 B2
Westcourt 8
off Basin St Upr 35 C2
Westcourt La 8 35 C2
Western Ind Est 12 40 A2
Western Parkway
Business Cen 12 40 B3
Western Parkway
Business Pk 12 40 B3
Western Rd 8 35 C3
Western Way 7 27 D3
Westfield Rd 6W 43 C2
Westgate Business
Pk 24 40 A3
Westhampton Pl 6W 43 C3
Westland Ct 2
off Cumberland St S 59 F4
Westland Row 2 59 F3
Westlink Ind Est 10 32 B3
Westmoreland Pk 6 44 B1
Westmoreland St 2 59 D3
Weston Av 14 52 B3
Weston Cl 14 52 B3
Weston Gro 14 52 B3
Weston Pk 14 52 B3
Weston Rd 14 52 B3
Weston Ter 14 52 B3
West Pk 5 15 C2
West Pk Dr 11 11 D3
Westpoint Ct Business
Pk 12 40 B1
West Rd 3 29 C3
West Row 1 58 C1
West Ter 8 33 D2
Westwood Av 11 9 D2
Westwood Rd 11 9 D2
Wexford St 2 36 A3
Wharton Ter 6
off Harolds Cross Rd 43 D1
Whitebank Rd 4 38 B2
Whitebarn Rd 14 52 A2
Whitebeam Av 14 45 C3
Whitebeam Rd 14 45 C3
Whitechurch
Abbey 7 14 51 C3
Whitechurch Pines 14 51 C3
Whitechurch Rd 14 51 C3
Whitechurch Rd 16 51 C3
Whitechurch
Stream 5 14 51 C3
Whitefriar Pl 8
off Aungier St 58 C4
Whitefriar St 8 58 C4
Whitehall Cl 6W 49 D1
Whitehall Gdns 12 42 A3
Whitehall Pk 12 49 D1
Whitehall Rd
(Rathfarnham) 14 52 A3
Whitehall Rd E 12 49 D1
Whitehall Rd W 12 49 D1
White Oak 14 53 C1
Whites La N 7 27 D3

Whites Rd 15 24 A2
Whitethorn Av 5 14 A2
Whitethorn Cl 5 13 D2
Whitethorn Cres 5 14 A2
Whitethorn Gro 5 14 A2
Whitethorn La 4
off Thorncastle St 37 D2
Whitethorn Pk 5 14 A2
Whitethorn Ri 5 14 A2
Whitethorn Rd 5 13 D2
Whitethorn Rd 14 45 C3
Whitton Rd 6 43 C3
Whitworth Av 3
off Whitworth Pl 28 A2
Whitworth Pl 3 28 A2
Whitworth Rd 1
off Seville Pl 29 C3
Whitworth Rd 9 27 D2
Wicklow La 2
off Wicklow St 59 D3
Wicklow St 2 59 D3
Wigan Rd 9 28 A2
Wilderwood Gro 6W 49 D2
Wilfield 4 46 A1
Wilfield Rd 4 46 A1
Wilfrid Rd 6W 43 D2
Willbrook Gro 14 51 C3
Willbrook Lawn 14 51 C3
Willbrook Pk 14 51 C3
Willbrook Rd 14 51 C3
Willbrook St 14 51 C3
Willfield Pk 4 46 A1
William's La 1
off Princes St N 59 D2
William's Pk 6 44 A1
William's Pl S 8 35 D3
William's Pl Upr 1 28 A2
William's Row 1
off Abbey St Mid 59 D2
William St N 1 28 A3
William St S 2 59 D4
Willington Av 6W 49 D1
Willington Ct 6W 49 D1
Willington Cres 6W 49 D1
Willington Dr 6W 49 D2
Willington Grn 6W 49 D1
Willington Gro 6W 49 D2
Willington Pk 6W
off Willington Gro 49 D2
Willow Bk D.L. 57 D3
Willowbank Pk 14 50 B3
Willow Business Pk 12 40 A1
Willowfield 4 46 A1
Willowfield Av 14 53 D2
Willowfield Pk 14 53 D2
Willow Ms 4 46 B2
Willow Pk Av 11 11 D1
Willow Pk Cl 11 11 C1
Willow Pk Cres 11 11 C1
Willow Pk Dr 11 11 D1
Willow Pk Gro 11 11 D1
Willow Pk Lawn 11 11 D1
Willow Pk Rd 11 11 D1
Willow Pl Boot. 55 C1
Willows, The 11 27 C1
Willows, The D.L. 56 A3
Willow Ter Boot.
off Rock Rd 55 C1
Wilson Cres Still. 54 A2
Wilson Rd Still. 54 A2
Wilsons Pl 2
off Grants Row 37 C2
Wilton Pl 2 36 B3
Wilton Ter 2 36 B3
Windele Rd 9 28 A1
Windgate Ri 13 23 D2
Windgate Rd 13 21 C3
Windmill Av 12 42 A2
Windmill Cres 12 42 A1
Windmill La 2 59 F2
Windmill Pk 12 42 A2
Windmill Rd 12 42 A2
Windsor Av 3 29 C2
Windsor Pl 2 36 B3
Windsor Rd 6 44 A2
Windsor Ter 8 43 D1
Windsor Ter D.L. 57 D3
Windsor Vil 3 29 C2
Windy Arbour Sta 14 52 B2
Winetavern St 8 58 B3
Winton Av 6 43 D3
Winton Rd 6 44 B1
Wolfe Tone Av D.L. 57 C3

Wolfe Tone Quay 7 35 C1
Wolfe Tone St 1 58 C2
Wolseley St 8 35 D3
Woodbank Av 11 9 D2
Woodbank Dr 11 9 D2
Woodbine Av Boot. 46 A3
Woodbine Cl 5 15 D1
Woodbine Dr 5 15 D2
Woodbine Pk 5 15 D2
Woodbine Pk Boot. 46 B3
Woodbine Rd 5 16 A1
Woodbine Rd Boot. 46 A3
Woodbrook Pk 16 50 A3
Woodcliff Hts 13 21 C3
Woodfield Av 10 33 D2
Woodfield Pl 10
off Woodfield Av 33 D2
Woodhaven 14 44 B3
Woodlands 6 51 D1
Woodlands, The 14 51 D1
Woodlands Av Still. 54 B3
Woodlands Dr Still. 54 B3
Woodlands Pk Black. 54 B2
Woodland Vil 6 44 B1
Woodlawn Cres 14 52 B2
Woodlawn Gro 14 52 B2
Woodlawn Pk 14 52 B2
Woodlawn Ter 14 52 B2
Wood Quay 8 58 B3
Woodside 3 31 C1
Woodside 14 51 D2
Woodside Dr 14 51 D2
Woodside Gro 14 51 D2
Woodstock Gdns 6 44 B2
Wood St 8 58 C4
Woodview Black. 55 C2
Woodview Cl 13 16 A1
Woodview Cotts 14 51 C2
Woodview Pk 13 16 A1
Woodville Rd 9
off Botanic Av 28 A1
Wynberg Pk D.L. 56 A3
Wynnefield Rd 6 44 A2
Wynnsward Dr 14 53 C1
Wynnsward Pk 14 53 C1

X

Xavier Av 3 29 C3

Y

Yale 14 53 D2
Yankee Ter Black. 55 D3
Yellow Rd 9 13 C2
Yewland Ter 6W 43 C3
York Av 6 44 A2
York Rd 4 37 D2
York Rd 6 44 A2
York Rd D.L. 57 C3
York St 2 58 C4
York Ter D.L. 57 C3

Z

Zion Rd 6 51 D1
Zoo Rd 8 34 B1